Adam Ferguson

The History of the Progress and Termination of the Roman Republic

Vol. II

Adam Ferguson

The History of the Progress and Termination of the Roman Republic
Vol. II

ISBN/EAN: 9783744694711

Printed in Europe, USA, Canada, Australia, Japan

Cover: Foto ©ninafisch / pixelio.de

More available books at **www.hansebooks.com**

THE

HISTORY

OF THE

PROGRESS AND TERMINATION

OF THE

ROMAN REPUBLIC.

BY

ADAM FERGUSON,

LL. D. F. R. S. E.

LATE PROFESSOR OF MORAL PHILOSOPHY IN THE UNIVERSITY OF
EDINBURGH; MEMBER OF THE ROYAL ACADEMY AT BERLIN,
OF THE ROYAL ACADEMY AT FLORENCE, OF THE ETRUS-
CAN SOCIETY OF ANTIQUARIES AT CORTONA,
AND OF THE ARCADIA AT ROME.

A NEW EDITION, IN FIVE VOLUMES,
REVISED AND CORRECTED.

WITH MAPS.

VOL. II.

EDINBURGH:
PRINTED FOR BELL & BRADFUTE; AND
G. G. & J. ROBINSON, LONDON.

1799.

CONTENTS

OF

VOLUME SECOND.

CHAP. X.

State of the Italian Allies, and the Views which now began to be entertained by them.—Appearance of Caius Gracchus.—Resolution to purge the City of Aliens.—Consulate and factious Motions of Fulvius Flaccus.—Conspiracy of Frigellæ suppressed.—Caius Gracchus returns to Rome.—Offers himself Candidate for the Tribunate.—Address of Cornelia.—Tribunate and Acts of Caius Gracchus.—Re-election.—Proposed to admit the Inhabitants of Italy on the Rolls of Roman Citizens.—Popular Acts of Gracchus and Livius.—The Senate begin to prevail.—Death of Caius Gracchus and Fulvius. Page 1

CHAP.

CHAP. XI.

State of Order and Tranquillity which followed the Suppression of the late Tumults.—Appearance of Caius Marius.—Foreign Wars.—Complaints against Jugurtha.—Appearance of the Cimbri.—War with Jugurtha.—Campaign and Treaty of Piso.—Jugurtha came to Rome with a Safe-conduct.—Obliged to retire from thence.—Campaign of Metellus.—Of Marius.—Jugurtha betrayed by Bocchus.—His Death, after the Triumph of Marius.—This General re-elected, in order to command against the Cimbri. - - Page 31

CHAP. XII.

Review of the Circumstances which revived the popular Party at Rome.—Further Account of Laws and Regulations under the Administration of this Party.—State of the Empire.—Fourth Consulate of Marius.—Continued Migrations of the barbarous Nations.—Defeated by Marius at Aquæ Sextiæ.—By Marius and Catulus in Italy. - - - - 78

CHAP. XIII.

Character and immoderate Ambition of Marius.—Death of Nonius.—Re-election of the Tribune Saturninus.—His Sedition and seizing the Capitol.—Death of Saturninus.—Reverse in the State of Parties.—Recall of Metellus.—Violent Death of the Tribune Furius.—Birth of Caius Julius Cæsar.—Lex Cæcilia Didia.—Blank in the Roman History.—Sylla offers himself Candidate for the Office of Prætor.—Edict of the Censors against the Latin

CONTENTS.

tin Rhetoricians.—Bullion in the Roman Treasury.—Present of a Group in Golden Figures from the King of Mauritania.—Acts of Livius Drusus.—Revolt of the Italian Allies.—Policy of the Romans in yielding to the Necessity of their Affairs.—The Laws of Plautius. - - Page 96

CHAP. XIV.

Triumph of Pompeius Strabo.—Progress of Sylla.—War with the King of Pontus.—Rise of that Kingdom.—Appointment of Sylla to command.—Policy of the Tribune Sulpicius.—Sylla's Commission recalled in favour of Marius.—His March from Campania to Rome.— Expels Marius and his Faction from the City.—His Operations in Greece.—Siege of Athens.—Battle of Chæronea.—Of Orchomenos.—Transactions at Rome.—Policy of Cinna. —Marius recalled.—Cinna flies, and is deprived.—Recovers the Possession of Rome.—Treaty of Sylla with Mithridates.—He passes into Italy.—Is opposed by numerous Armies.—Various Events of the War in Italy.— Sylla prevails.—His Proscription, or Massacre.—Named Dictator.—His Policy—Resignation—and Death. 136

CHAP. XV.

State of the Commonwealth and Numbers of the People.— Characters of Persons who began to appear in the time of Sylla.—Faction of Lepidus.—Sertorius harbours the Marian Party in Spain.—Is attacked by Metellus and Pompey.—His Death, and final Suppression of the Party.—First Appearance of C. Julius Cæsar.— Tribunes begin to trespass on the Laws of Sylla.—Progress of the Empire.—Preparations of Mithridates.—War with the Romans.—

Romans.—Irruption into Bithynia.—Siege of Cyzicus.—Raised.—Flight of Mithridates.—Lucullus carries the War into Pontus.—Rout and Dispersion of the Army of Mithridates.—His Flight into Armenia.—Conduct of Lucullus in the Province of Asia. Page 212

CHAP. XVI.

Escape and Revolt of the Gladiators at Capua.—Spartacus.—Action and Defeat of Lentulus the Roman Consul.—And of Cassius the Prætor of Gaul.—Appointment of M. Crassus for this Service.—Destruction of the Gladiators.—Triumph of Metellus and Pompey.—Consulship of Pompey and Crassus.—Tribunes restored to their former Powers.—Consulate of Metellus and Hortensius.—War in Crete.—Renewal of the War in Pontus and Armenia.—Defeat of Tigranes.—Negotiation with the King of Parthia.—Mutiny of the Roman Army.—Complaints of Piracies committed in the Roman Seas.—Commission proposed to Pompey.—His Conduct against the Pirates.—His Commission extended to Pontus.—Operations against Mithridates.—Defeat and Flight of that Prince.—Operations of Pompey in Syria.—Siege and Reduction of Jerusalem.—Death of Mithridates. - 247

CHAP. XVII.

Growing Corruption of the Roman Officers of State.—The Love of Consideration changed for Avarice, Rapacity, and Prodigality.—Laws against Extortion.—Cataline a Candidate for the Consulship.—Conspiracy with Autronius.—Competition for the Consulate.—Election of Cicero and Antonius.—Condition of the Times.—Agrarian Law of Rullus.—Trial of Rabirius.—Cabals of the Tribunes.—

CONTENTS.

Tribunes.—Of Cataline.—His Flight from the City.—Discovery of his Accomplices.—Their Execution. Page 318

CHAP. XVIII.

Character of the Times.—Philosophy.—Opposite Tenets and Votaries.— Proceedings of the Senate.—Tribunate of Metellus, Nepos, and of Cato.—Proposal to recall Pompey at the head of his Army frustrated.—His Arrival in Italy.—And Triumph. - - 358

CHAP. XIX.

Transactions at Rome, and in the Provinces.—Julius Cæsar appointed, in the quality of Proprætor, to his first Province of Lusitania.— Trial of Clodius.— Proposed Adoption into a Plebeian Family, to qualify him for the Office of Tribune.—Cæsar a Candidate for the Consulship.—The Triumvirate of Cæsar, Pompey, and Crassus. —Consulship of Cæsar.—Motion of Vatinius, to confer on Cæsar, for five Years, the Command in Gaul.—Marriage of Pompey to Julia.—Of Cæsar to Calpurnia.— Plot of Vettius. — Consulate of Lucius Calpurnius and A. Gabinius.—Attack made upon Cicero.—His Exile. 388

THE

THE

HISTORY

OF THE

PROGRESS AND TERMINATION

OF THE

ROMAN REPUBLIC.

John Campbell

CHAP. X.

State of the Italian Allies, and the Views which now began to be entertained by them.—Appearance of Caius Gracchus.—Resolution to purge the City of Aliens. — Consulate and factious Motions of Fulvius Flaccus. — Conspiracy of Frigellæ suppressed.—Caius Gracchus returns to Rome.—Offers himself Candidate for the Tribunate.—Address of Cornelia.—Tribunate and Acts of Caius Gracchus.—Re-election.—Proposed to admit the Inhabitants of Italy on the Rolls of Roman Citizens.—Popular Acts of Gracchus and Livius.— The Senate begin to prevail. — Death of Caius Gracchus and Fulvius.

THE eruption of Etna, and other particulars relating to the natural history of the earth, with the mention of which we concluded our last Chapter, were confidered as prodigies,

VOL. II.   A   or

or prefages of evils which were yet to afflict the republic of Rome. At this time indeed the State of Italy feemed to have received the feeds of much trouble, and to contain ample materials of civil combuftion. Ever fince paffing the Agrarian law, the Roman citizens, for whom no provifion had been made at their return from military fervice, or who thought themfelves partially dealt with in the colonies, the leaders of tumult and faction in the city, were now taught to confider land property as their joint inheritance. They were, in imagination, diftributing their lots, and felecting their fhares.

In the mean time, the inhabitants of the Municipia, or free towns, and their diftricts, who, not being Roman citizens, took part with the State as fubjects, had reafon to dread the rapacity of fuch needy and powerful fovereigns. They themfelves likewife began to repine under the inequality of their own condition. They obferved, that while they were fcarcely allowed to retain the poffeffions of their fathers, Rome, aided by their arms, had gained that extenfive dominion, and obtained that territory, about which the poor and the rich were now likely to quarrel among themfelves. And " the Italian allies," they faid, " muft bleed in " this conteft, no lefs than they have done in the " foreign or more diftant wars of the common- " wealth." They had been made, by the profeffions of Tiberius Gracchus, to entertain hopes that every diftinction in Italy would foon be removed,

moved, that every freeman in the country would be enrolled as a citizen of Rome, and be admitted to all the powers and pretenfions implied in that defignation. The confideration of this fubject, therefore, could not long be delayed; and the Roman Senators, already ftruggling with the claims of their fellow-citizens, had an immediate ftorm to apprehend from the allies.

Tranfitions equivalent to revolution had been fo frequent in this republic, and its progrefs from fmall beginnings to a great empire had been fo rapid, that the changes to which men are expofed, and the exertions of which they are capable, no where appear fo confpicuous, nor are they any where fo diftinctly marked.

In the firft ages of Rome, the diftinctive importance of a citizen appears not to have been fenfibly felt or underftood. Conquered enemies were removed to Rome, and their captivity confifted in being forced to be Romans, a condition to which they fubmitted with great reluctance. In that period it is not to be doubted that every foreigner fettling at Rome was welcome to take his place as a Roman citizen in the affembly of the People; that many were admitted into the Senate [1], and fome even were placed on the throne [2]. It is likely alfo, that the firft colonies confidered themfelves as detached from the city, and as forming cantons apart; for we find them, like the other

[1] The Claudian family were aliens.

[2] Tarquinius Prifcus was of Greek extraction and an alien from Tarquinii.

other States of Italy, occasionally at war with the Romans.

But when the sovereignty of Italy came to be established at Rome, and was there actually exercised by the collective body of the People, the inhabitants of the colonies, it is probable, laid claim to their votes at elections, and presented themselves to be inrolled in the Tribes. They felt their own consequence and their superiority over the Municipia, or free towns in their neighbourhood, to whom, as a mark of distinction and an act of munificence, some remains of independence had been left. Even in this state, the rolls of the People had been very negligently made up, or preserved. The Kings, the Consuls, the Censors, who were the officers, in different ages of the State, entrusted with the musters, gave the privilege of citizens to such as presented themselves, or to such as they were pleased to receive on the rolls. One Consul invited all the free inhabitants of Latium to poll in the assemblies of the People; another rejected them, and in time of elections forbad them the city. But notwithstanding this prohibition, aliens who had been brought to Rome even as captives, were suffered by degrees to mix with the citizens [1]. The inhabitants of the free towns, removing to Rome upon any creditable footing, found easy admission among the members of some tribe; but from the facility of this admission, the towns complained they were depopulated; and the Senate at last, sensible of the abuse,

[1] This happened particularly in the case of the Campanians.

abufe, endeavoured to fhut the gates of their city by repeated fcrutinies, and the prohibition of furreptitious enrolments: but in vain. The practice ftill continued, and the growing privilege, diftinction, and eminence of a Roman citizen, made that title become the great object of ambition to individuals, and to entire cantons. It had already been extended to diftricts whofe inhabitants were not diftinguifhed by any fingular merit towards the Roman State. In this refpect all the allies were nearly equal.; they had regularly compofed at leaft one half in every Roman army, and had borne an equal fhare in all the dangers and troubles of the commonwealth; and, from having valued themfelves of old on their feparate titles and national diftinctions, they began now to afpire to a fhare in the fovereignty of the empire, and wifhed to fink for ever their municipal defignations under the general title of Romans.

Not only the great power that was enjoyed in the affembly of the People, and the ferious privileges that were beftowed by the Porcian law, but even the title of citizen in Italy, of legionary foldier in the field, and the permiffion of wearing the Roman toga or gown, were now ardently coveted as marks of dignity and honour. The city was frequented by perfons who hoped feparately to be admitted in the Tribes, and by numbers who crowded from the neighbouring cantons, on every remarkable day of affembly, ftill flattering themfelves, that the expectations which Gracchus had

given

CHAP X.

U. C. 627.
Confuls;
M. Emilius Lepidus, L. Aurelius Oreftes.

given on this important fubject might foon be fulfilled.

In this ftate of affairs, the Senate authorifed Junius Pennus, one of the Tribunes, to move the People for an edict to prohibit, on days of election or public affembly, this concourfe of aliens, and requiring all the country towns in Italy to recall their denizens, who had left their own corporations to act the part of citizens at Rome.

On this occafion, Caius Gracchus, the brother of the late unfortunate Tribune, ftood forth, and made one of the firft exhibitions, in which he difplayed the extent of his talents, as well as made known the party he was likely to efpoufe in the commonwealth. Being about twenty years of age when the troubles occafioned by his elder brother had fo much difturbed the republic, and ended fo fatally for himfelf, this young man retired upon that cataftrophé from the public view, and made it uncertain whether the fufferings of his family might not deter him, not only from embracing like dangerous counfels, but even from entering at all on the fcene of political affairs. His retirement, however, he had employed in fuch ftudies as were then come into repute, on account of their importance, as a preparation for the bufinefs of the courts of juftice, of the Senate, or the popular affemblies; and the firft public appearance he made gave evident proof of the talents he had acquired for thefe feveral departments. His parts feemed to be quicker, and his fpirit more ardent,

than

OF THE ROMAN REPUBLIC.

than thofe of his brother Tiberius; and the people conceived hopes of having their pretenfions revived, and more fuccefsfully conducted, than they had been under any former leader. The caufe of the country towns, in which he now engaged, was fpecious, but as the part he took in it was likely to form a new and a numerous party, prepared for every factious attempt, and as he profeffed to make way for the promifcuous admiffion of ftrangers on the rolls of the People; a meafure which tended fo much to diftract the republic, to diminifh the confequence of thofe who were already citizens, the argument in favour of the refolution to purge the city of aliens prevailed, and an act to that purpofe now moved in the affembly of the People, accordingly paffed [1].

It deferves to be recorded, that amidft the inquiries fet on foot in confequence of this edict, or about this time, Perperna, the father of a late Conful [2], was claimed by one of the Italian corporations, and found not to have been a citizen of Rome. His fon, whom we have already mentioned, having vanquifhed and taken Ariftonicus, the pretended heir of Attalus, died in his command at Pergamus; he is accordingly faid to have been a rare example of the caprice of fortune, in having

[1] Sextus Pompeius Feftus in voce Republica. Cicero in Bruto in Officiis, lib. iii.

[2] Valerius Maximus, lib. iii. c. 4.

CHAP. having been a Roman Conful, though not a Ro-
X. man citizen. An example which may farther confirm what has been already obferved of the latitude
which officers took in conducting the Cenfus.

The fires of fedition which had fometime preyed on the commonwealth, were likely to break
out with increafing force upon the promotion of
Fulvius Flaccus to the dignity of firft magiftrate.

U. C. 628. This factious citizen had blown up the flame with
M. Plautius
Hipfius, M. Tiberius Gracchus, and having fucceeded him in
Fulvius
Flaccus. the commiffion for executing the Agrarian law,
never failed to carry the torch wherever matter of
inflammation or general combuftion could be
found. By his merit with the popular party he
had attained his prefent eminence, and was determined to preferve it by continuing his fervices.

Leges Ful- He accordingly began the functions of his office by
viæ. propofing a law to communicate the freedom of
the city to the allies or free inhabitants of Italy;
a meafure which tended to weaken the power of
the Senate, and to increafe the numbers of the People greatly beyond what could be convened in any
one collective body. Having failed in this attempt,
he fubftituted a propofal in appearance more moderate, but equally dangerous, That whoever claimed the right of citizen, in cafe of being caft by the
Cenfors, who were the proper judges, might appeal to the popular affembly [1]. This might have
conferred the power of naturalization on the leaders of faction; and the danger of fuch a meafure,
called

[1] Appian. de Bell. Civ. lib. i.

called upon the Senate to exert its authority and influence in having this motion alfo rejected.

CHAP.
X.

The Conful thus already entered on his popular career, uniting the power of fupreme magiftrate with that of a commiffioner for the execution of the Agrarian law, and likely to break through all the forms which had hitherto retarded or ftood in the way of this meafure, was with difficulty perfuaded to call a meeting of the Senate, and to take his place in that body. The whole, as foon as they were met, joined in reprefentations againft thefe dangerous meafures, and in a requeft that he would withdraw his motions. To thefe expoftulations he made no reply [1]; but an occafion foon afterwards offered, by which the Senate was enabled to divert him from thefe factious purfuits in the city. A deputation arrived from Marfeilles, then in alliance with Rome, to requeft the fupport of the republic againft the Salyii, a neighbouring nation, who had invaded their territories. The Senate gladly embracing this opportunity to find employment abroad for the Conful, decreed a fpeedy aid to the city of Marfeilles, and appointed M. Fulvius Flaccus to that fervice. Although this incident marred or interrupted for the prefent the political defigns of the Conful, yet he was induced, by the hopes of a triumph, to accept of the command which offered, and, by his abfence, to relieve the city for a while from the alarms which he had given. Caius Gracchus too was gone in the

[1] Val. Max. lib. ix. c. 5.

the rank of Proquæſtor to Sardinia; and the Senate, if they could by any pretence have kept thoſe unquiet ſpirits at a diſtance, had hopes of reſtoring the former order of the commonwealth.

In this interval ſome laws are ſaid to have paſſed reſpecting the office and conduct of the Cenſors. The particulars are not mentioned; but the object probably was, to render the magiſtrate more circumſpect in the admiſſion of thoſe who claimed to be numbered as citizens. Such at leaſt was likely to be the policy of the State in the abſence of demagogues, who, by propoſing to admit the allies on the rolls of the People, had awakened dangerous pretenſions in every corner of Italy. It ſoon appeared how ſeriouſly theſe pretenſions were adopted by the country towns; for the inhabitants already beſtirred themſelves, and were beginning to deviſe how they might extort by force what they were not likely to obtain with conſent of the original citizens of Rome. A ſuſpicion having ariſen of ſuch treaſonable concerts forming at Fregellæ [1], the Prætor Opimius had a ſpecial commiſſion to inquire into the matter, and to proceed as he ſhould find the occaſion required. Having ſummoned the chief magiſtrate of the place to appear before him, he received from this officer, upon a promiſe of ſecurity to his own perſon, full information of the combinations that had been forming againſt the government of Rome. So inſtructed, the Prætor aſſembled ſuch a force as was neceſſary to ſupport him

[1] A municipal town of the Liris, now Monte Corvo on the Garighano.

OF THE ROMAN REPUBLIC.

him in afferting the authority of the State; and thinking it neceffary to give a ftriking example in a matter of fo infectious and fo dangerous a nature, he ordered the place to be razed to the ground[1].

By this act of feverity, the defigns of the allies were for a while fufpended, and might have been entirely fuppreffed, if the factions at Rome had not given them frefh encouragement and hopes of fuccefs or impunity. This tranfaction was fcarcely paft, when Caius Gracchus appeared in the city to folicit the office of Tribune; and, by his prefence, revived the hopes of the allies. Having obferved, that the Proconful Aurelius Cotta, under whom he was acting as Proquæftor in Sardinia, inftead of being recalled, was continued in his command, and furnifhed with reinforcements and fupplies of every fort as for a fervice of long duration; and fufpecting, that this meafure was pointed againft himfelf, and proceeded from a defign to keep him at a diftance from the popular affemblies, he quitted his ftation in Sardinia, and returned to Rome without leave. Being called to account by the Cenfors for deferting his duty; he defended himfelf with fuch ability and force, as greatly raifed the expectations which had already been entertained by his party[2].

The law, he faid, required him only to carry arms ten years, he had actually carried them twelve years; although he might legally have quitted his ftation

CHAP. X.

U. C. 629.
C. Caffius Longinus,
C. Sextius Calvinus.

[1] Liv. lib. lx. Velleius Obfequens. Cic. lib. ii. De Inventione; De Finibus, v. Ibid. Rhetorius, lib. iv.

[2] Plutarch. in C. Gracchо.

CHAP. ſtation of Quæſtor at the expiration of one year,
X. yet he had remained in it three years. However
willing the Cenſors might have been to remove this
turbulent ſpirit from the commonwealth, they were
too weak to attempt any cenſure in this ſtate of his
cauſe, and in the preſent humour of the People.
They endeavoured, in vain, to load him with a
ſhare in the plot of Fregellæ; he ſtill exculpated
himſelf: and, if he had poſſeſſed every virtue of
a citizen, in proportion to his reſolution, application, eloquence, and even ſeverity of manners, he
might have been a powerful ſupport to the State.
In a ſpeech to the People, on his return from Sardinia, he concluded with the following remarkable
words: " The purſe which I carried full to the
" province, I have brought empty back. Others
" having cleared the wine caſks which they carried
" from Italy, bring them back from the provinces
" repleniſhed with ſilver and gold [1]."

In declaring himſelf a candidate for the office of
Tribune, Caius Gracchus profeſſed his intention to
propoſe many popular acts. The Senators exerted all their influence to diſappoint his views; but
ſuch were the expectations now entertained in
Italy, that multitudes crowded to the election in
greater numbers than could find place in the public
ſquare. His partizens handed and reached out their
ballots at the windows and over the battlements;
but Gracchus, though elected, was, in conſequence
of

[1] A. Gellius, lib. xv. c. 12.

of the oppofition he met with, only fourth in the CHAP. X.
lift [1].

Cornelia, the fifter of one Scipio Africanus, and the mother-in-law of the other, but ftill better known as the mother of the Gracchi, who, ever fince the death of her fon Tiberius, lived in retirement in Campania, upon hearing of the career which her fon, Caius, was likely to run, alarmed at the renewal of a fcene which had already occafioned her fo much forrow, expoftulated with him on the courfe he was taking; and, in an unaffected and paffionate addrefs, fpoke that ardent zeal for the republic, by which the more refpectable citizens of Rome had been long diftinguifhed.

This high-minded woman, on whom the entire care of her family had devolved by the death of her hufband, whilft the children were yet in their infancy, or under age, took care, with unufual attention, to have them educated for the rank they were to hold in the State, and did not fail even to excite their ambition. When Tiberius, after the difgrace of Mancinus, appeared to withdraw from the road of preferments and honours, "How "long," fhe faid, "fhall I be diftinguifhed as the "mother-in-law of Scipio, not as the mother of "the Gracchi?" This latter diftinction, however, fhe came to poffefs; and it has remained with her name, but from circumftances and events which this refpectable perfonage by no means appeared to defire. In one fragment of her letters to Caius,
which

[1] Plutarch, Appian, Orofius, Eutrop. Obfequens.

which is ftill preferved, " You will tell me," fhe faid, " that it is glorious to be revenged of our " enemies. No one thinks fo more than I do, if " we can be revenged without hurt to the repub- " lic; but if not, often may our enemies efcape. " Long may they be fafe, if the good of the com- " monwealth requires their fafety." In another letter, which appears to be written after his inten- tion of fuing for the Tribunate was declared, fhe accofts him to the following purpofe: " I take " the gods to witnefs, that, except the perfons " who killed my fon Tiberius, no one ever gave " me fo much affliction as you now do in this mat- " ter. You, from whom I might have expected " fome confolation in my age, and who, furely, of " all my children, ought to be moft careful not to " diftrefs me! I have not many years to live. Spare " the republic fo long for my fake. Shall I never " fee the madnefs of my family at an end? When " I am dead, you will think to honour me with a " parent's rites; but what honour can my memo- " ry receive from you, by whom I am abandoned " and difhonoured while I live? But, may the " gods forbid you fhould perfift! if you do, I " fear the courfe you are taking leads to remorfe " and diftraction, which will end only with your " life [1]."

Thefe remonftrances do not appear to have had any effect. Caius, upon his acceffion to the Tri- bunate,

[1] Fragmenta Corn. Nepotis ab Andrea Scotto collecta, edita cum fcriptis Corn. Nepotis.

bunate, proceeded to fulfil the expectations of his party. The Agrarian law, though still in force, had met with continued interruption and delay in the execution. It was even falling into neglect. Caius thought proper, as the first act of his magistracy, to move a renewal and confirmation of it, with exprefs injunctions, that there should be an annual diftribution of land to the poorer citizens [1]. To this he fubjoined, in the firft year of his office, a variety of regulations tending either to increafe his own popularity, or to diftinguifh his adminiftration. Upon his motion, public granaries were erected, and a law was made, that the corn should be iffued from thence monthly to the People, two parts in twelve under the prime or original coft [2].

This act gave a check to induftry, which is the beft guardian of manners in populous cities, or wherever multitudes of men are crowded together.

Caius likewife obtained a decree, by which the eftates of Attalus, king of Pergamus, lately bequeathed to the Romans, fhould be let in the manner of other lands under the infpection of the Cenfors; but the rents, inftead of being made part of the public revenue, fhould be allotted for the maintenance of the poorer citizens [3].

Another, by which any perfon depofed from an office

marginalia: CHAP. X. Lex Sempronia agraria. Lex frumentaria.

[1] Liv. lib. lx. Velleius, lib. ii. Hyginus de Limitibus. Appian, de vir. fis illuftribus.

[2] Semiffe et tricenti, for a half and a third, &c. Liv. Plutarch Appian. Ibid.

[3] Florus, lib. iii. c. 15. Cicer. in Verrem.

office of magiſtracy by the People, was to be deemed for ever diſqualified to ſerve the republic in any other ſtation. This act was intended to operate againſt Octavius, who, by the influence of Tiberius, had been degraded from the office of Tribune; and the act took its title from the name of the perſon againſt whom it was framed [1].

To theſe were joined, an act to regulate the conditions of the military ſervice [2], by which no one was obliged to enter before ſeventeen years of age, and by which Roman ſoldiers were to receive cloathing as well as pay [3]; poſſibly the firſt introduction of a uniform into the Roman legions: a circumſtance which, in modern times, is thought ſo eſſential to the character of troops, or the appearance of an army.

By the celebrated law of Porcius, which allowed of an appeal to the People, every citizen had a remedy againſt any oppreſſive ſentence or proceeding of the executive magiſtrate; but this did not appear to Gracchus a ſufficient reſtraint on the officers of State. He propoſed to have it enacted, that no perſon, under pain of a capital puniſhment, ſhould at all proceed againſt a citizen without a ſpecial commiſſion or warrant from the People to that effect. And he propoſed to give this law a retroſpect, in order to comprehend Popilius Lænas [4], who, being Conſul in the year after the troubles

[1] Privilegium in Octavium.　　[2] De militum commodis.
[3] Plutarch. in C. Graccho.—Lex Sempronia de libertate civium.
[4] Cicer. in Cluentio; pro Rabino; pro domo ſua.

OF THE ROMAN REPUBLIC.

troubles occasioned by Tiberius Gracchus, had, under the authority of the Senate alone, proceeded to try and condemn such as were accessory to that sedition. Lænas perceived the storm that was gathering against him, and chose to avoid it by a voluntary exile. This act was indeed almost an entire abolition of government, and a bar to the most ordinary measures, required for the peace of the commonwealth. A popular faction could withhold every power, which, in their apprehension, might be employed against themselves; and in their most pernicious designs had no interruption to fear from the Dictator named by the Senate and Consuls, nor from the Consul armed with the authority of the Senate for the suppression of disorders; a resource to which the republic had frequently owed its preservation. But as we find no change in the administration of justice upon this new regulation, it is probable that the absurdity of the law prevented its effect.

While Gracchus thus proposed to make all the powers of the State depend for their existence on the occasional will of the People, he meant also to render the assemblies of the People themselves more democratical, by stripping the higher classes of any prerogative, or influence they might derive from mere precedence, in leading the public decisions. The Centuries being hitherto called to vote in the order of their classes, those of the first or highest class, by voting first, set an example which influenced

enced the whole [1]. To obviate which for the future, the Centuries, by the ſtatute of Gracchus, were required, in every queſtion, to draw lots for the prerogative, or firſt place in the order of voting, and to declare their ſuffrage in the place they had drawn.

Under this active Tribune, much public buſineſs, that uſed to paſs through the Senate, was engroſſed by the popular aſſemblies. Even in the form of theſe aſſemblies, all appearance of reſpect to the Senate was laid aſide. The Roſtra, or platform on which the preſiding magiſtrate ſtood, was placed in the middle of an area, of which one part was the market-place, ſurrounded with ſtalls and booths for merchandize, and the courts of juſtice; the other part, called the Comitium, was open to receive the People in their public aſſemblies; and on one ſide of it, fronting the Roſtra, or bench of the magiſtrates, ſtood the Curia, or Senate-houſe. The People, when any one was ſpeaking, ſtood partly in the market-place, and partly in the Comitium. The ſpeakers directed their voice to the Comitium, ſo as to be heard in the Senate. This diſpoſition, Gracchus reverſed; and directing his voice to the Forum, or market-place, ſeemed to diſplace the Senate, and to deprive that body of their office as watchmen and guardians of the public order in matters that came before the popular aſſemblies [2].

At

---

[1] The firſt Century was called the Prerogativa.

[2] M. Varro de Re Ruſtica, lib. i. c. 2. Cic. de Amicitia. Plutarch. in vit. Caii Gracchi.

At the time that the Tribune Caius Gracchus engaged the minds of his contemporaries, and furnished history chiefly with these effects of his factious and turbulent spirit, it is observed, that he himself executed works of general utility; bridges highways, and other public accommodations throughout Italy. That the State having carried its arms, for the first time, beyond the maritime extremity of the Alps, happily terminated the war with the Salyii, a nation of Gaul, whose territory in the sequel became the first province of Rome in that country. And that, in consequence of what passed in this quarter, Caius Sextius, Consul of the preceding year, was authorised to place a colony in the neighbourhood of the hot springs, which, from his name, were called the Aquæ Sextiæ, and are still known by a corruption of the same appellation [1].

From Asia, at the same time, it was reported, that Ariarathes, the king of Cappadocia, and ally of the Romans, was murdered, at the instigation of Mithridates, king of Pontus, whose sister he had married; that the murdered Prince had left a son for whom Mithridates affected to secure the kingdom; but that the widowed queen having fallen into the hands of Nicomedes, king of Bythinia, this prince, in her right, had taken possession of Cappadocia, while Mithridates, in name of his nephew, was hastening to remove him from thence. On this subject a resolution was adopted in the assembly of the People at Rome, that both Nicomedes

[1] At Aix, in Provence.

CHAP.
X.
medes and Mithridates fhould be required immediately to evacuate Cappadocia, and to withdraw their troops. This refolution Caius Gracchus oppofed with all his eloquence and his credit, charging his antagonifts aloud with corruption, and a clandeftine correfpondence with the agents, who, on different fides, were now employed at Rome in foliciting this affair. "None of us," he faid, "ftand
"forth in this place for nothing. Even I, who de-
"fire you to put money in your own coffers, and to
"confult the intereft of the State, mean to be paid,
"not with filver or gold indeed, but with your
"favour and a good name. They who oppofe this
"refolution likewife covet, not honours from you,
"but money from Nicomedes; and they who fup-
"port it, expect to be paid by Mithridates, not by
"you. As for thofe who are filent, they, I be-
"lieve, underftand the market beft of all. They
"have heard the ftory of the poet, who being vain
"that he had got a great fum of money for re-
"hearfing a tragedy, was told by another, that
"it was not wonderful he had got fo much for
"talking, when I, faid the other, who it feems
"knew more than he was wifhed to declare, have
"got ten times as much for holding my tongue.
"There is nothing that a king will buy at fo
"great a price, on occafion, as filence [1]."

Such, at times, was the ftyle in which this popular orator was pleafed to addrefs his audience. Individuals are won by flattery; the multitude by buffoonry

[1] A. Gellius, lib. ii. c. 10.

buffoonry and fatire. From the tendency of this fpeech, it appears to have been the opinion of Gracchus, not that the Romans fhould fequefter the kingdom of Cappadocia for the heirs of Ariarathes, but that they fhould feize it for themfelves. The queftion, however, which now arofe relating to the fucceffion to this kingdom, laid the foundation of a tedious and bloody war, of which the operations and events will occur in their place.

Gracchus, on the approach of the election of Confuls, employed all his credit and influence to fupport Caius Fannius, in oppofition to Opimius, who, by his vigilance and activity in fuppreffing the treafonable defigns of the allies at Fregellæ, had incurred the difpleafure of the popular party; and Fannius being accordingly chofen, together with Cn. Domitius Ahenobarbus, Gracchus proceeded to offer himfelf as a candidate to be re-elected into the office of Tribune. In this he followed the example of his brother Tiberius in a ftep, which, being reckoned illegal as well as alarming, was that which haftened his ruin. An attempt had been fince made by Papirius Carbo to have the legality of fuch re-elections acknowledged; but this having failed, Caius Gracchus, with great addrefs, inferted in one of his popular edicts, a claufe declaring it competent for the People to re-elect a Tribune, in cafe he fhould need a continuation of his power in order to fulfil his public engagements. To avail himfelf of this claufe, he now declared, that his views in behalf of the

CHAP. X.

U. C. 639. C. Fannius, Cn. Domitius Ahenobarbus.

People

CHAP. X.

People were far from being accomplished. Under this pretence he obtained a preference to one of the new candidates, and greatly strengthened the the tribunitian power by the prospect of its repeated renewals, and duration for an indefinite time.

After his re-election, Caius, continuing his administration as before upon the same plan of animosity to the Senate, obtained a law to deprive that body of the share which his brother had left them in the courts of justice; and ordaining, that the judges, for the future, should be draughted from the Equestrian order alone, a class of men, who, being left out of the Senate, and of course not comprehended in the laws that prohibited commerce, had betaken themselves, as has been observed[1], to lucrative professions, were the farmers of the revenue, the contractors for the army, and, in general, the merchants who conducted the whole trade of the republic. Though they might be confidered as neutral in the disputes of the Senate and People, and therefore impartial where the other orders were biassed, there was no class of men, from their ordinary habits, more likely to prostitute the character of judges for interest or actual hire. This revolution in the courts of justice accordingly may have contributed greatly to hasten the approaching corruption of manners, and the disorders of the state.

Lex Sem-pronia Judiciaria.

Lex de Provinciis ordinandis.

The next ordinance prepared by Gracchus, or ascribed to him, related to the nomination of officers

[1] Page 278.

OF THE ROMAN REPUBLIC.

ficers to govern the provinces; and, if it had been strictly obferved, might have made fome compenfation for the former. The power of naming fuch officers was committed to the Senate, and the arrangements were to be annually made before the election of Confuls. This continued to be law, but was often over-ruled by the People².

In the fame year, the boldeft and moft dangerous project ever formed by any popular leader, that of extending the roll of Citizens to all the Italian allies, already attempted by Fulvius Flaccus, was again renewed by Caius Gracchus; and by the utmoft exertion of the vigilance and authority of the Senate, with great difficulty prevented.

The rumour of this project having brought multitudes to Rome, the Senate thought it neceffary to give the Confuls in charge, that on the day this important queftion was to come on, they fhould clear the city of all ftrangers, and not fuffer any aliens to remain within four miles of the walls. While this bufinefs remained in fufpence, Gracchus flattered the poorer citizens with the profpect of advantageous fettlements, in certain new colonies, of fix thoufand men each, which he propofed to plant in the diftricts of Campania and Tarentum, the beft cultivated and moft opulent parts of Italy, and in colonies, which he likewife propofed to fend abroad into fome of the richeft provinces.

B 4   Such

² Florus, lib. iv. c. 13. Salluft. de Bell. Jugurth. No. 621. Cicero de Provinciis Confularibus.

CHAP. X. Such settlements had been formerly made to occupy and secure some recent conquest abroad; they were now calculated to serve as allurements to popular favour, and as a provision, made by the leaders of faction, for their own friends and adherents at Rome.

The Senate, attacked by such popular arts, resolved to retort on their adversaries; and for this purpose encouraged Marcus Livius, another of the Tribunes, and probably jealous of Gracchus, to take such measures as should, if possible, supplant him in the favour of the People. Livius, accordingly, professing to act in concert with the Senate, proposed a number of acts: one to conciliate the minds of the allies, by giving them, while they served in the army, the same exemption from corporal punishment, which the Roman citizens had enjoyed.

Lex Livia de Tergo Civium Latini Nominis.

Another for the establishment of twelve different colonies, each of three thousand citizens. But what, possibly, had the greatest effect, because it appeared to exceed in munificence all the edicts of Gracchus, was an exemption of all those lands, which should be distributed in terms of the late Sempronian Law, from all quit-rents and public burdens, which had hitherto, in general, been laid on all possessions that were held from the public [1]. It was proposed to name ten commissioners to distribute lands thus unincumbered to the People; and three colonies are mentioned, Syllaceum, Tarentum, and Neptunia or Pestum, as having been actually

[1] Plutarch. Paulus Minutius de Legibus Romanis

actually sent abroad in this year, and probably on these terms.

About the same time it was decreed, that the city of Carthage should be rebuilt for the reception of a colony of six thousand Roman citizens. This decree bears the name, not of Sempronius or of Livius, but of Rubrius, another Tribune of the same year.

The Senate readily agreed to the settlement of these colonies, as likely to divide the popular favour, to carry off a number of the more factious citizens, and to furnish an opportunity likewise of removing from the city, for some time, the popular leaders themselves, under pretence of employing them to conduct and to settle the families destined to form those establishments. Accordingly, Caius Gracchus, and Fulvius Flaccus, late Consul, and now deeply engaged in all these factious measures, were destined to take charge of the new colonists, and to superintend their settlement [1].

In the mean time, the Senate, in the election of Opimius to the Consulship of the following year, carried an object of the highest importance to the reputation and interest of their party, and by the authority of this magistrate, conceived hopes of being able to combat the designs of Gracchus more effectually than they had hitherto done. Opimius was accordingly retained in the administration of affairs in Italy, while his colleague, Fabius, was appointed to command in Gaul.

CHAP. X.

Lex Rubria.

U. C. 632.
Con. L. O-
pimius, Q.
F-b, Max-
imus.

Caius

[1] Plutarch. Appian Orosius.

CHAP. X.

Caius Gracchus, having the prefumption to offer himfelf a third time candidate for the office of Tribune, was rejected, and had the mortification to find, that the authority of the Senate began to prevail; and, as they had credit enough to procure his exclufion from any fhare in the magiftracy, fo they might be able to fruftrate or reverfe many of the acts he had obtained in the purfuit or execution of his projects.

By the repulfe of Gracchus and his affociates, the ariftocratical party came to have a majority, even in the college of Tribunes. Queftions of legiflation were now likely to be determined in the affembly of the Centuries; and this circumftance alone, while the Senate was able to retain it, was equivalent to an entire reftitution of the ariftocratical government. The Centuries, under the leading of an active Conful, were likely to annul former refolutions with the fame decifion and rapidity with which they had been paffed. Much violence was expected, and the different parties, recollecting what had happened in the cafe of Tiberius Gracchus, and careful not to be furprifed by their antagonifts; for the moft part came to the place of affembly in bands, even under arms, and endeavoured to poffefs the advantage of the ground as in the prefence of an enemy.

Minucius, one of the Tribunes, in confequence of a refolution of the Senate, pretending that he was moved by fome unfavourable prefages, propofed a repeal or amendment of fome of the late popular

popular acts; and particularly, to change the deftination of the colony intended for Carthage, to some other place. This motion was ſtrenuouſly oppoſed by Fulvius Flaccus, and by Caius Gracchus, who treated the report of preſages from Africa as a mere fiction, and the whole deſign as proceeding from the inveterate hatred of the Nobles to the People. Before the aſſembly met, in which this queſtion was to be decided, the popular leaders attempted to ſeize the Capitol, but found themſelves prevented by the Conſul, who had already, with an armed force, ſecured that ſtation.

In the morning after they had received this diſappointment, the People being aſſembled, and the Conſul being employed in offering up the cuſtomary ſacrifices, Gracchus, with his party, came to their place in the Comitium. One of the attendants of the Conſul, who was removing the entrails of a victim, reproached Gracchus, as he paſſed, with ſedition, and in the petulance of a retainer to power, bid him deſiſt from his machinations againſt the government of the commonwealth. On this provocation, one of the party of Gracchus ſtruck the offender with his dagger, and killed him on the ſpot. The cry of murder ran through the multitude, and the aſſembly began to break up. Gracchus endeavoured to ſpeak, but could not be heard for the tumult; and all thoughts of buſineſs were laid aſide. The Conſul immediately ſummoned the Senate to meet; and having reported a murder committed in the place of aſſembly,

CHAP. X.
aſſembly, and what appeared to him the firſt act of hoſtility in a war, which the popular faction had prepared againſt the State, he received the charge that was uſual on perilous occaſions, to provide, in the manner which his own prudence ſhould direct, for the ſafety of the commonwealth. Thus authoriſed, he commanded the Senators and the Knights to arm, and made proper diſpoſitions to ſecure the principal ſtreets. Being maſter of the Capitol and Forum, he adjourned the aſſembly of the People to the uſual place on the following day, and cited the perſons accuſed of the murder that was recently committed, to anſwer for the crime which was laid to their charge.

In conſequence of this adjournment, and the Conſul's inſtructions, numbers in arms repaired to the Comitium at the hour of aſſembly, and were ready to execute ſuch orders as they might receive for the public ſafety. Gracchus and Fulvius refuſed to obey the citation they had received, and the Capitol being ſecured againſt them, they took poſt, with a numerous party in arms, on the Aventine Hill, which was oppoſite to the Capitol, and from which, though more diſtant, they equally looked down on the Circus, the Forum and the place of aſſembly.

Being again cited to appear at the Tribunal of the Roman People, they ſent a young man, one of the ſons of Fulvius, to capitulate with the Conſul, and to ſettle the terms on which they ſhould deſcend from their ſtrong-hold. To this meſſage
they

OF THE ROMAN REPUBLIC.

CHAP. X.

they were told, in return, that they muſt anſwer at the bar of the aſſembly, as criminals, not pretend to negociate with the republic, as equals; that no party, however numerous, was entitled to parley with the People of Rome; and to this anſwer the meſſenger was forbidden, at his peril, to bring any reply. The party, however, ſtill hoped to gain time, or to divide their enemies; and they ventured to employ young Fulvius again to repeat their meſſage. He was ſeized by the Conſul's order. Gracchus and Fulvius, with their adherents, were declared public enemies; and a reward was offered to the perſon who ſhould kill or ſecure them. They were inſtantly attacked, and, after a little reſiſtance, forced from their ground. Gracchus fled by the wooden bridge to the oppoſite ſide of the Tiber, and was there ſlain, either by his own hand, or by that of a faithful ſervant, who had undertaken the taſk of thus ſaving him in his laſt extremity from falling into the power of his enemies. Fulvius was dragged to execution from a bath where he attempted to conceal himſelf. The heads of both were carried to the Conſul, and exchanged for the promiſed reward.

In this fray the party of the Senate, being regularly armed and prepared for ſlaughter, cut off the adherents of Caius Gracchus and Fulvius in greater numbers than they had done thoſe of Tiberius; they killed about three thouſand two hundred and fifty in the ſtreets, and confined great numbers, who were afterwards ſtrangled in the priſons. The bodies of the ſlain, as the law ordained,

CHAP. ordained, in the cafes of treafon, being denied the
X. forms of a funeral, were caft into the river, and
their eftates confifcated [1].

The houfe of Fulvius was rafed, and the ground on which it ftood was laid open for public ufes; from thefe beginnings, it appeared that the Romans, who, in the purfuit of their foreign conquefts, had fo liberally fhed the blood of other nations, might become equally lavifh of their own.

[1] Appian. Plutarch. Orofius, lib. v. c. 11. Florus, lib. iii. c. 15. Auctor de Viris Illuftribus, c. 65.

CHAP. XI.

State of Order and Tranquillity which followed the Suppreſſion of the late Tumults.—Appearance of Caius Marius.—Foreign Wars.—Complaints againſt Jugurtha.—Appearance of the Cimbri.—War with Jugurtha.—Campaign and Treaty of Piſo.—Jugurtha came to Rome with a Safe-conduct.—Obliged to retire from thence.—Campaign of Metellus.—Of Marius.—Jugurtha betrayed by Bocchus.—His Death, after the Triumph of Marius.—This General re-elected, in order to command againſt the Cimbri.

THE popular party had, in the late tumults, carried their violence to ſuch extremes, as difguſted and alarmed every perſon who had any deſire of domeſtic peace; and in their ill-adviſed recourſe to arms, but too well juſtified the meaſures which had been taken againſt them. By this exertion of vigour, the Senate, and ordinary magiſtrates, recovered their former authority; affairs returned to their uſual channel, and the moſt perfect order ſeemed to ariſe from the late confuſions. Queſtions of legiſlation were allowed to take their riſe in the Senate, and were not carried to the People, without the ſanction of the Senate's authority. The legiſlative power was exerciſed in the aſſembly of the Centuries, and the prohibitory or defenſive function of the Tribunes, or repreſentatives of the People, without ſtopping the proceedings of government,

CHAP. XI. government, or substituting a democratical usurpation, was such as to check the abuses of executive power in the hands of the aristocracy. Even the judicative power, vested in the Equestrian order, promised to have a salutary effect, by holding a balance between the different ranks and distinctions of men in the republic.

Meanwhile the aristocratical party, notwithstanding the ascendant they had recently gained, did not attempt to rescind any of the regular institutions of Gracchus; they were contented with inflicting punishments on those who had been accessory to the late sedition, and with re-establishing such of the nobles as had suffered by the violence of the popular faction. Popilius Lænas, driven into exile by one of the edicts of Gracchus, or by the persecution to which it exposed him, was now recalled upon the motion of Calpurnius Piso one of the Tribunes [1].

U. C. 633.
Publius Manlius, and C. Papirius Carbo.

As the state of parties was in some measure reversed, Papirius Carbo, who wished to be of the winning side, thought proper to withdraw from that he had espoused; and, by the credit of those now in possession of the government, was promoted to the station of Consul; and yielded the first fruits of his conversion by defending the cause of his predecessor Opimius, who, at the expiration of his Consulate, was brought to trial for having put Roman citizens to death without the forms of law. Carbo, though himself connected with those who
suffered

[1] Cicero in Bruto.

suffered in that inftance, now pleaded the juftice and neceffity of the late military executions; and, upon this plea, obtained the acquittal of his client.

This merit on the part of Carbo, however, did not fo far cancel his former offences as to prevent his being himfelf tried and condemned in the following year, as an accomplice in the fedition of Gracchus. He was fuppofed to have been acceffary to the murder of Scipio; and his caufe not being warmly efpoufed by any party, he fell a facrifice to the imputation of this heinous crime. It is faid, that upon hearing his fentence pronounced, he killed himfelf.[i]

Octavius, one of the Tribunes of the prefent year, moved an amendment of the law obtained by Gracchus, refpecting the diftribution of corn from the public granaries, probably to eafe the treafury in part of that burden; but the particulars are unknown.

About this time appeared in the affemblies of the People the celebrated Caius Marius. Born of obfcure parents in the town of Arpinum, on the Liris[2], and formed amidft the occupations of a peafant[3], and the hardfhips of a legionary foldier, of ruftic manners, but of a refolute fpirit, and eager ambition. Without any other apparent title than that of being a denifon of Rome, he now laid claim to the honours of

CHAP. XI.

Lex Octavia Frumentaria.

---

[i] Valerius Max. lib. iii. c. 7. Cicero in Bruto.

[2] Juvenal. Sat. viii. Plin. lib. xxxiii. c. 11.

[3] The Garighano.

of the ſtate. He is remarkable for having ſuffered more repulſes in his firſt attempts to be elected into office, and for having ſucceeded more frequently afterwards, than any other Roman citizen during the exiſtence of the commonwealth.

Marius, after being diſappointed in his firſt canvas for the office of Tribune, ſucceeded in the following year. The acts which were paſſed under his Tribunate, and which bear his name, do not carry any violent expreſſions of party-ſpirit, nor give intimation of that inſatiate ambition with which he afterwards diſtreſſed his country; the firſt related to the conduct of elections, and provided ſome remedy for an evil which was complained of in the manner of ſoliciting votes. The ſpace between the rails, by which the citizens paſſed to give in their ballots, was ſo broad as to admit, not only thoſe who came to vote, but the candidates alſo, with their adherents and friends, who came to importune and to overawe the People in the very act of giving their ſuffrage. Marius propoſed to put an end to this practice, and to provide for the entire uninfluenced freedom of election, by narrowing the entrance, ſo that only the voters could paſs. A party of the Nobles, with Aurelius Cotta the Conful at their head, not knowing with what a reſolute ſpirit they were about to contend, being averſe to this reformation, prevailed on the Senate to withhold its aſſent, without which any regular queſtion on this ſubject could not be put to the People. But Marius,

Lex Maria de ſuffragiis.

in the character of Tribune, threatened the Consul with immediate imprisonment, if he did not move the Senate to recall its vote. The matter being reconsidered, Lucius Metellus, who was first on the Rolls, having given his voice for affirming the first decree, was ordered by Marius into custody; and there being no Tribune to intercede for him, must have gone to prison, if the dispute had not terminated by the majority agreeing to have the matter carried to the People, as Marius proposed, with the sanction of the Senate's authority.

In another of the acts of Marius the republic was still more indebted to his wisdom and courage, in withstanding an attempt of one of his colleagues to flatter the indigent citizens at the expence of the public treasury, by lowering the terms on which corn, in pursuance of an order recently obtained by Octavius, was distributed from the granaries. This was an ordinary expedient of Tribunitian faction. Marius opposed it as of dangerous consequence. And his conduct in this matter marked him out as one not to be awed by clamour, and a person, who, into whatever party he should be admitted, was destined to govern. The times indeed were likely to give more importance to his character as a soldier than as a citizen; and in that he was still farther raised above the censure of those who were inclined to revile or undervalue what were called his upstart pretensions[1].

[1] Plutarch, in Mario.

CHAP. XI.   From the time that the Romans firſt paſſed into the Tranſalpine Gaul, as auxiliaries to the republic of Marſeilles, they had maintained in that neighbourhood a certain military eſtabliſhment; and, by planting colonies at convenient ſtations, ſhewed their intention of retaining poſſeſſions on that ſide of the Alps. Betultus, or Betultich, a prince of the country, who was ſuppoſed to have a force at command of two hundred thouſand men, attempted to expel theſe intruders, but was defeated, firſt by the Proconſul Fabius, afterwards by Domitius Ahenobarbus, who found in their conflicts with this enemy the occaſion of their reſpective triumphs. This prince himſelf became a captive to Domitius, and was carried to Rome, where he was led in proceſſion, diſtinguiſhed by his painted arms and his chariot of ſilver, the equipage in which it was ſaid he uſually led his army to battle[1].

U. C. 633.   It appears that the Romans had availed themſelves of their poſſeſſions in Africa, to be ſupplied with elephants from thence, and theſe they employed in the firſt wars they made in Gaul; for the victory of Domitius is attributed to the effect that was produced by theſe animals[2].

Quintus Marcius ſucceeded Domitius in the command of the troops which were employed in Gaul, and continued to gain ground on the natives,

---
[1] Velleius Pater. Ammianus Marcell. lib. xv. fine. Pædianus in Verrinam Secundam   Val. Max. lib. v. c. 9.
[2] Seutonius in Vita Neronis.

tives, who took arms from different cantons fucceffively againſt him. He planted a colony at
Narbo, to ſtrengthen the frontier of the newly-
acquired province on one fide; and, as the Romans had hitherto always paſſed by fea into that
country, he endeavoured to open a paſſage by the
Alps, in order to have a communication by land
with Italy on the other. In the courſe of theſe
operations the Stæni, an Alpine nation that obſtructed his march, was entirely cut off.

About this time the Roman generals obtained
their triumphs on different quarters, in the Bali-
ares and in Dalmatia; as well as in Gaul: and the
republic did not meet for ſome years with an enemy able to refiſt her power, except on the fide
of Thrace and the Iſter or Danube, where a Proconſul of the name of Cato was defeated; and
where a refiſtance was for ſome years kept up by
the natives.

But of the foreign affairs which now occupied
the attention of the Romans, the moſt memorable
was that which aroſe from the conteſt of pretenders
to the crown of Numidia, which, by the death of
Micipſa, the ſon and ſucceſſor of Maſſiniſſa, came to
be difpoſed of about this time. The late king had
two ſons, Adherbal and Hiempſal. He had likewife
adopted Jugurtha, the natural ſon of his brother
Manaſtabal, whom he had employed at the head of
his armies, thinking it ſafer to gain him by good
offices, than to provoke him by a total excluſion
from favour. This monarch had formed a project,

ject, frequent in barbarous times, but always ruinous, to divide his territories; and he hoped that, while he provided for his own sons, he should secure to them, from motives of gratitude, the protection and good offices of Jugurtha, whom he admitted to an equal share with them in the partition of his kingdom. The consequences of this mistaken arrangement soon appeared in the distractions that followed, and which arose from the ambition of Jugurtha, who, not content with his part of the kingdom, aspired to make himself master of the whole. For this purpose he formed a secret design against the lives of both the brothers, of whom the younger, Hiempsal, fell into a snare, which was laid for him, and was killed. Adherbal, being more cautious, obliged his crafty enemy to declare himself openly, took the field against him with all the forces he could raise, but was defeated, and obliged to take refuge in the Roman province, and from thence thought proper to pass into Italy, in order to lay his complaints before the Senate and People of Rome.

Massinissa, the grandfather of this injured prince, had given effectual aid to the Romans in their wars with Carthage; and, upon the final reduction of that republic, was rewarded with a considerable part of its spoils. From this time forward the Romans expected, and the kings of Numidia actually paid to them, a deference in the manner of a vassal or tributary prince to his sovereign lord. Upon the faith of this connection with

OF THE ROMAN REPUBLIC. 39

with Rome, Adherbal now carried his complaints to that city; and Jugurtha, knowing how ready the Romans were, in the character of arbitrators, to confider themfelves as the fovereign among nations, thought proper to fend a deputation on his own part, to counteract the reprefentations of his rival.

This crafty Numidian had ferved under Scipio at the fiege of Numantia, where he had an opportunity of obferving the manners and difcipline of the Romans, and accommodated himfelf to both. He was equally diftinguifhed by his implicit fubmiffion to command, as by his impetuous courage, and by the ability of his conduct in every emergence. He had even then probably directed his views to the fucceffion which was likely to fall into weak or incapable hands, and faw of what confequence the Romans might prove in deciding his fortunes. He had ftudied their character, and had already marked out the line he was to follow in conducting his affairs with them. They appeared to be a number of fovereigns affembled together, able in council and formidable in the field; but, in comparifon to the Africans in general, open, undefigning and fimple. With the pride of monarchs they began, he imagined, to feel the indigence of courtiers, and were to be moved by confiderations of intereft rather than force. His commiffioners were now accordingly furnifhed with ample prefents, and with the means of gratifying the principal perfons at Rome in a manner that was fuited to their respective ranks and to their influence in the state.

In the choice of this plan Jugurtha, like most politicians that refine too much, had formed a system with great ingenuity, and spoke of it with a specious wit; but had not taken into his account the whole circumstances of the case in which he engaged. Rome, he used to say, was a city to be sold. But he forgot that, though many Romans could be bought, no treasure was sufficient to buy the republic; that to buy a few, made it necessary for him to buy many more; that as he raised expectations, the number of expectants increased without limit; that the more he gave, the more he was still expected to give; that in a state which was broke into factions, if he gained one party by his gifts, that alone would be sufficient to rouse up another against him. And accordingly, after lavishing his money to influence the councils of Rome, he was obliged to have recourse to arms at last, and to contend with the forces of the republic, after he had exhausted his own treasure in attempting to corrupt her virtue.

Although this adventurer had his abettors at Rome, such was the injustice of his cause, or the suspicion of treachery in those who espoused it, that they durst not openly avow their intentions. They endeavoured to suspend the resolutions which were in agitation against him, and had the matter referred to ten commissioners who should go into Africa, and in presence of the parties settle the differences

OF THE ROMAN REPUBLIC. 41

differences which subsisted between them. There indeed he was supposed to have practised his art on the Roman commissioners with better success than he had experienced with the Senate and People. He prevailed upon these commissioners to agree to a partition of the kingdom, and to favour him in the lot which should be assigned to himself: knowing that force must ultimately decide every controversy which might arise on the subject, he made choice, not of the richest, but of the most warlike division; and indeed had already determined that, as soon as the Romans were gone from Africa, he should make an end of the contest by the death of Adherbal; trusting that, by continuing to use the specific which it was said he had already applied, he might prevail on the Romans to overlook what they would not, on a previous request, have permitted.

CHAP. XI.

He accordingly, soon after the departure of the Roman commissioners, marched into the territories of Adherbal, shut him up in the town of Cirta; and, while the Romans sent him repeated messages to desist, still continued the blockade, until the mercenaries of Adherbal, tired of the hardships they were made to endure, advised, and, by their appearing ready to desert, forced him to commit himself to the mercy of Jugurtha, by whom he was immediately slain.

By these events, in about seven years from the death of Micipsa, Jugurtha attained the object which he had so long desired; but the arts which
procured

CHAP. XI.

procured him a crown, likewife rendered his ftate infecure. He was difappointed in his expectation to pacify the Romans. The money he dealt went into the pockets only of a few, but his crimes roufed the indignation of the whole People. Practifed ftatefmen or politicians are feldom directed in their conduct by mere feelings of injuftice refpecting wrongs of a private nature. They have, or affect to have, reafons of ftate to fet the confideration of individuals afide. The greater part of the Roman Senate accordingly, whether acting on maxims of policy, or, according to the fcandal of the times, won by the prefents of Jugurtha, received the complaints which were lodged againft him with indifference; but the affembly of the People, moved by the cries of perfidy and murder which were raifed by the Tribunes, received the reprefentations of his conduct with indignation and rage. Thefe paffions were inflamed by oppofition to the Nobles, who were fuppofed to favour the murderer. Neither the moft deliberate Statefman nor the moft determined partizan of Jugurtha durft appear in his caufe, nor propofe to decline a war with that prince, although it was likely to be attended with confiderable difficulties; and was to be undertaken at a time when a cloud hung over Italy itfelf on the fide of Gaul, a quarter from which the Italians always expected, and often experienced, the moft terrible ftorms.

U. C. 627. About the time that Adherbal laid his complaints againft Jugurtha before the Senate of Rome,

a

a new enemy had appeared. The north of Europe, or of Asia, had cast off a swarm of its people, which, spreading to the south and to the west, was first descried by the Romans on the frontier of Illyricum, and presently drew their attention to that side. The horde thus in motion was said to consist of three hundred thousand fighting men, accompanied by their families of women and children, and covering the plains with their cattle. The Consul Papirius Carbo was ordered to take post in Illyricum, to observe the motions of this tremendous host. Alarmed by their seeming to point towards the district of Aquileia, he put himself, with too little precaution, in their way; and, unable to withstand their numbers, was overwhelmed as by a tempest.

This migrating nation the Romans have called by the name of Cimbri, without determining from whence they came. It is said that their cavalry amounted to no more than fifteen thousand; that it was their practice to despise horses, as well as the other spoils of an enemy, which they generally destroyed: and from this circumstance it may be argued, that they were not of Scythian extraction, nor sprung from those mighty plains in the northern parts of Asia, where military force has from time immemorial consisted of cavalry, and where the animal they mounted was valued above every other species of acquisition or property; and that they must have been bred rather amongst mountains and woods, where the horse is not of equal service. On their helmets,

CHAP. mets, which were crested with plumes, they car-
XI. ried the gaping jaws of wild beasts. On their
bodies they wore breast-plates of iron, had shields
painted of a conspicuous colour; and carried
two missile javelins or darts, and a heavy sword.
They collected their fighting men, for the most
part, into a solid column, equally extending every way: in one of their battles, it was reported, that the sides of this square extended thirty stadia, or between three and four miles. The
men of the foremost ranks were fastened together with chains locked to their girdles, which
made them impenetrable to every attack, and
gave them the force of a torrent, in sweeping ob-
structions before them. Such were the accounts,
whether well or ill founded, with which the Romans were alarmed on the approach of this tremendous enemy.

Although, by the defeat of Carbo, Italy lay
open to their devastations, yet they turned away
to the north and to the westward, and keeping the
Alps on their left, made their appearance again in
the neighbourhood of Narbonne, or province of
Transalpine Gaul, and from thence passed over the
Pyrenees, alarming the Roman settlements in
Spain, and keeping Rome itself in suspence, by
the uncertainty of the track they might afterwards
choose to pursue.

U. C. 642.
Pub. Cor-
nelius, Sci-
pio Nasica.
L. Culpur-
nius, Piso,
Festis.

Such was the state of affairs, when the popular
cry and generous indignation of the Roman People forced the State into a war with Jugurtha.
The

The neceffary levies and fupplies for this fer- CHAP. XI.
vice were ordered. The Conful Pifo was deftined to command, and Jugurtha could no longer
doubt that the force of the Roman republic was
to be employed againft himfelf; yet in hopes
to avert the ftorm, and relying on the arts he had
formerly practifed, which were faid to confift in
the diftribution of prefents and money, he fent
his own fon, with two proper affiftants, in quality
of ambaffadors to Rome. As foon as their arrival
was announced to the Senate, a refolution of this
body paffed, that unlefs they brought an offer
from Jugurtha to furrender his perfon and his
kingdom at difcretion, they fhould be required in
ten days to be gone from Italy.

This refolution being made known to the fon of
Jugurtha, he prefently withdrew, and was foon
followed by a Roman army, which had been already prepared to embark for Africa. The war
was conducted at firft with great vivacity and
fuccefs: but Jugurtha, by offering great public
conceffions or private gratifications, prevailed on
the Conful to negociate. It was agreed, that,
upon receiving a proper hoftage on the part of the
Romans, the king himfelf fhould repair to their
camp, in order to conclude the treaty. In the articles which were made public, the king agreed to
furrender himfelf at difcretion, and to pay a large
contribution in horfes, corn, elephants, and money;
but in fecret articles, which were drawn up at the
fame time, the Conful engaged that the perfon of

the

CHAP. XI. the king should be safe, and that the kingdom of Numidia should be secured to him.

During these transactions the time of the expiration of Piso's command drew near, and he himself was called into Italy to preside at the approaching elections. His report of the treaty with Jugurtha was received with suspicion, and the cry of corruption resumed by the popular party. " Where is this captive?" said the Tribune Memmius; " if he have surrendered himself, he will " obey your commands; send for him; question " him in respect to what is past. If he refuse to " come, we shall know what to think of a treaty " which brings impunity to Jurgurtha, princely " fortunes to a few private persons, mortification " and infamy to the Roman republic." Upon this motion the Prætor Cassius Longinus, a person of approved merit and unshaken integrity, was hastened into Africa, with positive instructions to bring the king of Numidia to Rome. By the safe conduct which Cassius brought on the part of the republic, and by his own assurances of protection, Jugurtha was prevailed on to commit himself to the faith of the Romans. He accordingly laid aside his kingly state, dismissed his attendants, and set out for Italy, determined to appear as a suppliant at Rome. Upon his arrival, being called into the public assembly, Memmius proposed to interrogate him on the subject of his supposed secret transaction with certain members of the Senate; but here Bebius, another of the Tribunes, interposed interpofed his negative; and, notwithftanding that the People exclaimed, and even menaced, this Tribune perfifted. And before this obftruction to the further examination of Jugurtha could be removed, an incident took place, which occafioned his fudden departure from Italy.

CHAP. XI.

Maffiva, the fon of Guluffa, being the grandfon and natural reprefentative of Maffiniffa, and the only perfon befide Jugurtha who remained of the royal line of Numidia, had been perfuaded by Albinus, the Conful elected for the enfuing year, to ftate his own pretenfions before the Roman Senate, and to lay claim to the crown. Jugurtha, though at Rome, and in the power of thofe who were likely to refent any infult that was offered to their government, gave a fpecimen of the bold and fanguinary counfels to which he was inclined, employing againft his competitor the ordinary arts of an African court, had him affaffinated. The crime was traced to its author, but the fafe conduct he had received could not be violated; and he was only commanded, without delay to depart from Italy. On this occafion he left Rome with that memorable faying; " Here is a city to be fold, if any buyer can be " found."

The Conful Albinus foon followed Jugurtha, to take the command of the Roman army in Africa; and being eager to perform fome notable action before the expiration of his year, which was faft approaching, he preffed on the king of Numidia, with all the forces he could affemble in the province;

U. C. 64. M. N. nu- cius Rufus, and Po.tu- mius Albi- nus.

CHAP. XI.

vince; but found that he had to do with an enemy who had the art to elude his impetuosity, and from whose apparent conduct no judgment could be formed of his real designs. This artful warrior often advanced with a seeming intention to hazard a battle, when he was most resolved to decline it; or he himself precipitantly fled, when his design was to rally and take advantage of any disorder his enemy might incur in a too eager pursuit. His offers of submission, or his threats, were equally fallacious; and he used, perhaps in common with other African princes, means to mislead his antagonist, which Europeans, antient as well as modern, have in general condemned. He made solemn capitulations and treaties with a view to break them, and considered breach of faith no more than a feint or an ambush, as a stratagem licensed in war. The Europeans have always termed it perfidy to violate the faith of a treaty, the Africans held it stupidity to be caught in the snare.

By the artifices of Jugurtha accordingly, or by the remissness of those who were opposed to him, the war was protracted for another year, and the Consul, as the time of election drew near, was recalled, as usual, to preside in the choice of his successor. At his arrival the city was in great agitation. The cry of corruption, which had been raised against many of the Nobles, on account of their supposed correspondence with Jugurtha, gave an advantage to the popular party, and they determined

mined to improve it, by raising prosecutions to the ruin of persons, either odious to the People, or obnoxious to the Equestrian order, who then had the power of judicature in their hands[1]. Three inquisitors were accordingly named by special commission to take cognizance of all complaints of corruption that should be brought before them; and this commission was instantly employed to harass the Nobility, and to revenge the blood which had been shed in the late popular tumults. Lucius Calpurnius Piso, Bestia, C. Cato, Spurius Albinus, and L. Opimius, all of consular dignity, fell a sacrifice on this occasion to the popular resentment. The Tribune Mamilius, upon whose motion this tribunal had been erected, with his associates, apprehending that, upon the expiration of their trust, the heat of the prosecutions might abate, moved the People that they might be continued in their office; and, upon finding themselves opposed by the influence of the Senate and the ordinary magistrates, they suspended, by virtue of their tribunitian prerogative, the election of Consuls, and for a whole year kept the republic in a state of absolute anarchy.

In this interval Aulus Albinus, who had been left by his brother, the late Consul, in the command of the army in Africa, determined to improve the occasion by some memorable action. He left his quarters in the winter, and marched far into the country, hoping that by force or surprise

[1] Cicero de Claris Oratoribus. Salust. in Bell. Jugurth.

prise he might possess himself of the Numidian treasures and military stores. Jugurtha encouraged him in this design, affected fear, retired with precipitation wherever the Romans presented themselves; and, to increase the presumption of their general, sent frequent messages to implore his pity.

He at the same time endeavoured to open a correspondence with Thracians and other irregulars, by whom the Roman army was attended. Some of these he corrupted; and, when he had drawn his enemy into a difficult situation, and prepared his plan for execution, he suddenly advanced in the night; and the avenues to the Roman station being occupied, as he expected, by the Thracians and Ligurians whom he had corrupted, and by whom he was suffered to pass, he surprised the legions in their camp, and drove them from thence in great confusion to a neighbouring height, where they enjoyed during the night, some respite from the attacks of the enemy; but without any resource for subsistence, or hopes of recovering their baggage.

In the morning Jugurtha desired to confer with the Prætor; and representing how much the Romans, deprived of their provision and equipage, were then in his power, made a merit of offering them quarter, on condition that they would conclude a treaty of peace, and in ten days evacuate his kingdom.

These terms were accordingly accepted: but the capitulation, when known at Rome, gave occasion

casion to much indignation and clamour. It was voted by the Senate not to be binding, and the Conful Albinus, in order to repair the lofs of the Public, and to reftore the credit of his own family, made hafty levies, with which he propofed to renew the war in Numidia. But not having the confent of the Tribunes to this meafure, he was obliged to leave his forces behind him in Italy, and joined the army in perfon without being able to bring any reinforcement. He found it in no condition to face the enemy, and was contented to remain inactive until a fucceffor fhould be named in the province.

CHAP. XI.

Refentment of the difgraces incurred in Numidia, and fear of invafion from the Cimbri, who, having traverfed Spain and Gaul, were ftill on their march, appear to have calmed for a little time the animofity of domeftic factions at Rome. The confular elections were fuffered to proceed; and the choice of the People falling on Quintus Cæcilius Metellus and M. Junius Silanus, the firft was appointed to the command of the army in Numidia, the fecond to obferve the motions of the Cimbri on the frontiers of Gaul, and to turn them afide, if poffible, from the territory of Rome. About this time thofe wandering nations had fent a formal meffage to the Romans, defiring to have it underftood on what lands they might fettle [1], or rather, over what lands they might pafs in migration with their families and herds. No return being

U. C. 644.
Q. Cæcilius Metellus Numidicus, M. Junius Silanus.

[1] Florus, lib. iii. Liv. lib. lxv.

being made to this application by the Senate, they continued to wander, and opening their paſſage by force, overcame in battle the Conſul Silanus, and, probably without intending to retain any conqueſt, paſſed on their way wherever the aſpect of the country tempted their choice.

Metellus proceeded to Africa with a conſiderable reinforcement; and, having ſpent ſome time in reſtoring the diſcipline of the army, which had been greatly neglected, and in training his new levies to the duties and hardſhips of the ſervice, he directed his march to the enemy's country, and in his way had frequent meſſages from the king of Numidia, with profeſſions of ſubmiſſion and of a pacific diſpoſition: So much, that when the Roman army entered on the territory of this prince, they found the country every where prepared to receive them in a friendly manner; the people in tranquillity, the gates of every city left open, and the markets ready to ſupply them with neceſſaries.

Theſe appearances, with the known character of Jugurtha, creating diſtruſt, only excited the vigilance of Metellus. They even provoked him to retort on the Numidian his own inſiduous arts. He accordingly tampered with Bomilcar and the other meſſengers of Jugurtha to betray their maſter, and promiſed them great rewards if they would deliver this offender into the hands of the Romans either living or dead.

Jugurtha, not confidering that his known character

CHAP.
XI

racter for falſehood muſt have deſtroyed the credit of all his own profeſſions, even if he ſhould at any time think proper to make them ſincere, and truſting to the effect of his ſubmiſſive meſſages in rendering the enemy ſecure, made a difpofition to profit by any errors they ſhould commit, and hoped to circumvent and deſtroy them on their march. For this purpoſe he waited for them on the deſcents of a high mountain, over which they were to paſs in their way to the Muthul, a river which helped to form the ſituation of which he was to avail himſelf. He accordingly lay concealed by its banks until the enemy actually fell in to the ſnare he had laid for them. And although the effect was not anſwerable to his hopes, he maintained, during the greater part of a day, with the advantage of ground and of numbers, a conteſt with troops who poſſeſſed, againſt his irregulars, a great ſuperiority of order, diſcipline, and courage; but not having found the Romans, as he expected, in any degree off their guard, he was in the event of that day's action, obliged to depart with a few horſe to a remote or interior part of his kingdom.

This victory obtained over Jugurtha, appeared to be an end of the war. His army was diſperſed, and he was left with a few horſemen, who attended his perſon, to find a place of retreat, or to chuſe a new ſtation at which to re-aſſemble his forces, if he meant to continue the war.

. The Numidians were inured to action. The frequent wars of that continent, the wild and unſettled fettled ftate of their own country, made the ufe of horfes and of arms familiar to them: but fo void was the nation of military policy, and its people fo unaccuftomed to any permanent order, that it was fcarcely poffible for the king to fight two battles with the fame army. If victorious, they withdrew with their plunder; if defeated, they fuppofed all military obligations at an end: and in either cafe, after an action, every one fled where he expected to be fooneft in fafety, or moft at liberty to avail himfelf of the fpoil he had gained.

Metellus, after the late engagement, finding no enemy in the field, was for fome time uncertain to what part of the kingdom Jugurtha had directed his flight. But having intelligence that he was in a new fituation affembling an army, and likely to form one ftill more numerous than any he had yet brought into the field, tired of purfuing an enemy on whom defeats had fo little effect, he turned away to the richer and more cultivated parts of the kingdom. Here the plunder of the country might better repay his labour, and the king, if he ventured to defend his own territory, might more fenfibly feel his defeats. Jugurtha perceiving this intention of the Roman general, drew the forces he had affembled towards the fame quarter, and foon appeared in his rear.

While Metellus was endeavouring to force the city of Zama, Jugurtha affaulted his camp, and, though repulfed from thence, took a poft, by which he made the fituation of the Romans, between

the

the town on one fide, and the Numidian army on the other, fo uneafy, as to oblige them to raife the fiege.

This the Numidian prince thought a proper opportunity to gain fome credit to his pacific profeffions. He made an offer accordingly to furrender at difcretion, and actually delivered up great part of his arms and military ftores; but this purpofe, if ever fincere, he foon retracted, and again had recourfe to arms.

The victory which had been obtained in Africa flattered the vanity of the Roman People, and procured to Metellus, in the quality of Proconful, a continuation of his former command. The troops he had pofted in Vacca being cut off by the inhabitants, he made hafty marches in the night, furprifed the place, and, without having allowed the authors of that outrage more than two days to enjoy the fruits of their perfidy, amply revenged the wrong they had done to the Roman garrifon.

But the fuccefs of Metellus did not haften the ruin of Jugurtha fo much as his own mifconduct, in the jealous and fanguinary meafures which he now took to fupprefs plots and confpiracies either real or fuppofed to be formed againft his life, by perfons the moft in his confidence.

Bomilcar, ftill carrying in his mind the offers which had been made to him by Metellus, and willing to have fome merit with the Romans, into whofe hands he and all the fubjects of Jugurtha were likely foon to fall, formed a defign againft his

his master, and drew Nabdalsa, a principal officer in the Numidian armies, to take part in the plot. They were discovered in time to prevent the execution of their design, but they made Jugurtha from thenceforward consider the camp of his own army as a place of danger to himself, rendered him distrustful, timorous, and unquiet; frequently changing his company and his quarters, his guards and his bed. Under these apprehensions, by which his mind was considerably disordered and weakened, he endeavoured, by continual and rapid motions, to make it uncertain where he should be found; and he experienced at last, that private assassination and breach of faith, although they appear to abridge the toils of ambition, are not expedient even in war; that they render human life itself, for the advantages of which war is undertaken, no longer eligible or worthy of being preserved. Weary of his anxious state, he ventured once more to face Metellus in the field, and being again defeated, fled to Thala, where he had left his children and the most valuable part of his treasure. This city too, finding Metellus had followed him, he was obliged to abandon, and, with his children and his remaining effects, fled from Numidia, first to the country of the Getuli, barbarous nations, that lived among the mountains of Atlas, south of Numidia, and whom he endeavoured to arm in his cause. From thence he fled to Bocchus king of Mauritania, whose daughter he had married; and having

OF THE ROMAN REPUBLIC. 57

ing perſuaded this prince to conſider his quarrel with the Romans as the common cauſe of all monarchies, who were likely in ſucceſſion to become the prey of this arrogant and inſatiable Power, he prevailed on the king of Mauritania to aſſemble an army, and to attempt the relief of Numidia.

Jugurtha, in conjunction with his new ally, directed his march to Cirta, and the Roman general perceiving his intention, took poſt to cover that place. But while he was endeavouring, by threats or perſuaſions, to detach the king of Mauritania from Jugurtha, he received information from Rome, that he himſelf was ſuperſeded in the command of the army; and from thenceforward, under pretence of meſſages and negotiations that were paſſing between the parties, protracted the war, and poſſibly inclined to leave it with all its difficulties entire to his ſucceſſor. His diſmiſſion was the more galling to himſelf, that it was obtained in favour of Caius Marius, who, having ſerved under him in this war, had with great difficulty, and not without ſome expreſſion of ſcorn on the part of his general, obtained leave to depart for Rome, where he meant to ſtand for the Conſulſhip. He accordingly appeared in the capacity of candidate for this honour, and by vaunting, inſtead of concealing, the obſcurity of his birth; by inveighing againſt the whole order of Nobility, their dreſs, their city manners, their Greek learning, their family images, the ſtreſs they laid on the virtue of their anceſtors to compenſate

CHAP.
XI.

CHAP. XI. penfate the want of it in themfelves; but more efpecially by arraigning the dilatory conduct of Metellus, and by promifing a fpeedy iffue to the war, if it fhould be entrufted to himfelf; a promife, to which the force and ability he had fhewn in all the ftations he had hitherto filled, procured him much credit; he fo far won upon the People, that, in oppofition to the intereft of the Nobles, and to the influence of all the leading men of the Senate, he prevailed in the election His promotion was in a particular manner offenfive to Metellus, whofe reputation he had attacked, and to whom, by an exprefs order of the People, in contempt of a different arrangement made by the Senate, he was now to fucceed.

U. C. 646.
L. Caffius
Longinus,
C. Marius.

Upon the nomination of Marius, the party who had oppofed his preferment, did not attempt to withhold the reinforcements which he afked for the fervice in which he was to command. They even hoped to increafe his difficulties, by fuffering him to augment the military eftablifhment of his province. The wealthier or more refpectable clafs of the People alone were yet admitted into the legions; and being averfe to fuch diftant fervices, were likely to conceive a diflike to the perfons by whom they were dragged from home. Marius, therefore, in making his levies, his opponents fuppofed, might lofe fome part of the popular favour which he now enjoyed, and become lefs formidable to his rivals in the State. But this crafty and daring adventurer, by flighting the laws which
excluded

excluded the necessitous citizens from serving in the legions, found in this class of the People, a numerous and willing recruit. They crowded to his standard, and filled up his army without delay, and even without offence to those of a better condition, who were pleased with the relief they obtained from this part of their public burdens.

This circumstance is quoted as a remarkable and dangerous innovation in the Roman State, and is frequently mentioned among the steps which hastened its ruin. The example, no doubt, with its consequences, may instruct nations to distinguish the military operations required at a distance, from the more important object of preservation and home-defence; so that in declining the distant service, the more respectable orders of the People may not think it necessary to abandon themselves to depredation at home. In the first ages of Rome, the citizens in political convention, were styled the Army of their Country, and such in every age is the army in whose hands the freedom of nations is secure. From the date of these levies at Rome, the sword began to pass from the hands of those who were interested in the preservation of the republic, into the hands of others who were willing to make it a prey. The circumstances of the times were such, indeed, as to give warning of the change. The service of a legionary soldier abroad, was become too severe for those of the People who could live at their ease, and it now opened to the necessitous a principal

cipal road to profit, as well as honour. Marius, to facilitate his levies, was willing to gratify both; and thus gave beginning to the formation of armies who were ready to fight for or againſt the laws of their country, and who, in the ſequel, ſubſtituted battles in the ſtreets of Rome, for the bloodleſs conteſts which, in the early ages of Rome, had ariſen from the diviſions of party.

The new Conſul, unrivalled in the favour of the People, obtained whatever he required; and, being completely provided for the ſervice to which he was deſtined, embarked for Africa, and with a great reinforcement, in a few days arrived at Uttica. Upon his arrival, the operations of the war were reſumed, and carried into the wealthieſt provinces of Numidia, where he encouraged his army with the hopes of ſpoil. The new levies though compoſed of perſons hitherto untrained and even excluded from the military ſervice, were formed by the example of the legions already in the field, and who were now well apprifed of their own ſuperiority to the African armies. Bocchus and Jugurtha, upon the approach of this enemy, thought proper to ſeparate, and took different routes into places of ſafety in the more difficult and inacceſſible parts of the country.

This ſeparation was made at the ſuggeſtion of Jugurtha, who alleged that, upon their appearing to deſpair, and to diſcontinue all offenſive operations, the Roman general would become more ſecure, and more open to ſurpriſe. But Marius,
without

without abating his vigilance, preffed where the enemy gave way, over-ran the country, and took poffeffion of the towns they had left. To rival the glory which Metellus had gained in the reduction of Thala, he ventured on a like enterprife, in the face of fimilar difficulties, by attacking Thapfa, a place furrounded with defarts, and in the midft of a land deftitute of water, and of every refource for an army. Having fucceeded in this defign, he ventured, in his return to attack another fortrefs, in which, the place being fuppofed impregnable, the royal treafures were lodged. This ftrong hold was placed on a rock, which was every where, except at one path that was fortified with ramparts and towers, faced with fteep and inacceffible cliffs. The garrifon permitted the firft approaches of the Romans with perfect fecurity, and even derifion. After fome fruitlefs attacks, Marius, under fome imputation of folly in having made the attempt, was about to defift from the enterprife, when a Ligurian, who had been ufed to pick fnails on the cliffs over which this fortrefs was fituate, found himfelf, in fearch of his prey, and by the growing facility of the afcent, led to a height from which he began to have hopes of reaching the fummit. He accordingly furmounted all the difficulties in his way; and the garrifon being then intent on the oppofite fide of the fortrefs to which the attack was directed, he returned unobferved. This intelligence he carried to Marius, and undertook to be the guide

of

of a detachment of chosen men, with an unusual number of trumpets and instruments of alarm, who were ordered to follow his directions. Marius himself, to divert the attention of the besieged, and, on receiving a signal agreed upon from within, to be ready to make a vigorous and decisive assault, advanced to the walls. The Ligurian proceeded, though with much difficulty, to fulfil the expectations he had given. The soldiers who followed him were obliged to untie their sandals and their helmets, to fling their shields and their swords, and, at difficult parts of the rock, could not be persuaded to advance until their guide had repeatedly passed and repassed in their sight, or had found stumps and points of the stone at which they could fasten ropes to aid their ascent. The summit was to be gained at last by climbing a tree which, being rooted in a cleft of the rock, grew up to the edge of the precipice. By the trunk of this tree the whole party passed, and, being as high as its branches could carry them, landed at last on the summit. They instantly sounded their trumpets and gave a sudden alarm. The besieged, who had been drawn to an opposite part of the walls to resist the enemy who there menaced an attack, were astonished with this sound in their rear, and soon after, greatly terrified with the confused flight from behind them of women, children, and men unarmed, and being at the same time vigorously pressed at their gates, were no longer able to resist, suffered the Romans to force

their

their way at this entrance, and in the end to become mafters of the fort.

While Marius was engaged in the fiege of this place, he was joined by the Quæftor Sylla, who had been left in Italy to bring up the cavalry, which were not ready to embark at the departure of the Conful. This young man was a Patrician, but of a family which had not, for fome generations, borne any of the higher offices of State. He himfelf partook in the learning which then fpread into Italy, from a communication with the Greeks, and had paffed the early part of his life in town-diffipation or in literary ftudies, of which the laft, though coming into fafhion at this time at Rome, was confidered as a fpecies of corruption almoft equal to the firft. He was yet a novice in war, but having an enterprifing genius, foon became an object of refpect to the foldiers, and of jealoufy to his general, with whom he now laid the foundation of a quarrel ftill more fatal to the commonwealth than that which had fubfifted between the prefent and preceding commander in this fervice.

The king of Numidia, ftung by the fenfe of what he had already loft, and expecting no advantage from any further delays, determined, in conjunction with his ally, to make a vigorous effort, and to oblige Marius, who was then moving towards his winter quarters, yet to hazard a battle for the prefervation of what he had acquired in the preceding campaign. The king of Mauritania,

nia, upon the late events of the war, had been inclined to return to his neutrality, or to enter on a separate treaty with the Romans; but being promised a third part of the kingdom of Numidia, in case the enemy were expelled from thence, or if the war should be otherwise brought to a happy conclusion, he once more advanced with his army, and joined Jugurtha.

The prosperous state of the Romans, undisturbed for some time by any opposition from an enemy in the field, inspired them with some degree of negligence or security, by which they were exposed to surprise. Near the close of a careless march, and about an hour before the setting of the sun, they found themselves entering among scattered parties, who, without any settled order, increased in their numbers, occupied the fields through which the Romans were to pass, and seemed to intend, by assailing them on every side, to begin the night with a scene of confusion, of which they might afterwards more effectually avail themselves in the dark. In an action begun under these disadvantages, Jugurtha flattered himself, that the Roman army might be entirely defeated, or, in a country with which they were not acquainted, and in circumstances for which they were not at all prepared, being unable to effect a retreat, be obliged to surrender at discretion.

The king, with his usual intrepidity and conduct, profited by every circumstance which presented itself in his favour. He brought the troops,

of which his army was compofed, whether Getu- CHAP.
lians or Numidians, horfe or foot, to harafs the XI.
enemy in their different ways of fighting, and
wherever they could moft eafily make their attacks.
Where a party was repulfed, he took care to replace it ; and fometimes affected to remit his ardour, or to flee with every appearance of panic, in
order to tempt the Romans to break from their
ranks. Marius, notwithftanding, with great dex-
terity and prefence of mind, maintained the form
of his march ; and, before night, got poffeffion of
fome heights on which he could reft with fafety.
He himfelf, with the infantry, chofe that which
had the fteepeft afcent, and ordered Sylla, with the
cavalry, to take his poft on a fmaller and more ac-
ceffible eminence below. That his pofition might
not be known to the enemy, he prohibited the
lighting of fires, and the ufual founding of trumpets at the different watches of the night. The
Numidians had halted on the plain where night
overtook them, and were obferved, at break of day,
repofing in great fecurity, and without any feem-
ing apprehenfion of danger from an enemy, who
was fuppofed to be flying, and who, on the preceding day, had, with fome difficulty, efcaped from
their hands. In this fituation, Marius refolved to
attack them, and gave orders, which were paffed
through the ranks, that, at a general found of the
trumpets, every man fhould ftand to his arms, and
with a great fhout, and beating on his fhield, make
an impetuous affault on the enemy. The defign,
accordingly,

CHAP. XI.

accordingly, succeeded. The Numidians, who on former occasions had often affected to flee, were driven into an actual route. Great numbers fell in the flight, and many ensigns and trophies were taken.

After this victory, Marius, with his usual precautions, and though it might be supposed that the enemy were dispersed, without remitting his vigilance, directed his march to the towns on the coast, where he intended to fix his quarters for the winter. Jugurtha, well apprised of his route, proposed again to surprise him before he should reach the end of his journey; and, for this purpose, avoided giving him any premature or unnecessary cause of alarm. He deferred his attack until the Roman army was arrived in the neighbourhood of Cirta, supposed to be the end of their labours, and near to which it was probable they would think themselves secure from any further attempts of their enemy. In the execution of this design, he, with the greatest ability, conducted his troops to the place of action, and there too made every effort of conduct and resolution. But the match being unequal, he was obliged to give up the contest; and, with his sword and his armour all bathed in blood, and almost alone, is said to have left a field, in which, for the first time, he had taken no precautions for re-assembling an army, and on which his Numidians were accordingly routed, in appearance, to rally no more.

Upon

Upon these repeated defeats, Bocchus despaired of the fortunes of Jugurtha, and sent a deputation to Marius, requesting a conference with himself, or with some of his officers. He obtained an interview with Sylla and Manlius; but, upon their arrival, had taken no fixed resolution, and was still kept in suspence, by the persuasion of those of his court who favoured the interest of Jugurtha. Marius, being continued in his command, resumed the operations of the war, and was about to attack the only place which yet remained in the hands of the enemy. When the king of Mauritania, alarmed by this circumstance, took his resolution to sue for peace, he sent a deputation of five chosen persons, first to the quarters of Marius, and, with this general's permission, ordered them to proceed from thence to Rome. These deputies, being admitted into the Senate, made offers of friendship in the name of their master; but were informed, in return, that he must give proofs of his friendly disposition to the Romans, before they could rely on his professions, or listen to any terms of peace. When this answer was reported to Bocchus, he was not at a loss to understand that the Romans wished him to deliver up the king of Numidia into their hands; and seems to have conceived the design of purchasing peace, even on these terms. Sylla being already personally known to him, he made choice of this officer, as the person with whom he would treat, and desired he might be sent to his quarters. The Roman Quæstor accordingly set out

CHAP.
XI.
U. C. 647.
C. Attilius
Serannus,
Quintus
Servilius
Cæticq.

out with a small party. On the way he was met by Volux, the son of the king of Mauritania, with a thousand horse: him he considered as of doubtful intention, whether destined to act as a friend or an enemy; but coming with professions of friendship from the king his father, and with orders to escort the Roman Quæstor, they proceeded together. On the second day after this junction, Volux came in haste to the quarters of Sylla, and informed him, that the advanced party had discovered Jugurtha posted on their route, with numbers through which they might not be able to force their way, and earnestly pressed the Roman officer to endeavour his own escape in the night.

Sylla could no longer disguise his suspicions, and, sensible that he had imprudently, without hostage or other security, ventured too far on the faith of an African prince, proudly refused to alter his march; desired that the Mauritanian prince, if he thought proper, should depart; but informing him, at the same time, that the Roman people would know how to avenge so public an insult, and would not fail to punish the perfidy of the king his father. Volux, in return, made strong protestations of innocence; and as the Roman Quæstor could not be prevailed on to save himself by flight, this prince insisted to remain, and to share in his danger. They accordingly kept on their way, passed in the view of Jugurtha with his party, who, though disposed to offer violence to the Romans, had yet some measures to preserve with the king of Mauritania,

whose

whose son was in company; and thus while, contrary to his usual character, he remained undecided, the prey escaped him, or got out of his reach.

Jugurtha sent persons of confidence immediately to counteract the negotiations of Sylla at the court of Bocchus; and each of these parties solicited the king of Mauritania to betray the other. The Numidian endeavoured to persuade him, that, with such an hostage as Sylla in his hands, he might still expect some honourable terms from the Romans; and Sylla, on the other part, represented, that, as the king of Mauritania had offended the Romans, by abetting the crimes of Jugurtha, he must now expiate his guilt by delivering him over to justice. It was the inclination of this prince to favour his Numidian ally; but it was his interest, as well as his intention, to gain the Romans. While he was still in suspence, he gave equal encouragement to both parties; and, without being finally determined what he should do, appointed the Roman Quæstor and the king of Numidia to meet him without any escort, or number of men in arms on either side, reserving, for himself, to the last moment the power of determining against the one or the other. By the time, however, that the parties were met, he had taken his resolution, had placed a body of his own troops in ambush, and, before any conference took place, gave a signal, which his men understood to be for seizing Jugurtha. The Numidians, who attended their king, were slain; he himself was put in chains, and delivered up to the

Roman Quæstor. Sylla, with the exultation of a successful hunter, received this lion in his toils; and, though he lived to perform much greater actions; still appears to have valued himself most on the event of this transaction. He boasted so much of his prize, that he became, from that moment, an object of jealousy to Marius, and was considered as a person advancing too fast in the same career of renown [*]. It was understood among the Romans, that the commander in chief, upon any service, in any division or province of the empire, enjoyed the triumph for victories gained, even in his own absence, by his lieutenants, or by those who served under his command; and Marius probably thought that Sylla took more to himself than was due upon this occasion. The desire of being the person who put the finishing hand to any matter of great public concern, however accomplished, was not peculiar to these officers. It was an effect of the Roman policy in making the rewards of distinction depend so much on events, without regard to the means which were employed to produce them. A circumstance, from which the citizens of this republic were as desirous of having the reputation of successful adventures affixed to their names, as courtiers in modern Europe are desirous of titles, or covet badges of honour and marks of their sovereign's favour.

The war being thus at an end, Marius appointed a thanksgiving; and, while he was offering the customary

[*] Plutarch. in Mario et in Sylla.

customary sacrifices, the news arrived from Rome that the People had dispensed with the law in his favour, and again had elected him Consul for the following year. This choice was determined by the great alarm which the Romans had taken on the approach of the barbarous nations, who, like a meteor, had, for some years, traversed the regions of Europe, and, with uncertain direction, were said to destroy wherever they moved. The Romans had repeatedly stood in their way, and had provoked a resentment, which these barbarians were supposed, in haste, to wreck upon Italy. They were at first heard of under the name only of Cimbri; but were now known to consist of many nations, under the appellations of Ambrones, Teutones, Tectosagi, and others; and had gained accessions of force by the junction of the Tigurini, and other Gaulish nations, who, either by choice or compulsion, were made a part in this mighty host, whose movements the Romans considered as now chiefly directed against themselves.

CHAP. XI.

Besides the armies commanded by the Consuls Carbo and Silanus, which had fallen victims to this barbarous enemy, other considerable bodies, under Scaurus and Cassius, had perished by their hands; and other misfortunes, from the same quarter, were coming apace. At the time that Marius had finished the war with Jugurtha, Quintus Servius Cæpio, having the former year commanded in Gaul, where he destroyed or pillaged the city of Tolosa, and made a great booty, consisting, according to Justin,

U. C. 648.
P. Rutilius Rufus, Cn. Mallius.

CHAP. XI. of one hundred thousand pounds weight of gold, and one million five hundred thousand pounds weight of silver, was now, in his turn, to meet with this torrent of wandering nations; the Conful Mallius or Manilius had orders to join him; and all the troops they could affemble were but too few to withftand fuch an enemy. Thefe generals united their forces on the Rhône, but without a proper difpofition to act in concert; they were accordingly defeated in battle; eighty thoufand Romans, amongft whom were the two fons of the Conful Manilius, were killed in the action; forty thoufand attendants of the army were maffacred in cold blood. Both camps were taken.

After this victory, the lords of the Cimbri, being affembled in council, called before them Aurelius Scaurus, formerly a Roman Conful, lately fecond in command over one of their vanquifhed armies, and now a prifoner. They queftioned him with refpect to the forces in Italy, and the route to be taken acrofs the Alps: To thefe queftions he made anfwer, That it would be in vain for them to invade that country; that the Romans, on their own territory, were invincible. And, in return to thefe words, it is faid, that a Barbarian ftruck the prifoner with his dagger to the heart. It is further faid of this barbarous council, that they came to a refolution to fpare no prifoners, to deftroy the fpoils of the flain, to caft all the treafures of gold and filver into the neareft river, to deftroy all horfes with their faddles and furniture, and to fave no

booty

booty whatever. It muſt be confeſſed, that in this, their reſolutions were guided by a policy well accommodated to the manner of life they had choſen. Wealthy poſſeſſions frequently diſqualify even ſettled nations for the toils of war, but to hordes in continual migration, the accommodations of luxury and ſloth, would be certain impediments and the means of ruin[1].

Theſe accounts of impending enemies, and of the diſaſters which befel the Roman armies which ventured to encounter them, were received at Rome with amazement and terror. The citizens changed their dreſs, and aſſumed the military habit. Rutilius, the Conſul, who had remained in the adminiſtration of affairs in Italy, had inſtructions from the Senate to array every perſon that was fit to bear arms. No one who had attained the military age was exempted. It is mentioned, that the ſon of the Conſul himſelf was turned into the ranks of a legion. There was little time to train ſuch levies; and the uſual way was thought inſufficient. The fencing-maſters, employed to train gladiators for the public ſhews, were brought forth, and diſtributed to inſtruct the citizens in the uſe of their weapons[2]. But the expedient, on which the People chiefly relied for deliverance from the dangers which threatened them, was the repeated nomination of Marius to command againſt this terrible enemy.

This officer, upon hearing of his re-election, ſet out for Italy, and, with his legions and their captives,

[1] Oroſius, lib. v. c. 16. Eutrop. lib. v.   [2] Valer. Max. lib. ii. c. 3.

tives, made his entrance at Rome in triumph; a spectacle, of which Jugurtha, in chains, with his unfortunate children, were the principal figures. When the proceſſion was over, the captive king was led to a dungeon, under orders for his immediate execution. As he was about to be ſtripped of his ornaments and robes, the executioner, in haſte to pluck the pendants from his ears, tore away the fleſh, and thruſt him naked into a circular aperture into which he deſcended with a ſmile, ſaying, "What a cold "bath is here?" He pined about ſix days under ground, and expired. A king and an able commander would, in ſuch a ſituation, have been an object of reſpect and of pity, if we did not recollect, that he was the murderer of Adherbal and Hiempſal, the innocent children of his benefactor; and if we did not receive ſome conſolation from being told, that his own children, who were likewiſe innocent, were exempted from the lot of their father, and honourably entertained in Italy.

Marius, in this triumph, is ſaid to have brought into the treaſury three thouſand and ſeven pounds, or thirty thouſand and ſeventy ounces of gold, and fifty-ſeven thouſand ſeven hundred and fifty ounces of ſilver; and in money, two hundred and eighty-ſeven thouſand denarii [1]. He entered the Senate, contrary to cuſtom, in his triumphal robes, probably to inſult the Nobles, who uſed to deſpiſe him as a perſon of obſcure extraction, born in a country town, and of a mean family: but finding that

---

[1] About L. 10,000.

that this was confidered as an act of petulance, and generally condemned, he withdrew and changed his drefs.

CHAP. XI.

The kingdom of Numidia was difmembered; part was put into the poffeffion of Bocchus as a reward for his late fervices; and part referved for the furviving heirs of Maffiniffa.

As the law refpecting the Confulate now ftood, no one could be elected in abfence, nor re-elected into this office, till after an interval of ten years. Both claufes were difpenfed with in favour of Marius, under pretence of continuing him at the head of the army; but as he might ftill have remained in his ftation, and have rendered the fame fervices to the State in the quality of Proconful, his re-election may be afcribed to his own ambition, and to his jealoufy of other rifing men in the State. Being reputed head of the popular party, his perfonal elevation was an object of zeal to the Tribunes of the People, and was intended to mortify thofe who affected the diftinctions of antient family. Contrary to the ufual form, and without cafting lots, for the affignation of his Province, he was preferred to his colleague in the appointment to command in Gaul. Having his choice of all the armies at that time in Italy, he took the new levies, lately affembled and difciplined by Rutilius, in preference to the veterans, who had ferved in Africa under Metellus and himfelf. It is probable that he was determined in this choice, more by his defire to gratify the veterans, who wifhed

U. C. 649.
Confuls;
C. Marius
2do, C.
Flavius
Fimbria.

to

to be discharged, in order to enjoy the fruits of their labours, than by the consideration of any supposed superiority in the discipline to which the new levies had been trained [1].

Upon the arrival of Marius in his province, it appeared, that the alarm taken for the safety of Italy was somewhat premature. The Barbarians in their battles only meant to maintain the reputation of their valour, or to keep open the track of their migrations. They had found the lands, from about the higher parts of the Danube and the Rhine, through Gaul and across the Pyrenees into Spain, and to the ocean, convenient for their purpose, and sufficiently extensive. They had not yet meditated any war with the Romans, or other nation in particular; but did not decline any contest where they met with resistance. At present they continued their migrations to the westward, without attempting to cross the Alps, or seeming to have knowledge of nations who inhabited the peninsula of Italy within those mountains.

We have nothing recorded in history concerning the movements of these wandering hordes, during the two subsequent years, except what is related of their adventure with Fulvius, a Roman Prætor, probably in Spain, who, in return for hostilities committed in his province, having made a feint to draw the attention of their warriors elsewhere, surprised and sacked their camp. Under the apprehension, however, of their return towards Gaul

[1] Frontius de Stragemat. lib. iv. c. 2.

Gaul and Italy, Marius continued to be elected Conful, and was repeatedly named to the command of the army that was deftined to oppofe them. His party at Rome had, at this time, befides the exigency which juftified their choice of fuch a leader, many other advantages againft their antagonifts, and maintained the ufual conteft of envy in the lower people againft the pride of nobility with great animofity and zeal.

CHAP.

CHAP. XII.

Review of the Circumstances which revived the popular Party at Rome.—Further Account of Laws and Regulations under the Administration of this Party.—State of the Empire.—Fourth Consulate of Marius.—Continued Migrations of the barbarous Nations.—Defeated by Marius at Aquæ Sextiæ.—By Marius and Catulus in Italy.

THE Senate had, for some time after the suppression of the troubles which were raised by Fulvius and the younger Gracchus, retained its authority, and restrained the Tribunes of the People within ordinary bounds; but by the miscarriages of the war in Numidia, and the suspicions which arose against them, on the subject of their transactions with Jugurtha, they again lost their advantage. It is difficult to ascertain the real grounds of these suspicions. Salust seems to admit them in their utmost extent, and represents the whole order of nobility as mercenary traders, disposed to sell what the Republic entrusted to their honour. That the presents of Jugurtha were sometimes accepted, and had their effect, is not to be doubted; but that the aristocracy of Rome, during its temporary ascendant, was so much corrupted, as the relation of this historian implies, is scarcely to be credited. Such a measure of corruption must have rendered the State a prey to every rival that was in condition to mislead its councils, and is not consistent

consistent with that superiority which the Romans then generally possessed in their negotiations, as well as in their wars. The charge itself favours too much of that envy with which the lower class of the People at all times interpret the conduct of their superiors, and which at the time when Salust wrote his history, was greatly countenanced by the partizans of Cæsar, in order to vilify and traduce the Senate. We cannot, however, oppose mere conjecture to the positive testimony of Salust, corroborated by some suspicious circumstances in the transactions of the times. Among these we may recollect the patronage which Jugurtha met with at Rome, contrary to the general sense of the People, and the uncommon presumption of guilt implied in the degradation of so many members as were about the same time, by the authority of the Censors, Q. Cæcilius Metellus and Cn. Domitius Ahenobarbus [1], expelled from the Senate.

Whatever may have been the real occasion of the cry then subsisting against the Nobles, we have seen that the popular party, availing themselves of it, and giving it all manner of countenance, found means to recover great part of the power they had formerly lost. The Tribunes, having obtained the establishment of a special commission for the trial of those who had received any bribes from Jugurtha, the people mistook their own act

in

---

[1] It is already mentioned, that thirty-two Senators were struck off the rolls by these magistrates. Epitom. Liv. lib. 62.

CHAP. XII. in constituting a court of inquiry, as sufficient to evince the reality of the crime. The prosecutions which continued to be carried on for two years, upon this supposition, served more than the subject of any former dispute to exasperate and to alienate the minds of men from each other, and from the public. Questions were more of a private than of a public nature, and occupied the worst of the human passions, envy, malice, and revenge. One party learned to cherish falsehood, subornation, and perjury; the other lived in continual and degrading fear of having such engines employed against themselves.

The People, in their zeal to attack the Nobility under any pretence, made no distinction between errors and crimes; and, contrary to the noble spirit of their ancestors, treated misfortune, incapacity, and treachery, with equal rigour. One Tribune had extended the use of the secret ballot in giving judgment on certain offences or misdemeanors [1]; another, upon this occasion, took away all distinctions, or introduced the same cover of secrecy in the trial of capital crimes [2]: insomuch, that a judge draughted from among the parties then at variance, could, without being accountable, indulge his malice or partial favour, so as to affect the life as well as the honour of a fellow citizen [3], to whom he bore any spite.

Laws were made to promote the interest, as well as to gratify the animosity, of the lower people.

By

---

[1] Lex Cassia Tabellaria.   [2] Lex Cælia Tabellaria.
[3] Cicer. de Legibus, lib. iii.

OF THE ROMAN REPUBLIC.

By the Agrarian law of Gracchus, no one could possess above a certain measure in land; but in order to render the surplus of property to be surrendered immediately useful to the People, it was permitted, by an amendment of the law made during the low state of the aristocratical party, that persons holding more than the legal measure, might retain their possession, but subject to a rent to be collected for the benefit of the poorer citizens; and thus it was provided, that without discontinuing the practice of faction, or removing into what was considered as a species of exile in the country, the favourites of the party should be accommodated, and reap the fruits of sedition and idleness, while they continued to pursue the same course of life in the city [1].

CHAP. XII.

It was proposed, by the Consul Servilius Cæpio, that the Senate, whose members were personally so much exposed to prosecutions, should have their share likewise in composing the courts of justice, a privilege of which, by the edict of Gracchus, they had been deprived [2]. In whatever degree this proposal was adopted, it was again expressly rejected upon the motion of Servilius Glaucia. And Cæpio soon after experienced, in his own person, the animosity of the popular faction: Being tried for miscarriage in his battle with the Cimbri, he was condemned by the judges, and afterwards, by a separate act obtained by Cassius, one of the Tribunes, declared, in consequence

U. C. 647.
Lex Servilia de Judiciis.

[1] Appian. de Bell. Civ. lib. i.   [2] Valer. Max. lib. v. c. 9.

of that sentence, disqualified to hold a place in the Senate [1].

Besides the transactions already mentioned, the following particulars, overlooked in the hurry of recording military operations and events, may serve still further to characterize the times. M. Junius Silanus was tried for misconduct against the enemy; M. Emilius Scaurus, first on the roll of the Senate, was brought to trial for contempt of religion; but both acquitted. The ardour for these prosecutions and popular regulations, continued without abatement, until the second Consulate of Marius, when M. Marcius Philippus, one of the Tribunes, moved to revive the law of Tiberius Gracchus respecting the division of estates in land, which, from this circumstance, should appear had never been executed; and, in his speech to support this motion, affirmed, that there were not then two thousand families in Rome possessed of any property in land whatever [2]. This motion, however, was withdrawn.

Among the crimes which the populace were now so eager to punish, fortunately that of peculation or extortion in the provinces was one. To facilitate complaints on this subject, not only persons having an immediate interest in the case, but all to whom any money or effects injuriously taken might have otherwise come by inheritance, were intitled to prosecute for this offence; and any alien, who convicted a Roman citizen of this crime, so

---

[1] Asconius Pædianus in Corneliana Ciceronis.
[2] Cicer. de Officiis, lib. ii.

as to have him ſtruck off the rolls of the People, was intitled himſelf to be inrolled inſtead of the citizen diſplaced [1].

Domitius one of the Tribunes, attacked the ariſtocratical conſtitution even of the prieſthood, and endeavoured to transfer the right of election to vacant places from the order itſelf to the People; but ſuperſtition, which often continues to influence the bulk of mankind after reaſon has failed, here ſtood in his way. The cuſtom was againſt him; and in ſuch matters, religion and cuſtom are the ſame. The People, therefore, it was confeſſed by the mover of this reform, could not without profanation pretend to elect a prieſt; but a certain part of the People might judge of the candidates, and inſtruct the college itſelf in the choice to be made [2]. The ſame artifice, or verbal evaſion, had been already admitted in the form of electing the Pontifex Maximus, preſented to the order, not by the People at large, but by ſeventeen of the Tribes who were drawn by lot [3].

Lex Domitia de Sacerdotiis.

During this period, a charge of depravity, worſe than that which was brought againſt thoſe who were employed in the State, might with equal juſtice be directed againſt thoſe who were loudeſt in raiſing the cry of corruption; for liberty, on the part of the populace, was conceived to imply a freedom from every reſtraint, and to juſtify licenſe and contempt of the laws. The gratuitous aids which were given to the People, enabled

---

[1] Cicero in Balbiana. [2] Aſconius in Corneliana Ciceronis.
[3] Cicero de Lege Agraria.

abled them to subsist in idleness and sloth; the wealth that was passing to Rome in the hands of traders, contractors, and farmers of the revenue, was spent in profusion. That which was acquired by officers in one station of command in the provinces, was lavished in public shews, in the baiting of wild beasts and fights of gladiators, to gain the People in the canvass for further preferments: And from all these circumstances we may conclude, that if there be reason to regret or detest the abuses incident to monarchy, and the luxury of courts, there is surely no less in the brutal taste and dissolute manners incident to a populace, acknowledged in democracy the sovereign or supreme disposer of preferments and honours.

The severities which were practised in certain cases, the sumptuary laws which were provided to restrain dissipation, were but feeble aids to stop up the source of so much disorder. It is mentioned, as an instance of severity which the times required, that some vestals were questioned for a breach of that sacred obligation to chastity, under which they were held up as a pattern of manners to the sex at Rome; that three of them were condemned, and, together with so many Roman knights, the supposed partners in their guilt, suffered extreme punishment; but no two things are more consistent than superstition and vice. A temple was on this occasion erected to the goddess Venus, under what may to us appear a new title, that of the Reformer[1];

prayers

---

[1] Venus Verticordia.

OF THE ROMAN REPUBLIC.

CHAP. XII.

prayers were to be offered up in this temple, that it might please the goddess of Love to guard the chastity of Roman women [1]. And from this we may apprehend, that the devotions paid to this deity, were in some instances of a purer kind than we are apt to imagine.

The term luxury is somewhat ambiguous; it is put for sensuality or excess in what relates to the uses or gratifications of animal nature; and for the effect of vanity, in what relates to the decorations of rank and fortune. The luxury of the Romans, in the present age, was probably of the former kind, and sumptuary laws were provided, not to restrain vanity, but to govern the appetites for mere debauch. About the time that Jugurtha was at Rome, the sumptuary law of Fannius received an addition, by which Roman citizens were not only restricted in their ordinary expence, but the legal quantities and species of food were distinctly prescribed. The whole expence of the table was restricted to thirty asses [2] a-day, and the meat to be served up, to three or four pounds, dried or salted. There was no restriction in the use of herbs or vegetables of any sort [3]. According to A. Gellius, the law permitted, on certain days, an expence of an hundred asses; on wedding-days, two hundred. It is remarkable, that this law continued to have its effect on the tables

[1] Orosius, lib. v. c. 15. Jul. Obsequens. Ovid. Fast. lib. v.
[2] About two shillings.
[3] Macrobius Satur. lib. ii. c. 17.

tables of Roman citizens after Cicero was a man [r]. The Epicures of his time were obliged to make up, in the cookery of their vegetable diet, what was defective in that species of food.

About the time of the commencement of the Numidian war, the People, according to the Cenſus, amounted to four hundred and three thouſand four hundred and thirty-ſix citizens, fit to carry arms. At this time it was that the Cenſors, Quintus Cæcilius Mettellus, and Cn. Domitius Ahenobarbus, as already mentioned, expelled thirty-two members from the Senate.

While the Romans were intent on the war which ſubſiſted in Africa, they were not exempted from like trouble in other parts of their empire. In Spain particularly, hoſtilities, at intervals, were ſtill renewed. There, in trying to quell a revolt of the natives, a Roman Prætor was killed; in another encounter, the forces employed againſt the natives, were cut off; and a freſh army was tranſported from Italy, to ſecure the Roman poſſeſſions.

Hoſtilities were likewiſe continued on the frontier of Macedonia, by the Scordiſci, Triballi, and other Thracian nations; and the Proconſul Rufus, by his victories in this quarter, obtained a triumph.

During this period, in the Conſulſhip of Attilius Serranus, and Q. Servilius Cæpio, the year after the firſt Conſulſhip of Marius, were born two illuſtrious

---

[r] Epiſt. ad Familiar. lib. vii. ad Gallum.

illustrious citizens, M. Tullius Cicero, and Cneius Pompeius Strabo, afterwards distinguished by the appellation of Pompey the Great. And with the mention of these names we are now to open the scene in which persons, on whom the fate of the Roman empire was to depend, made their several entries into life, or into public business, and in which they began to pass through an infancy or a youth of danger, to an old age of extreme trouble, which closed with the subversion of that constitution of government under which they were born.

CHAP. XII.

Marius having, without any memorable event, passed the year of his second Consulship on the frontier of Narbonne Gaul, was, by the People, still under the same apprehension of the Cimbric invasion, re-elected, and destined to remain in his station. This year likewise the Barbarians turned aside from the Roman province, and left the republic at leisure to contend with enemies of less consideration, who appeared in a different quarter. Athenio, a slave in Sicily, having murdered his master, and broken open the prisons or walled inclosures in which slaves were commonly confined at work, assembled a number together, and being himself clothed in a purple robe, with a crown and sceptre, affected a species of royalty, while he invited all the slaves of the island to assume their freedom under his protection. He acquired strength sufficient to cope with Servilius Casca, the Roman Prætor, and actually forced him in his camp. He likewise defeated the succeeding Prætor, Licinius Lucullus;

U. C. 650. Caius Marius, tio. L. Aurelius Orestes.

lus[1]; and was, in the third year of his insurrection, with great difficulty, reduced by the Consul Aquilius. This revolt was at its height in this year of the third Consulship of Marius, and the rebels being surrounded in their strong holds, and obliged to surrender for want of provisions, it was quelled in the second year after this Consulship[2]. The whole is mentioned now, that it may not recur hereafter to interrupt the series of matters more important.

About the same time the Romans had been obliged to equip a naval armament under Marcus Antonius, known by the appellation of the Orator, against the Cilician pirates, who had lately infested the seas. All that we know of this service is, in general, that it was performed with ability and success[3].

From Macedonia, Calpurnius Piso reported, that the victory he had gained over the Thracians had enabled him to penetrate to the mountains of Rhodope and Caucasus.

Such was the state of the empire when Caius Marius arrived from his province in Gaul, to preside at a new election of Consuls. He was himself again, by the voice of the People, called upon to resume his trust; but he affected, with an appearance of modesty, to decline the honour. His partizans were apprised of the part he was to act, and were accordingly prepared, by their importunities, to force him

---

[1] Florus, lib. iii. c. 19. [2] Ibid. lib. iv. c. 19.
[3] Ibid. lib. iii. c. 6. Cicero de Oratore, lib. 1.

him into an office which he certainly did not mean to decline. Among these, Apuleius Saturninus, at this time himself candidate for the office of Tribune, charged Marius with treachery to his country in propofing to defert the republic in times of fo much danger; and with his reproaches feemed to prevail fo far as to render this favourite of the People paffive to the will of his fellow-citizens, who wifhed to re-inftate [1] him in his former command.

In this fourth Confulate, the courage and military fkill of Marius came to be actually exerted in his province. The barbarous nations, after their return from Spain, began to appear in feparate bodies, each forming a numerous and formidable army. In one divifion the Cimbri and Tectofages had paffed through the whole length of Gaul to the Rhine; from thence proceeded by the Danube to Noricum or Auftria, and by the paffes of Carinthea, or by the valley of Trent, might have an eafy accefs to Italy. The Conful Lutatius Catulus was ftationed on the Athefis, near the defcent [2] of the Alps, to obferve the motions of this body.

In another divifion, the Ambrones and the Teutones, between the Garonne and the Rhône, hung on the frontier of the Roman province, and gave out, that they meant, by another route of the mountains, to join their allies who were expected on the Po.

Upon the approach of this formidable enemy in the divifion to which he was oppofed, Marius took poft on the Rhône at the confluence
of

U. C. 651.
Caius Marius 4to, L. Lutatius Catulus.

---

[1] Plutarch in Mario.   [2] Now the Adige.

of this river with the Isere, and fortified his camp in the most effectual manner. The Barbarians, reproaching him with cowardice for having taken these precautions, sent, agreeably to their own notions of war, a formal challenge to meet them in battle; and having had for answer, That the Romans did not consult their enemies to know when it was proper to fight, they were confirmed in their usual contempt, ventured to leave the Roman army behind, and proceeded in separate divisions to look out for a passage into Italy. Marius followed; with rapid marches, overtook them in their progress, and even dispersed over the country, without precaution or order; some of them near to the Roman colony of Sextius [1], and far removed from each other. Having found them under such disadvantage, and in such condition as exposed them to slaughter, with scarcely any means of resistance, he put the greater part to the sword. Thus, one part of the hordes, who had for years been so formidable to the Romans, were now entirely cut off. Ninety thousand prisoners, with Teutobochus, one of their kings, were taken, and two hundred thousand were said to be slain in the field [2], accounts which, with some others relating to this war, we may suspect to be exaggerated.

The news of this victory arriving at Rome, while it

---

[1] Now Aix, in Provence.

[2] Plutarch. in Mario. Orosius, lib. v. c. 16. Florus, lib. iii. c. 3. Vellejus. Eutropius.

it was known that a second swarm of the same hive, not less formidable than the first, still hung on the approaches to Italy, it was not to be doubted that the command and office of Consul would still be continued to Marius. The populace, incited by some of the factious Tribunes, joined, with the other usual marks of their attachment to this favourite leader, that of disrespect and insolence to those who were supposed to be his opponents and rivals. Of these, Metellus Numidicus, whom he had supplanted in the command of the army against Jugurtha, was the chief. This respectable citizen, being now in the office of Censor, one Equitius, an impostor of obscure or slavish extraction, offered himself to be enrolled as a citizen, under the popular designation and name of Caius Gracchus, the son of Tiberius. The Censor, doubting his title, called upon Sempronia, the sister of Gracchus, to testify what she knew of this pretended relation; and, upon her giving evidence against him, rejected his claim. But the populace, ill-disposed to Metellus, on account of his supposed disagreement with Marius, took this opportunity to insult the Censor in the discharge of his office; attacked his house, and obliged him to take refuge in the Capitol. Even there the Tribune Saturninus would have laid violent hands on his person, if he had not been protected by a body of the Roman Knights, who had assembled in arms to defend him. This tumult was suppressed, but not without bloodshed.

While

CHAP. XII.

U. C. 653.
Caius Marius 5to, M. Aquilius.

While the popular faction was indulging in these marks of dislike to Metellus, they proceeded to bestow the honours which they intended for Marius, and chose him for a fifth time Consul, in conjunction with M. Aquilius. His late splendid successes against one division of the wandering Barbarians justified this choice, and pointed him out as the fittest person to combat the other, which was still expected from the banks of the Danube, to attempt the invasion of Italy. Catulus, the late colleague of Marius, commanding the troops that were stationed on the Athesis, to cover the access to Italy from what is now called the Tyrol and the valley of Trent, was destined to act in subordination to the Consul, who had given orders to hasten the passage of his victorious army from the other extremity of the Alps and the Rhône.

Catulus had taken post near Verona, thrown a bridge over the Athesis, and, in order to command the passage of that river, had fortified stations on both its banks. While he was in this posture, and before the junction of Marius, the enemy arrived in his neighbourhood. The amazing works which they performed might serve to confirm the report of their numbers. They obstructed with mounds of timber and earth the channel of the Athesis, so as to force it to change its course; and by this means, instead of themselves passing the river, they threw it behind them in their march. They continued to float such quantities of wood towards the bridge which Catulus had constructed, that the stream being

OF THE ROMAN REPUBLIC. 93

being obstructed, the bridge itself, unable to sustain such a pressure, with all the timber which was accumulated before it, was entirely carried off. The troops of Rome, on seeing such proofs of the numbers and strength of their enemy, were seized with a panic. Many deserted their colours, some fled even to the city itself, without halting. The Proconsul, to hide his disgrace, thought proper to order a retreat; and by this order, seeming to authorise what he could not prevent, endeavoured to save in part the credit of his army.

The level country on the Po was in this manner laid open to the incursions of the Barbarians. The inhabitants of Italy were greatly alarmed: and the Roman People passed an act of attainder against all those who had abandoned their colours. Marius, who had been at Rome while he expected the arrival of his army from Gaul, suspended the triumph which had been decreed to himself by the Senate, now went to receive the legions on their approach, and hastened to rally and to reinforce the army of Catulus.

Upon their junction, those who had lately fled from the plains of Verona recovered their courage, and the generals determined, without loss of time, to hazard a battle. It is said that the Barbarians of this division were still ignorant of the disaster which had befallen their confederates on the other side of the Alps, and had sent the Roman army a defiance or a challenge to fight; but that, being informed of their loss, when they

CHAP. XII.

they were about to engage, they made their attack with less than their usual ferocity or confidence. Catulus received them in front. Marius made a movement to assail them in flank; but as the field was darkened by the clouds of dust which every where rose from the plain, he missed his way, or could not fall in with the enemy till after they had been repulsed by Catulus, and were already put to flight. The rout, as usual, was extremely bloody; an hundred and fifty thousand were said to be slain; sixty thousand submitted to be taken. The remainder of this mighty host, even the women and children, perished by their own hands; and in this manner a race of barbarous nations who had migrated through Europe, perhaps for ages before they encountered with the Romans, now appear to have been entirely cut off [1].

On receiving the news of this victory at Rome, the city resounded with joy, and the People, in every sacrifice they offered up, addressed themselves to Marius as to a god. He had been constantly attended in this war by Sylla, who, though already an object of his jealousy, still chose to neglect the preferments of the city, and to serve in the camp. In the victory, now to be celebrated, Marius was no more than partner with Catulus, and impatient, as he will soon appear of any competition for power, did justice to his colleague in this particular, admit-

ting

[1] Plutarch. in Mario et Sylla. Orosius, lib. v. c. 16. Florus, lib iii. c. 3. Velleius. Eutrop. Appian in Celtica.

ting him equally to partake in the triumph which enfued. In this proceffion there were not any carriages loaded with gold, filver, or precious fpoils of any fort; but, inftead of them, the fhattered armour and broken fwords of a ferocious enemy; the furer marks of an honour juftly won, and of a more important fervice performed. Thefe were tranfported in waggon-loads, and piled up in the Capitol.

CHAP. XIII.

Character and immoderate Ambition of Marius.—Death of Nonius.—Re-election of the Tribune Saturninus.—His Sedition and seizing the Capitol.—Death of Saturninus.—Reverse in the State of Parties.—Recall of Metellus.—Violent Death of the Tribune Furius.—Birth of Caius Julius Cæsar.—Lex Cæcilia Didia.—Blank in the Roman History.—Sylla offers himself Candidate for the office of Prætor.—Edict of the Censors against the Latin Rhetoricians.—Bullion in the Roman Treasury.—Present of a Groupe in Golden Figures from the King of Mauritania.—Acts of Livius Drusus.—Revolt of the Italian Allies.—Policy of the Romans in yielding to the Necessity of their Affairs.—The Laws of Plautius.

CHAP. XIII.

UPON the extinction of the wandering nations which had now for some time molested the empire, there was no foreign enemy to endanger the peace of Italy. The wars in Thrace and in Spain had no effect beyond the provinces in which they subsisted. The insurrection of the slaves in Sicily, by the good conduct of Aquilius the Consul, to whom that service had been committed, was near being quelled.

Marius, being now returned to the city, might have quitted the paths of ambition with uncommon distinction and honour. An ordinary Consulate, after his having been so often called upon, in times of extreme danger, as the perfon moft likely to fave his country, could make no addition to his glory. His being fet afide in times of fecurity and leifure, on the contrary, muft have been the moft honourable and flattering comment that could have been made on his former elections.

But there is reafon to believe, that immoderate thirft of power, and extreme animofity to his rivals, not genuine elevation of mind, were the characteriftics of Marius. His ambition had hitherto paffed for an averfion to ariftocratical ufurpations. But his affected and furious contempt of family diftinctions, too often the offspring of fenfibility to the want of fuch honours, by clafhing with the eftablifhed fubordination of ranks in his country, became a fource of difaffection to the State itfelf. He formed views upon the Confulate yet a fixth time; and inftead of the moderation, or the fatiety of honours with which he formerly pretended to be actuated, when he hoped to be preffed into office, he now openly employed all his influence, even his money, to procure a re-election; and in the event prevailed, together with Valerius Flaccus. He had warmly efpoufed the intereft of this candidate againft Metellus, from animofity to the competitor, whofe great authority, placed in oppofition to himfelf, he dreaded, more than from any regard or predilection for Flaccus. And now being chofen, in order the more to ftrengthen himfelf in the exercife of his power, he entered into concert with the Tribune Apuleius Saturninus, and,

U. C. 653. Caius Marius 6to, L. Val. Flaccus.

and, it is probable, agreed to support this factious demagogue in his pretensions to remain in office for another year; a precedent which had taken place only in the most factious times of the republic, and which was in itself more dangerous than any other re-election whatever. The person of the Tribune being sacred, his will was absolute, there was no check to his power besides the fear of being called to account at the expiration of his term; and if this fear were removed by the perpetuity of office, it was a power yet more formidable than that of the Dictator, and to be restrained only by the divisions which might arise among those who were joined together in the exercise of it.

The faction now formed by Marius and the Tribune Saturninus, with their adherents, was farther strengthened by the accession of the Prætor Glaucia. This person, while in office, and as he sat in judgment, had received an affront from Saturninus, in having his chair of state broken down, for presuming to occupy any part in the attention of the People, while an assembly called by the Tribune was met. He nevertheless chose to overlook this insult, in order to be admitted a partner in the consideration and power which was likely to devolve on these popular leaders.

Upon the approach of the tribunitian elections, the Senate and Nobles exerted themselves to prevent the re-election of Saturninus; and nine of the new candidates were, without any question, declared

declared to be duly elected in preference to him. The tenth place too, was actually filled by the election of Nonius Sufenas, whom the aristocracy had supported with all its influence. But the party of Apuleius, enraged at their disappointment, had recourse to violence, forced Nonius, though already vested with the sacred character of Tribune, to take refuge in a work-shop, from whence he was dragged by some of the late soldiery attached to Marius, and slain. The assembly broke up with the cry of murder, and every sober person, though reputed of the popular party, retired from the scene under the strongest impressions of affliction and terror.

Marius had reason to apprehend some violent resolution from the Senate, and was in no haste to assemble that body. Mean time his associate Glaucia, in the night, at the head of a party armed with daggers, took possession of the Capitol and place of assembly, and, at an early hour in the morning, pretending to observe all the forms of election, announced Apuleius again Tribune, in the place that was vacated by the murder of Nonius. This furious demagogue was accordingly reinstated in the sacred character, which, though recently violated by himself, was still revered by the bulk of the People. He was continually attended by a new set of men who infested the streets, freemen of desperate fortune, whom Marius, contrary to the established forms of the constitution, had admitted into the legions, these

CHAP. XIII. were grown fierce and infolent, as partners in the victories of their general, and were now made to expect that, in cafe the popular party fhould prevail, they themfelves were to have comfortable fettlements, and eftates in land.

Under the dread of fo many affaffins, who confidered the Nobles as enemies to their caufe, Marius with his faction was become mafter of the commonwealth. The better fort of the People was deterred from frequenting the public affemblies, and no one had courage to propofe, that any inquiry fhould be made into the death of the Tribune Nonius, in whofe perfon the facred law had been again fet at nought [1].

Lex Agraria. Apuleius haftened to gratify his party by moving popular acts. One to feize, in name of the Public, thofe lands beyond the Po which had lately been overrun and defolated by the barbarous nations, and to diftribute them in lots to the poorer citizens [2].

Another, by which it was enacted, that in the province of Africa a hundred jugera a man fhould be diftributed to the veterans [3]: that new fettlements fhould be made in Greece, Macedonia, and Sicily: and that the money taken from the temple at Tolofa [4] fhould be employed in the purchafe

of

---

[1] Appian de Bell. Civil. lib. i. Plutarch. in Mario, lib. lxix. Valer. Max. lib. ix. c. 7. Orofius, lib. v. c. 57. Florus, lib. iii. c. 16.

[2] Appian de Bell. Civil. lib. i.

[3] Aut. de Viris Illuftribus in Saturnino.

[4] Now Thouloufe.

of lands for a like purpofe: that wherever thefe colonies fhould be planted, Marius fhould have a power to infcribe, at each of the fettlements, the names of any three aliens into the lift of citizens¹. That the price, hitherto paid at the public granaries, fhould be difcontinued, and that corn fhould be diftributed gratis to the People.

Lex Frumentaria.

Upon the intention to obtain the laft of thofe laws being known, Q. Servilius Cæpio, one of the Quæftors, reprefented, that if fuch a law fhould pafs, there would be an end to induftry, good order and government in the city; and that the treafury of Rome would not be fufficient to defray the expence. He exhorted the Senate to employ every meafure to defeat this ruinous project. And this body accordingly made a refolution, that whoever attempted to obtain the law in queftion fhould be deemed an enemy to his country. But Apuleius was not to be reftrained by the terrors of this refolution. He proceeded to propofe the law in the ufual form, and had planted the rails and balloting urns for the People to give their votes, when Cæpio, with a body of his attendants, had the courage to attack the Tribune, broke down the fteps, and overfet the balloting urns; an action for which he was afterwards impeached upon an accufation of treafon, but by which, for the prefent, he difappointed the defigns of the faction².

Apuleius, to extend the power of the popular affemblies,

---

¹ Aut. de Viris Illuftribus in Saturnino.
² Aut. Rhetoricorum ad Herennium.

assemblies, and to remove every obstruction from his own designs, brought forward a number of new regulations. One to confirm a former statute, by which the acts of the Tribes were declared to have the force of laws. Another, declaring it to be treason for any person to interrupt a Tribune in putting a question to the People. A third, obliging the Senate to confirm every act of the Tribes within five days after such act had passed, and requiring every Senator, under pain of a fine, and of being struck off the rolls, to take an oath to abide by these regulations. While these motions were under debate, some one of the party who opposed them, in order to stop the career of this factious Tribune, observed that it thundered; a circumstance which, upon the ordinary maxims of the Roman Augurs, was sufficient to suspend any business in which the People were engaged, and to break up their assembly. "If you be not silent," said Apuleius to the person who observed that it thundered, "you will also find that it hails." The assembly accordingly, without being deterred by this interposition of the auspices, passed acts to the several purposes now mentioned. The power of the Senate was thus entirely suppressed, their part of the legislature being reduced to a mere form, and even this form they were not at liberty to withhold. Marius called them together, and proposed that they should consider what resolution they were to take with respect to a change of so much importance,

and

and particularly with respect to the oath which was to be exacted from the Senators, binding or obliging themselves to abide by the regulations now made. The old warrior is said, on this occasion, to have practised an artifice by which he imposed on many of those who were present, and which afterwards furnished him with a pretence for removing his enemy Metellus from the councils of state. He declared himself with great warmth against taking the oath, and by his example led other Senators to express their dislike. Metellus, in particular, assured the assembly, that it was his own resolution never to come under any such engagement.

While the Senators relied on the concurrence of Marius in refusing the oath, the time appointed for administring it nearly approached; and this Consul, after the third day was far spent, assembled the Senate, set forth the dangerous state of the commonwealth; at the same time expressed his own fears of the disturbances that might arise if the Senate refused to gratify the People in this matter, and while multitudes were assembled in the streets to know the issue of their councils, he required that the oath should be administred. He himself took it, to the astonishment of the Senate, and to the joy of the populace, who, being assembled by Apuleius, sounded applause through the streets. Metellus alone, of all who were present, refused to comply, and withstood all the intreaties of his friends, who represented the danger with which he was threatened. "*If it were al-ways safe to do right,*" he said, "*who would ever do wrong? But good men are distinguished, by choosing to do right even when it is least for their safety to do so.*"

On the following day the Tribune Saturninus entered the Senate, and, not being stopped by the negative of any of his own colleagues, the only power that could restrain him, dragged Metellus from his place, and proffered an act of attainder and banishment against him, for having refused the oath which was enjoined by the People. Many of the most respectable citizens offered their aid to defend this illustrious Senator by force; but he himself declined being the subject of any civil commotion, and went into exile.

While the act, which afterwards passed for his banishment was preparing, he was heard to say, " If the times should mend, I shall recover my station; if not, it is good to be absent from hence." He fixed his abode at Smyrna, conducted his retirement with great dignity during his exile, and probably felt as he ought, that any censure inflicted by men of a vile or profligate character, whatever title they assumed, whether of Nobles or People, or of the State itself, was an honour.

In these transactions elapsed the second year, in which Apuleius filled the office of Tribune; and, being favoured by a supineness of the opposite party contracted in a seeming despair of the republic, he he prevailed yet a third time in being vefted with this formidable power. To court the favour of the People, he affected to credit what was alleged concerning the birth of Equitius; and, under the name of Caius Gracchus, fon of Tiberius, had this impoftor affociated with himfelf in the office of Tribune. The name of Gracchus, in this fituation, awakened the memory of former hopes and of former refentments. The Popular party had deftined Glaucia for the Confulate, and appear to have left Marius out of their councils. This will perhaps account for the conduct with which he concluded his adminiftration in the prefent year.

At the election which followed, the intereft of the Nobles was exerted for Marcus Antonius and C. Memmius. The firft was declared Conful, and the fecond was likely to prevail over Glaucia; when, in the midft of the crowds that were affembled to vote, a fudden tumult arofe; Memmius was befet and murdered; and the greater part of the People, alarmed at fo ftrange an outrage, were feized with a panic, and fled.

In the night, it being known, that Glaucia, Saturninus, and the Quæftor Saufeius, were together in fecret conference, all the citizens who yet retained any regard for the commonwealth affembled, in dread of what fo defperate a faction might attempt. All the voices were united againft Saturninus, the fuppofed author of fo many diforders and murders. It was propofed, without delay, to feize his perfon, either living or dead: but

being

being put upon his guard, by the appearance of a storm so likely to break on his head, he thought proper, with the other leaders of his party and their retainers in arms, to seize the Capitol, there to secure themselves, and to overawe the assembly of the People. It was no longer to be doubted that the republic was in a state of war. Marius, who had fomented these troubles from aversion to the Nobles, would have remained undetermined what part he should act. But the Senate being met, gave the usual charge to himself and his colleague to avert the danger with which the republic was threatened; and both these officers, however much they were disposed to favour the sedition, being in this manner armed with the sword of the commonwealth, were obliged to employ it in support of the public authority. The Senators, the Knights, and all the citizens of rank repaired in arms to their standard. Antonius, Consul elected for the following year, in order to prevent the entry of disorderly persons from the country to join the faction, was stationed in the suburbs with an armed force [1]. The Capitol was invested in form, and appears to have held out some days; at the end of which, in order to oblige the rebels to surrender, the pipes that supplied them with water were cut off [2]. This had the intended effect. They

---

[1] Cicero pro C. Rabirio. Et si Caius Marius quod fistulas quibus aqua suppetabatur Jovis optimi maximi temlis ac sedibus precidi imperarat.

[2] Plutarch. in Caio Mario; τυς γαρ οχιτυς απικοψεν.

They submitted on such terms as were proposed to them; and Marius being inclined to favour, had them only confined to the hall of the Senate till farther orders. In the mean time a great party of citizens, who were in arms for the defence of their families, impatient of delay, and thinking it dangerous to spare such daring offenders, beset them instantly in their place of confinement, and put the whole to the sword [1].

It was reported, though afterwards questioned upon a solemn occasion [2], that Caius Rabirius, a Senator of distinction, having cut off the head of Apuleius, according to the manners of the times, carried it as a trophy, and had it presented for some days at all the entertainments which were given on this occasion, or at which he himself was a guest.

This was the fourth tribunitian sedition raised to a dangerous height, and quelled by the vigour and resolution of the Senate. Marius, who had been obliged to act as the instrument of Government on this occasion, saw his projects baffled, and his credit greatly impaired. Plutarch relates, that he soon after withdrew from the city for some time, on pretence of a desire to visit the province of Asia, where his active spirit became busy in forming the project of new wars, for the conduct of which he was

---

[1] Plut. in Mario. Appian de Bell. Civil. lib. i. Oros. lib. v. c. 17. Flor. lib. iii. Aut. de Viris Illust. Cicero in Sextiana in Catal. lib. i. Philip. lib. viii. et pro Caio Rabirio.

[2] At the trial of Rabirius, when, some years afterwards, he was accused of having killed Saturninus.

was much better qualified than for the administration of affairs in peace.

Upon the suppression of this dangerous sedition, the commonwealth was restored to a state which, compared to the late mixture of civil contention and military execution, may have deserved the name of public order. One office of Consul was still vacant; and the election proceeding without disturbance, Posthumius Albinus was joined to Antonius. Most of the other elections had also been favourable to the Nobles; and the majority even of the Tribunes of the People recovered from the late diforders were inclined to respect the Senate and the Aristocracy, as principal supports of the commonwealth.

The first effect of this happy disposition was a motion to recal Metellus from banishment. In this measure two of the Tribunes, Q. Pompeius Rufus and L. Porcius Cato concurred. But Marius having opposed it with all his influence, and Publius Furius, another of the Tribunes, having interposed his negative, it could not at that time be carried into execution. Soon after, however, the same motion being renewed by the Tribune Callidius, and Furius having repeated his negative, Metellus, son of the exile, in presence of the People, threw himself upon the ground, and, embracing the Tribune's knees, besought him not to withstand the recal of his father. The young man, from this action, afterwards acquired the Sirname of *Pius*; and the Tribune, insolently spurning this suppliant, as he lay on the ground, served

his

his cauſe by that act of indignity perhaps more effectually than he could have done by lending a favourable ear to his requeſt. The People, ever governed by their preſent paſſions, were moved with tenderneſs and with indignation. They proceeded, without regard to the negative of Furius, under emotions of ſympathy for the ſon, to recal the exiled father. The meſſenger of the republic ſent to announce this act of the People to Metellus, found him at Tralles in Lydia, among the ſpectators at a public ſhow. When the letters were delivered to him, he continued to the end of the entertainment without breaking the ſeals; by this mark of indifference, treating the favour of a diſorderly populace with as much contempt as he had ſhown to their cenſure.

The Senate, in conſequence of the diſtaſte which all reaſonable men had taken to the violence of the oppoſite party, having got the aſcendant at Rome, were gratified, not only with the teſt of ſuperiority they had gained in the recal of Metellus, but in the downfal alſo of ſome of the Tribunes who had been active in the late diſorders. Publius Furius, now become an object of general deteſtation, fell a ſacrifice to the law of Apuleius, which declared it treaſon to interrupt a Tribune in putting a queſtion to the People. Being accuſed by Canuleius, one of his colleagues, of violating this law, he was by the populace, who are ever carried by the torrent, and prompt for execution, prevented from making his defence; and, though a Tribune in office, was put to death. Decianus, another of these officers, in supporting the charge against Furius, happened to speak with regret of the death of Saturninus, a crime for which he incurred a prosecution, and was banished [1]. So strong was the tide of popularity now opposite to its late direction, and so fatal as precedents even to their own cause frequently are the rules by which violent men think to obtain discretionary power to themselves. The murder of Nonius was a precedent to justify the execution of Apuleius, and both were followed by that of Furius. The law which had for its object the support of Apuleius in any measure of disorder or licence, was now employed to support his enemies against himself and his faction.

Amidst these triumphs of the aristocratical party, Sextus Titius, one of the Tribunes, still had the courage to move a revival of the Agrarian law of Gracchus. The proposal was acceptable in the assembly of the People [2]: And the edict was accordingly passed. But it was observed, that while the People were met on this business, two ravens were fighting in the air above the place of assembly, and the College of Augurs, on pretence of this unfavourable omen, annulled the decree [3]. Titius, the author of it, was soon after condemned for having in his house the statue of Saturninus [4].

The

---

[1] Val. Max. lib. viii. c. 1.   [2] Julius Obsequens.
[3] Cicero de Legibus, lib. ii.
[4] Ibid. pro C. Rabirio. Ibid. de Orator. lib. ii. c. 28.

The Conful Acquilius returned from Sicily; and having had an ovation or proceffion on foot for the reduction of the Sicilian flaves, was on the following year brought to trial for extortion in his province. He called no exculpatory evidence, nor deigned to court the favour of his judges. But when about to receive fentence, M. Antonius, who had pleaded his caufe, tore open the veft of his client, and difplayed to the court and the audience the fcars which he bore in his breaft, and which were the marks of wounds received in the fervice of his country. Upon this fpectacle, a fudden emotion of pity or refpect decided againft the former conviction of the court, and unfixed the refolution which, a few moments before, they had taken to condemn the accufed.

Among the events which diftinguifhed the Confulate of M. Antonius and A. Poftumius Albinus, may be reckoned the birth of Caius Julius Cæfar, for whofe ambition the feeds of tribunitian diforder now fown were preparing a plentiful harveft. This birth, it is faid, was ufhered in with many prefages and tokens of future greatnefs. If, indeed, we were to believe, that Nature in this manner gives intimation of impending events, we fhould not be furprifed that her moft ominous figns were employed to mark the birth of a perfonage who was deftined to change the whole face of the political world, and to lay Rome herfelf, with all the nations fhe had conquered, proftrate under the dominion of caprice and force, a ftate

CHAP. XIII.

of degradation which, by its natural effects, served to turn back into the loweſt ebb of ignorance and meanneſs the tide of mental attainment which had flowed for ſome ages in an oppoſite direction.

U. C. 655.
Q. Cæcilius Metellus Nepo,
T. Didius.

Antonius and Albinus were ſucceeded in office by Q. Cæcilius Metellus and Titus Didius. The war ſtill continued in Spain, and the conduct of it fell to the lot of Didius. Upon his arrival in the Province, Dolabella, the Proprætor, ſet out on his return to Rome, and, for his victories in Spain, obtained a triumph. Metellus remained in the adminiſtration of affairs in Italy.

Lex Cæcilia Didia.

The legiſlation of the preſent year is diſtinguiſhed by an act in which both Conſuls concurred, and which is therefore marked in the title with their joint names. The Roman People had frequently experienced the defect of their forms in the manner of enacting laws. Factious Tribunes had it in their power to carry motions by ſurpriſe, to include in the ſame law a variety of regulations, and, by obliging the People to paſs or reject the whole in one vote, frequently obtained, under the favour of ſome popular clauſe, acts of a very dangerous tendency. To prevent this abuſe, it was now enacted, upon the joint motion of the Conſuls Cæcilius and Didius, that every propoſed law ſhould be made public three market days before it could receive the aſſent of the People; that all its different clauſes ſhould be ſeparately voted: and that it ſhould be lawful for the People

ple to felect a part, if they were not inclined to adopt the whole [1].

This law had a falutary tendency; and, though far from fufficient to prevent a return of the late evils, it ferved for a time to obftruct the courfe of tribunitian violence: but while the fource was open, any mere temporary obftruction could only tend to increafe the force with which it occafionally burft over every impediment of law or good order that was placed in its way. And the inefficacy of meafures taken upon the fuppreffion of the late dangerous fedition to eradicate the evil, fhews the extreme difficulty with which men are led, in moft cafes, to make any great or juft reformation.

It is fomewhat fingular, that about this time, in the midft of fo much animofity of the People to the Senate and Nobles, this fuperior and probably more opulent clafs of the citizens were the patrons of aufterity, and contended for fumptuary laws, while the popular Tribunes contended for licenfe and the abolition of former reftraints. " What is your liberty," faid the Tribune Duronius to the People, (while he moved for a repeal of the fumptuary law of Fannius), " if you may not enjoy what is your " own; if you muft be directed by rule and " meafure; if you muft be ftinted in your plea-" fures?—Let us fhake off, I pray you, thefe " mufty remains of antiquity, and make free to " profit

---

[1] Cic. Philip. v. Pro domo fua. Epift. ad Atticum. lib. ii.

"profit by what we and our fathers have gained [1]."

For the petulance of these expressions, this Tribune was, by the judgment of the Censors, on the following year, expelled from the Senate; and he took his revenge by prosecuting the Censor Antonius for bribery in canvassing for the very office he now held.

Cn. Cornelius Lentulus and Publius Licinius Crassus being raised to the Consulate, the latter was appointed to relieve Didius in Spain, and the other to succeed Metellus in Italy. There is, during some years, a considerable deficiency in the materials from which our accounts are collected; little more is recorded than the succession of Consuls, with the number of years that elapsed, and a few particulars, that ill supply the interval, of what passed in the city, or in the series of important affairs abroad. So far as these particulars, however, can be referred to their respective dates, it will be proper, while we endeavour to mark the lapse of time, to record them in the order in which they are supposed to have happened.

In the present year are dated two remarkable acts of the Senate; one to prohibit recourse to magic, another to abolish the practice of human sacrifices [2]: the first proceeding, perhaps, from credulity in the authors of the law; the other implying some remains of a gross and inhuman superstition, which was still entertained by the People, though rejected by the Government [3].

In

---

[1] Val. Max. lib. ii. c. 9. [2] Plin. lib. xxx. c. 1.
[3] Dion. Cassius, lib. xlii. p. 226.

In the following Consulate the kingdom of Cyrené was bequeathed to the Romans by Ptolomy Appion, the late king. But, as this People professed themselves to be the general patrons of liberty, where this blessing was not forfeited by some act of ingratitude or perfidy in their allies, they did not avail themselves of this legacy, leaving the subjects of Cyrené to retain for some time the independence of their nation with a species of popular government; and in this condition they were allowed to act the part of a separate State, until, under a general arrangement respecting all the dependencies of the Roman empire, the territories of Cyrené, among the rest, were reduced to the form of a province.

The following Consuls gave its name and its date to an act of the People, nearly of the same tenor with some of those which were formerly passed for the exclusion of aliens. The inhabitants of Italy still continued the practice of repairing in great numbers to Rome, if not in expectation of obtaining in a body the prerogative of citizens, at least in hopes of intruding themselves individually, as many of them separately did, into some of the Tribes, by which persons of this extraction came by degrees, from voting at elections, to be themselves elected into the higher offices of State.

Times of faction were extremely favourable to this intrusion of strangers. Different leaders connived at the enrolment of those who were likely to favour their respective parties. And the factious

CHAP. XIII.

U. C. 655.
L. Licinius
Crassus.
Q. Mucius
Scævola.
Lex Licinia Mucia
de Civibus
regendis.

CHAP. XIII.
tious Tribunes, however little they may have favoured the general claim of the allies to be admitted as Romans, fondly espoused their cause, as matter of opposition to the Senate, and as likely to open a more spacious field for their own operations; as they expected to raise the storm of popular animosity and tumult with the more ease, in proportion as the numbers of the People increased. By the act of Licinius and Mucius, nevertheless, a scrutiny was set on foot, and all who, without a just title, ventured to exercise any privilege of Roman citizens, were remitted to their several boroughs [1].

In this Consulate is likewise dated the trial of Servilius Cæpio, for his supposed misconduct about ten years before in his command of the army against the Cimbri. He had exasperated the popular faction, by opposing the act of Saturninus for the gratuitous distribution of corn, and his enemies were now encouraged to raise this prosecution against him. The People gave sentence of condemnation, and violently drove from the place of assembly two of the Tribunes who ventured to interpose their negative in his favour. Authors, according to Valerius Maximus, have differed in their accounts of the sequel; some affirming that Cæpio, being put to death in prison, his body was dragged through the streets as that of a traitor, and cast into the river; others, that he was, by the favour

[1] Ascon. in Orat. pro Cornelio Majest. reo.

vour of Antiſtius, one of the Tribunes, refcued, or enabled to make his efcape¹.

C. Norbanus, who was faid to be author of the riot which occaſioned the condemnation of Cæpio, and the fuppofed cruel execution of that citizen, was on the following year brought to trial himſelf for mal-adminiſtration and fedition in office; but, by his own popularity, and the addrefs of the orator Antonius, who pleaded his caufe, was acquitted².

The war in Spain ſtill continued; and the Romans, having gained confiderable victories, fent ten commiffioners, to endeavour, in concert with Craffus and Didius, to make fuch arrangements as might tend to the future peace of thofe provinces: but in vain; hoſtilities were again renewed in the following year.

L. Cornelius Sylla, who had been Quæſtor in the year of Rome fix hundred and forty-fix, now, after an interval of about fourteen years, and without having been Edile, ſtood candidate for the office of Prætor. Whether his neglect of political honours, during this period, proceeded from idlenefs, or from want of ambition, is uncertain. His character will juſtify either conſtruction, being equally fufceptible of diffipation, and of the difdain of ordinary diſtinctions. The People, however, refufed to gratify him in his defire of paſſing on to the office of Prætor without being Edile; as they were refolved to be gratified with the magnificent

U. C. 660.
C. Val.
Flaccus,
M. Hierennius.

¹ Val. Max. lib. iv. c. 7.   ² Cicero de Orator. lib. ii.

CHAP.
XIII.
ficent shows of wild beasts, which his supposed correspondence with the king of Mauritania enabled him to furnish. But to remove this objection to his preferment, he gave out, that as Prætor he should exhibit the same shows which were expected from him as Edile: and having, in the following year, persisted in his suit, he was accordingly elected, and fulfilled the expectations of the People; insomuch, that he is said to have let loose in the Circus one hundred maned or male lions, and to have exhibited the method of baiting or fighting them by Mauritanian huntsmen[1]. Such was the price which candidates for preferment at Rome were obliged to pay for the suffrage of the People.

In this variable scene, where so many particular men excelled in genius and magnanimity, while measures of State were affected by the caprice of a disorderly multitude, P. Rutilius, late Quæstor in Asia, exhibited a spectacle more than sufficient to counterbalance the lions of Sylla; and, if it were permitted in any case whatever to treat our country with disdain, furnished an instance to be applauded of the just contempt with which the undeserved resentments of corrupt and malicious men may be slighted. Having reformed many abuses of the equestrian tax-gatherers in the province which he governed, he was himself brought before the tribunal of an equestrian jury, to be tried for the crime he had restrained in others.

In

[1] Plin. lib. viii. c. 16.

In this situation he declined the aid of any friend, told the judges he would make no defence; but stated the particulars by which he had offended his prosecutors, left the court to decide, and, being condemned, retired to Smyrna, where he ever after lived in great tranquillity, and could not be prevailed on, even by Sylla in the height of his power, to return to Rome[1]. Great as the State and Republic of Rome was become, unmerited disgrace was certainly a just object of contempt or indifference, to the worthy person on whom it was inflicted.

The Proconsuls, Didius and Crassus, were permitted to triumph for victories obtained in Spain, but had not been able to establish the peace of that country. The conduct of the war which broke out afresh in one of the provinces was committed to Valerius Flaccus, and that of the other to Perperna, one of the Consuls. Flaccus, near the town of Belgida, obtained a great victory, in which were slain about twenty thousand of the enemy; but he could not prevail on the canton to submit. Such of the People as were inclined to capitulate, having met to deliberate on terms, were beset by their fellow-citizens, and the house in which they were assembled being set on fire, they perished in the flames.

The war having been likewise renewed with the Thracians on the frontiers of Macedonia, Geminius, who commanded there in the quality of Proprætor,

U. C. 661.
C. Claudius Pulcher,
M. Perperna.

[1] Val. Max. lib. vi. c. 17. Liv. lib. lxx. Orosius, lib. v. c. 17. Cic. de Orator. et in Bruto: Pædianus in Divinationem. Velleius, lib ii.

praetor, was defeated, and the province over-run by the enemy.

The Praetor Sylla, at the expiration of his office, was sent into Asia with a commission to restore Ariarathes to the kingdom of Cappadocia, which had been seized by Mithridates, and to restore Pylamenes to that of Paphlagonia, from which he had been expelled by Nicomedes king of Bythinia. The Praetor having successfully executed both these commissions, continued his journey to the Euphrates, where he had a conference, and concluded a treaty with an ambassador from Ariarathes king of the Parthians [1].

From an edict of the Censors, Cn. Domitius Ahenobarbus and C. Licinius Crassus, condemning the schools of Latin rhetoric [2], it appears that the Romans, during this period, still received with reluctance the refinements which were gradually taking place in the literary as well as in the other arts. "Whereas information," said the Censors in their edict, "has been lodged before us that "schools are kept by certain persons, under the "title of Latin rhetoricians, to which the youth "of this city resort, and at which they pass entire "days in frivolity and sloth; and whereas our an- "cestors have determined what their children "should learn, and what exercises they ought to "frequent: these innovations on the customs and "manners of our forefathers being, in our opi- "nion,

---

[1] Plutarch. in Sylla. Appian in Mithridatico. Justin, lib. xxxiii. Strabo, lib. xii.
[2] Cicer. de Orator, lib. iii. c. 24.

"nion, offensive and wrong, we publish these
"presents, that both masters and scholars, given
"to these illicit practices, may be duly apprised
"of our displeasure¹." Cicero being now fourteen years of age, and employed in acquiring that eloquence for which he became so famous, was probably involved in this censure, as frequenting the schools which, by this formal edict of the magistrate, were condemned.

In the Consulate of Marcius Philippus and Sext. Julius Cæsar, according to Pliny, there were in the Roman treasury sixteen hundred and twenty-eight thousand eight hundred and twenty-nine pondo² of gold³, or between sixty and seventy or eighty millions Sterling. In the same year a present sent from the king of Mauritania had nearly produced a civil war in the commonwealth, or at least inflamed the passions from which that calamity soon after arose. Bocchus, in order to remind the Romans of the merit he had acquired by delivering Jugurtha into their hands, had caused this scene to be represented in a groupe of images of gold, containing his own figure, that of Jugurtha, and that of Sylla, to whom the unhappy prince was delivered up. Marius, under whose auspices this transaction had passed, being provoked at having no place in the groupe by which it was represented, attempted to pull down the images after they had been erected in the place of their destination

U. C. 662.
Lucius Marcius Philippus, Sextus Julius Cæsar.

---
1 A. Gellius, lib. xv. c. 11.   2 The Roman pondo of ten ounces.
3 Plin. Harduen, lib. xxxiii. c. 3.

destination in the Capitol. Sylla was equally solicitous to have them remain; and the contest was likely to end in violence, if matters of greater moment had not arisen to occupy the ardent and vehement spirit of these rivals.

The expectations of all parties at Rome, and throughout Italy, were now raised by the projects of Livius Drusus, an active Tribune, who, in order to distinguish himself, brought forward many subjects of the greatest concern to the public. He acted at first in concert with the leading men of the Senate, and was supported by them in order to obtain some amendment in the law as it then stood respecting the courts of justice. The Equestrian order had acquired exclusive possession of the judicature. The Senators wished to recover at least a share in that prerogative; and Drusus, in order to gratify them, moved for an act of which the tendency was, to restore the Senators to their place in forming the courts of justice; and to prevent opposition from the Equestrian order, he proposed, at once, to enrol three hundred knights into the Senate; and that the Senators, who appear at this time to have amounted to no more than three hundred, might not withstand this increase of their numbers, he left to each the nomination of one of the new members; proposing, that from the six hundred so constituted, the lists of judges should be taken [1]. Many of the knights were reconciled

[1] Appian. de Bell. Civ. lib. i. Aut. de Viris Illustribus, c. 66. Cicero pro Clientio.

OF THE ROMAN REPUBLIC. 223

ciled to this arrangement, by the hopes of be- CHAP.
coming Senators; but the order, in general, seem XIII.
to have confidered it as a fnare laid to deprive
them of their confequence in the government of
their country; and individuals refufed to accept
of a place in the Senate, at the hazard of fo great
and fo fudden a change in the conftitution of the
State, and in the condition of an order from which
they derived their confequence [1].

This Tribune likewife propofed an act to de- Lex Numbafe the filver coin, by mixing an eighth of alloy. maria.
But the part of his project which gave the greateft alarm, was that which related to the indigent
citizens of Rome, and to the inhabitants of Italy
in general.

With a view to gratify the poorer citizens he Lex de Coloniis.
propofed, that all the new fettlements, projected
by the law of Caius Gracchus, fhould now be carried into execution. The Conful, Marcus Perperna, having ventured to oppofe this propofal,
was, by order of the Tribune, taken into cuftody;
and fo roughly treated in the execution of this
order, that, while he ftruggled to difengage himfelf, the blood was made to fpring from his noftrils. "It is no more than the pickle of the tur-
" tle-fifh [2]," faid the Tribune, a fpecies of delicacy, in which, it feems, among other luxuries of
the

[1] Appian. de Bell. Civ. lib. i. Aut. de Viris Illuftribus, c. 66. Cicero pro Clientio.

[2] Ex turdis maria. Aut. de Viris Illuftribus, in L. Druf. Val. Max. lib. ix. c. 4. Florus.

CHAP. XIII.

the table, this Conful was fuppofed frequently to indulge himfelf.

Lex de Civitate Sociis danda.

For the allies of Italy, Livius Drufus propofed to obtain the favourite object on which they had been fo long intent, their admiffion on the rolls of Roman citizens. In all his other propofals, he had the concurrence of fome party in the commonwealth, and by perfuafion, or force, had obtained his purpofe; but in this he ftruck at the perfonal confideration of every citizen, and was oppofed by the general voice of the People.

This Tribune ufed to boaft, that he would exhauft every fund from which any order of men could be gratified, and leave to thofe who came after him, nothing to give but the air and the earth[1]. The citizens in general, however, were become tired of his favours, and the people of Italy were ill-difpofed to requite the merit of a project, which, though in their favour, he had not been able to execute.

Soon after the motion which Drufus made for this great and alarming innovation, he was fuddenly taken ill in the public affembly, and Papirius Carbo, another of the Tribunes, made a fhort fpeech on the occafion, which, among a people prone to fuperftition, and ready to execute whatever they conceived to be awarded by the gods, probably haftened the fate of his falling colleague: " O Marcus Drufus!" he faid, " the father I call, not this degenerate fon; thou " who ufedft to fay, The commonwealth is facred,
" whoever

[1] Florus, lib. iii. c. 17.

"whoever violates it is sure to be punished. The temerity of the son may soon evince the wisdom of the father." A great shout arose in the assembly, and Drusus[1], being attended to his own house by a numerous multitude, received in the crowd a secret wound of which he died[2]. All his laws were soon after repealed, as having passed under unfavourable auspices. But the inhabitants of Italy were not to be appeased under their late disappointment, and discontents were breaking out in every part of the country, which threatened to end in some great convulsion.

In this state of public alarm, some prosecutions were raised by the Tribunes, calculated merely to gratify their own private resentments, and tending at the same time to excite extreme animosities. Q. Varius Hybrida obtained a decree of the People, directing, that inquiry should be made by whose fault the allies had been made to expect the freedom of the city. In consequence of an inquest set on foot for this purpose, L. Calphurnius Bestia, late Consul, and M. Aurelius Orator, and other eminent men, were condemned[3]. Mummius Achaicus was banished to Delos. Emilius Scaurus, who had long maintained his dignity as *Princeps*, or first on the roll of the Senate, was cited on this occasion before the People as a person involved in the same guilt. Quintus Varius, the

---

[1] Cicero in Bruto, p. 63.
[2] Velleius, lib. ii. c. 13, 14. Appian. Florus, lib. iii. c. 17.
[3] Appian. Val. Max. lib. viii. c. 4. Cicero in Bruto.

the Tribune, who accused him, being a native of Spain, Scaurus was acquitted upon the following short defence: " Q. Varius, from the banks of " the Sucro, in Spain, says, That M. Emilius " Scaurus, first in the roll of the Senate, has en- " couraged your subjects to revolt; Varius main- " tains the charge; Scaurus denies it; there is no " other evidence in this matter: choose whom you " will believe¹."

The year following, Varius himself was tried, and condemned in terms of his own act; and while these prosecutions suspended all other civil affairs, and even interrupted the measures required for the safety of the public, the inhabitants of Italy were forming dangerous combinations, and were ready to break out in actual rebellion. They were exasperated with having their suit not only refused, but in having the abettors of it at Rome considered as criminals. They deputed commissioners to meet at a convenient place, to concert their measures, and were speedily advancing to the effect of some violent resolutions.

The Romans took their first suspicion of a dangerous design in agitation among their allies, from observing that they were exchanging hostages among themselves. The Proconsul Servilius, who commanded in the Picenum, having intelligence of such proceedings from Asculum, repaired thither, in order, by his presence, to prevent any commotion; but

---

1 Cicero pro M. Scauro filio. Aut. de Viris Illustribus, c. 72. Quintilian. lib. v. c. 12. Val Max. lib. iii. c. 7.

but his coming, in reality, haftened the revolt. His remonftrances and his threats made the inhabitants fenfible that their defigns were known, and that the execution of them could no longer be in fafety delayed. They accordingly took arms, and put to the fword the Proconful Servilius himfelf, with his lieutenant, and all the Roman citizens who happened to be in the place. The alarm immediately fpread throughout all the towns that were concerned in the plot; and, as upon a fignal agreed, the Marfi, Peligni, Veftini, Marcini, Picentes, Ferentanæ, Hirpini, Pompeiani, Venufini, Apuli, Lucani, and Samnites, took arms, and in this menacing pofture, fent a joint deputation to Rome, to demand a participation in the privilege of citizens; of which they had, by their fervices, contributed fo largely to increafe the value.

In anfwer to this demand they were told by the Senate, That they muft difcontinue their affemblies, and renounce their pretenfions; otherwife, that they muft not prefume to fend any other meffage to Rome.

War being thus declared, both parties prepared for the conteft. The allies pitched upon Corfinium for the capital of what they denominated the *Italian Republic:* they inftituted a Senate of five hundred members; elected two Confuls, with other civil and military officers of ftate, to replace the political government at Rome, from which they now withdrew their allegiance. They muftered

tered in separate bodies and under different leaders, one hundred thousand men in arms [1]. The Romans now found themselves in an instant brought back to the condition in which they had been about three hundred years before; reduced to a few miles of territory round their walls, and beset with enemies more united, and more numerous than ever had assailed them at once on the same ground. But their city was likewise enlarged, their numbers increased, and every individual excellently formed to occupy his place in the State, either as a warrior or a citizen. All of them assumed, upon this occasion, the sagum or military dress; and being joined by such of the Latins as remained in their allegiance, and by such of their colonies, from different parts of Italy, as continued to be faithful, together with some mercenaries from Gaul and Numidia, they assembled a force equal to that of their revolted subjects.

The Consuls were placed at the head of the two principal armies; Lucius Julius Cæsar, in the country of the Samnites [2], and Rutilius, in that of the Marsi [3]. They had under their command the most celebrated and experienced officers of the republic; but little more is preserved to furnish an account of the war besides the names of the Roman commanders, and those of the persons opposed to them. Rutilius was attended by Pompeius Strabo, the father of him who afterwards bore

---

[1] Diodorus, lib. xxxvii. Eclog. 1.
[2] Now part of the kingdom of Naples.
[3] Contiguous part of the Ecclesiastical State.

bore the title of Pompey the Great; Cæpio, Perperna, Meſſala, and Caius Marius, of whom the laſt had already ſo often been Conſul. Lucius Cæſar had, in the army which he commanded, Lentulus, Didius, Craſſus, and Marcellus. They were oppoſed by T. Afranius, P. Ventidius, Marcus Egnatius, Q. Pompedius, C. Papius, M. Lamponius, C. Judacilius, Hircus, Aſſinius, and Vetius Cato, at the head of the allies. The forces were ſimilar in diſcipline and in arms. The Romans were likely to be inferior in numbers and in reſources, but had the advantage in reputation, authority, and in the fame of their leaders, employed in the higheſt ſtations, and inured to command. But ſo well had the allies taken their meaſures, and with ſo much animoſity did they enter into a quarrel which they had been meditating for ſome years, that the Romans appeared at firſt unequal to the conteſt, and were ſurpriſed and overcome in ſundry encounters.

The detail of theſe operations is imperfectly recorded; and does not furniſh the materials of a relation either intereſting or inſtructive. We muſt therefore content ourſelves with little more than a liſt of actions and events, together with the general reſult.

One of the Conſuls, Lucius Cæſar, in the firſt operation of the war, was defeated by Vetius Cato near Eſernia, and had two thouſand men killed in the field. The town of Eſernia was immediately inveſted, and ſome Roman officers of diſtinction were obliged to make their eſcape in the diſguiſe

CHAP. disguise of slaves. Two Roman cohorts were cut
XIII. off at Venafrum, and that colony fell into the
hands of the enemy. The other Consul, Rutilius,
was likewise defeated by the Marsi, and fell in the
field, with eight thousand men of his army. His
colleague was called to the city to preside at the
election of a successor; but being necessarily detained with the army, the office continued vacant
for the remainder of the campaign, while the army acted under the direction of the late Consuls,
Marius and Cæpio.

The corpse of Rutilius, and of other persons of
rank, being brought to the city in order to have
the honours of a public funeral, seemed to spread
such a gloom, as to suggest a resolution in the Senate, which is probably wise on all such occasions, that for the future the dead should be buried where they fell.

In the mean time, Lucius Cæsar obtained a victory in the country of the Samnites; and the Senate, in order to compose the minds of the People,
which in this war were agitated to an uncommon
degree, as if this victory had suppressed the revolt,
resolved, that the sagum, or military dress, should
be laid aside ⁱ.

U. C. 664.
Cn. Pomp.
Strabo,
L. Porcius
Cato.

The usual time of the Consular elections being
come, Cn. Pompeius Strabo and Porcius Cato were
named. The first gained a complete victory over
the Marsi; and, notwithstanding an obstinate defence,

ⁱ Liv. lib. lxxiv. Appian. Orosius, lib. v. c. 18. Florus, lib. iii. c. 18.
Velleius, Eutropius.

fence, reduced the city of Asculum, where the first hostilities took place, and where the Romans had suffered the greatest outrage. The principal inhabitants of the place were put to death, the remainder were sold for slaves. The other Consul, Cato, was killed in an attack upon the entrenchments of the Marsi; and although Marius and Sylla, in different quarters, had turned the fortune of the war against the allies, yet the event still continued to be extremely doubtful.

The Umbrians, Etruscans, and inhabitants of other districts of Italy, who had hitherto hesitated in the choice of their party, took courage from the perseverance and success of their neighbours, and openly joined the revolt. The more distant parts of the empire were soon likely to receive the contagion: they were already, by the obstruction they met with in carrying supplies of provisions or revenue, severed from the capital, and they were likely to withdraw on the first opportunity, the allegiance which they were supposed to owe as conquered provinces.

Mithridates, the king of Pontus, did not neglect the occasion that was offered to him; in this distraction of affairs in Italy; he put all his forces in motion, expelled Nicomedes from Bythinia, and Ariobarzones from Cappadocia, and thus himself became master of the greater part of the Lesser Asia.

In this extremity it appeared necessary at Rome to compose the disorders of Italy, and no longer

CHAP. XIII. to withstand the request of the allies; but the Senate had the address to make the intended concessions seem to be an act of munificence and generosity, not of weakness or fear.

The Latins, who had continued in their allegiance, were, in consideration of their fidelity, admitted to all the privileges of Roman citizens. The Umbri and Tuscans, who either had not yet declared, or who had appeared the least active in the quarrel, were next comprehended; and some other inhabitants of Italy, observing, that they were likely to obtain by favour what they endeavoured at so great a risk to extort by force, grew remiss in the war, or withdrew from the league, that they might appear to be forward in the general return to peace.

The Marsi, Samnites, and Lucanians, who had been the principal authors of the revolt, or who had acted with most animosity in the conduct of it, continued for some time to be excluded from the privilege to which they aspired, and which the Romans would not be forced to bestow. But the civil war, which soon after broke out among the citizens themselves, terminated either in the extirpation of those obstinate aliens, and in the settlement of Roman colonies in their stead, or gave them an opportunity, under favour of the party they espoused, of gaining admittance to the freedom of Rome: so that, in a few years, all the inhabitants of Italy, from the Rubicon to the

Straits

Straits of Meſſina, were inſcribed on the rolls of the People, and a conſtitution of ſtate, which had been already overcharged by the numbers who partook of the ſovereignty, was now altogether overwhelmed; or if this change alone were not ſufficient to deſtroy it, was not likely long to remain without ſome notable or fatal reverſe. Aſſemblies of the People, already ſufficiently tumultuary, being now conſidered as the collective body of all the Italians, were become altogether impracticable, or for the moſt part could be no more than partial tumults, which, for particular purpoſes, aſſumed this title, in the ſtreets of Rome, or the contiguous fields; inſomuch that when we read of the authority of the Senate being ſet aſide by an order of the People, we may venture to conceive all government ſuſpended at the ſuit of the party or faction who had the populace of the town at their call, rather than any regular tranſaction of ſtate.

Licinius Craſſus and L. Julius Cæſar were choſen Cenſors, in order to make up the new rolls of the People. This, it is likely, was found to be a difficult and tedious work. It became neceſſary to ſcrutinize the rolls of every ſeparate borough, in order to know who were entitled to be added to the liſt of Roman citizens; and this difficulty was further increaſed in conſequence of a law deviſed about this time by Papirius Carbo, in which it was enacted, that not only the natives and ancient denizens of Italy, but all who ſhould, for the future, obtain the freedom of any Italian borough,

CHAP. XIII.
if they had a refidence in Italy, and lodged their claim to the Prætor fixty days, fhould, by that act, become citizens of Rome¹; fo that the prerogative of the Roman People continued to be in the gift of every feparate corporation, as well as in that of the State itfelf.

The number of the aliens admitted on the rolls, at this mufter, is not recorded; but it was probably equal to that of the ancient citizens, and might have inftantly formed a very powerful and dangerous faction in the State, if effectual meafures had not been taken to diminifh or guard againft the effect of their influence. For this purpofe, the new citizens were not mixed promifcuoufly with the mafs of the People, but confined to eight particular Tribes²; and of confequence, could influence only eight votes in thirty-five.³; and the ancient citizens were ftill poffeffed of a great majority. But this artifice did not long efcape the attention of thofe who were aggrieved by it, and became, in the fequel, fubject of farther difpute.

Meantime, while the Romans were meditating, or actually making, this important change in the ftate of their commonwealth, they found leifure for matters of lefs moment, in which they endeavoured to provide

---

1 Cicero pro Archia Poëta.

2 Velleius Paterculus, lib. ii c. 20.

3 Hiftorians mention this particular, as if eight new Tribes were added to the former thirty-five; but the continual allufion of Roman writers, to the number thirty-five, will not allow us to fuppofe any augmentation. Cicero de Lege Agraria 2da, c. 8.

provide for the peace of the city, and the administration of justice.

Plautius, one of the Tribunes, obtained a new law for the selection of judges, by which it was enacted, That each Tribe should annually set apart fifteen citizens, without any distinction of rank; and that, from the whole so named, the judges in all trials that occurred within the year should be taken [1]. This law appeared to be equitable, as it gave, with great propriety, to all the different classes of men in the commonwealth, an equal right to be named of the juries; and to every party concerned, an equal chance of being tried by his peers.

Lex Plotia de Judiciis.

The same Tribune likewise obtained a law for the preservation of the public peace, by which it was declared capital to be seen in any place of public resort, with a weapon, or instrument of death; to occupy any place of strength in the city; to offer violence to the house of any person, to disturb any private company; to interrupt any meeting of the Senate, assembly of the People, or court of justice. To these clauses Catulus subjoined another, in which he comprehended persons surrounding the Senate with an armed force, or offering violence to any magistrate [2].

Lex Plotia de Vi.

[1] Pedianus in Cornelianam Ciceronis.

[2] Cicero pro Cælio, et de Aruspicum Responso.

CHAP. XIV.

Triumph of Pompeius Strabo.—Progress of Sylla. —War with the King of Pontus.—Rise of that kingdom.—Appointment of Sylla to command.—Policy of the Tribune Sulpicius.—Sylla's Commission recalled in favour of Marius.—His March from Campania to Rome.—Expels Marius and his Faction from the City.—His Operations in Greece. —Siege of Athens.—Battle of Chæronea.—Of Orchomenos.—Transactions at Rome.—Policy of Cinna.—Marius recalled.—Cinna flies, and is deprived.—Recovers the Possession of Rome.—Treaty of Sylla with Mithridates.—He passes into Italy. —Is opposed by numerous Armies.—Various Events of the War in Italy.—Sylla prevails.—His Proscription, or Massacre.—Named Dictator. —His Policy—Resignation—and Death.

CHAP. XIV.

THE social war, though far from being successful on the part of the Romans, concluded with a triumphal procession; and the Senate, though actually obliged to yield the point for which they contended, thought proper, under pretence of advantages gained on some particular occasions, to erect a trophy. They singled out Pompeius Strabo for the pageant in this ceremony; either because he had reduced Asculum, where the rebellion first broke out, or because a victory obtained by him had most immediately preceded the peace. But the most remarkable circumstance

in

in this procession was, its being, in shew, a triumph of the old citizens over the new, but in reality a triumph of the latter. Ventidius Bassus, being a prisoner in the war, and led as such in the present triumph, was now, though in the form of a captive, in fact introduced to share in the prerogatives of a Roman; he was, in the sequel, promoted to all the honours of the State; and, in the quality of a victorious general, came to lead a procession of the same kind with that in which he himself had made his first entry at Rome as a captive [1].

Sylla, by his conduct and his successes wherever he had borne a separate command in this war, gave proof of that superior genius by which he now began to be distinguished. By his magnanimity on all occasions, by his great courage in danger, by his imperious exactions from the enemy, and by his lavish profusion to his own troops, he obtained, in a very high degree, the confidence and attachment of soldiers; and yet in this, it is probable, that he acted merely from temper, and not from design, or with any view to the consequence. With so careless and so bold a hand did this man already hold the reins of military discipline, that Albinus, an officer of high rank, and next in command to himself, being killed by the soldiers in a mutiny, he treated this outrage as a trifle, saying, when the matter was reported to him, That the

[1] Val. lib. vi. c. 9. Gellius, lib. xv. c. 4. Plin, lib. 7. c. 43. Dio Cassius, 43. fine.

the troops would atone for it when they met with the enemy[1]. With great merits recently displayed, he repaired to the city, laid claim to the Consulate, and was accordingly chosen, in conjunction with Quintus Pompeius Rufus.

It was thought necessary still to keep a proper force under arms in Italy, until the public tranquillity should be fully established. The army, which had acted under Cneius Pompeius Strabo, Consul of the preceding year, was destined for this service; and Quintus Rufus was appointed to the command of it.

The war with Mithridates, king of Pontus, however, was the principal object of attention; and this province, together with the army then lying in Campania, fell to the lot of Sylla.

The monarchy of Pontus had sprung from the ruins of the Macedonian establishments in Asia; and, upon their entire suppression, was become one of the most considerable kingdoms of the East.

Mithridates had inherited from his ancestors a great extent of territory, reaching in length, according to the representation of his ambassador quoted by Appian, twenty thousand stadia, above two thousand miles. He himself had joined to it the kingdom of Colchis, and other provinces on the coasts of the Euxine sea. His military establishment amounted to three hundred thousand foot, and forty thousand horse, besides auxiliaries from Thrace, and from that part of Scythia which lies on

[1] Plutarch. in Sylla.

on the Meotis and the Tanais, countries over which he had acquired an afcendant approaching to fovereignty. He had pretenfions likewife on the kingdoms of Bithynia and Cappadocia, which he had hitherto relinquifhed from deference to the Romans; or of which he had poftponed the effect until he fhould be prepared to cope with this formidable power. All his pretenfions, indeed, like thofe of other monarchies or ftates of any denomination, were likely to extend with his force; and to receive no limitation but from the defect of his power. And fuch were his refources, and his perfonal character, that if he had encountered on the fide of Europe with an enemy lefs able than the Romans were to withftand his progrefs, it is probable that in his hands the empire of Pontus might have vied with that of the greateft conquerors recorded in hiftory.

About the time that the focial war broke out in Italy, Caffius Longinus, Manius Acquilius, and C. Oppius were, in different characters, ftationed in the province of Afia, and had taken under their protection every power in the country that was likely to oppofe the king of Pontus in his progrefs to empire.

Nicomedes, who had been recently reftored to the crown of Bithynia, made hoftile incurfions under the encouragement of his Roman allies, even into the kingdom of Pontus itfelf. And the king, having made fruitlefs complaints on this fubject to the Roman governors in Afia; and thinking
that

that the distracted state of Italy furnished him with a favourable opportunity to slight their resentment, he sent his son Ariarathes into Cappadocia with a force to expel Ariobarzanes, though an ally of the Romans, and to possess that kingdom. He took the field himself, and sent powerful armies, under his generals, against Nicomedes, and his Italian confederates, who, on their part, had assembled all the force of their province and of their allies, to the amount of an hundred and twenty thousand men, in different bodies, to defend their own frontier, or to annoy their enemy.

Mithridates fell separately upon the different parties which were thus forming against him; and having defeated Nicomedes, and afterwards Manius, obliged the Roman officers, with their ally, to retire; Cassius to Apamea, Manius towards Rhodes, and Nicomedes, to Pergamus. His fleet, likewise, consisting of three hundred gallies, opened the passage of the Hellespont, took all the ships which the Romans had stationed in those straits; and he himself soon after in person traversed Phrygia and the Lesser Asia, to the sea of Cilicia and Greece. In all the cities of the Lesser Asia, where the people, as usual upon a change of masters, now openly declared their detestation of the Roman dominion, he was received with open gates. He got possession of the person of Oppius, by means of the inhabitants of Laodicea, where this general had taken refuge with a body of mercenaries. These were allowed to disband; but Oppius himself

self was conducted as a prisoner to the head-quarters of Mithridates, and, in mockery of his state as a Roman governor, was made to pass through the cities in his way, with his fasces or ensigns of magistracy carried before him.

Manius Acquilius likewise fell into the hands of the enemy, was treated with similar scorn; and with a barbarity which nothing but the most criminal abuse of the power he lately possessed could have deserved or provoked. Being carried round the cities of Asia mounted on an ass, he was obliged at every place to declare, that his own avarice had been the cause of the war; and he was at last put to death by the pouring of melted gold into his throat.

While Mithridates thus overwhelmed his enemies, and was endeavouring to complete his conquest of Asia by the reduction of Rhodes, he ordered his general Archelaus to penetrate by the way of Thrace and Macedonia into Greece.

Such was the alarming state of the war, when the Romans, having scarcely appeased the troubles in Italy, appointed L. Cornelius Sylla, with six legions that lay in Campania, to embark for Greece, in order, if possible, to stem a torrent which no ordinary bars were likely to withstand.

But before Sylla or his colleague could depart for their provinces, disorders arose in the city, which, however secure from the approach of foreign enemies, brought armies to battle in the streets,

streets, and covered the pavements of Rome with the slain.

Publius Sulpicius, Tribune of the People, with a singular boldness and profligacy, ventured to tamper with the dangerous humours which were but ill suppressed in the event of the late troubles; and, unrestrained by the sad experience of civil wars and domestic tumults, lighted the torch anew, and kindled the former animosity of the popular and Senatorian parties. The severe measures hitherto taken by the Senate and Magistrates against the authors of sedition had, in some instances, been effectual to snatch the republic out of the hands of lawless men, and to suspend for a while the ruin which threatened the commonwealth; but the examples so given, instead of deterring others from a repetition of the same crimes, appear only to have admonished the factious leaders to take more effectual precautions, and to make the necessary provision of armed force before they embarked in designs against the State. They accordingly improved and refined by degrees on the measures which they successively took against the Senate; and when the Tribune Sulpicius began to act, the arrangements he made were equal to a system of formal war. This Tribune, according to Plutarch, had three thousand gladiators in his pay; and in despite of the law of Plautius, had ever at his beck a numerous company of retainers, armed with daggers and other offensive weapons; these he called his *Anti-senate;* and kept in readiness to be employed in attempts,

which

which he was at no pains to difguife, againſt the authority of the Senate itſelf. He moved the People to recal from exile all thoſe who had withdrawn from the city, on occaſion of the former diſorders, and to admit the new citizens, and enfranchiſed ſlaves, to be enrolled promiſcuouſly in all the Tribes without regard to the late wiſe limitation of the Senate's decree, by which they were reſtricted to a few. By the change which he now propoſed, the citizens of leaſt conſideration might come to have a majority, or irreſiſtible ſway in the public deliberations. The Tribunes would become maſters in every queſtion, and fill up the rolls of the People in the manner that moſt ſuited their intereſt.

This preſumptuous man himſelf undertook to procure the freedom of the city for every perſon who applied to him, and boldly received premiums in the ſtreets for this proſtitution of the privileges and powers of his own conſtituents.

The more reſpectable citizens, and even the magiſtrates, in vain withſtood theſe abuſes. They were overpowered by force, and frequently driven from the place of aſſembly. In this extremity they had recourſe to ſuperſtition, and by multiplying holidays, endeavoured to ſtop or to diſconcert their antagoniſts. But Sulpicius, with his party, laid violent hands on the Conſuls, in order to force them to recal theſe appointments. Young Pompey, the ſon of the preſent Conſul, and ſon-in-law to Sylla, was killed in the fray. Sylla himſelf,

though

though withdrawn from the tumult, feeling that he was in the power of this desperate faction, and being impatient to get into a situation in which he could more effectually counteract their fury, chose for the present to comply with their demands [1].

In the midst of these violences, the city being under an actual ;usurpation or tyranny, Sylla repaired to the army in Campania, with a resolution to pursue the object of his destination in Asia, and to leave the Tribunitian storms at Rome to spend their force. But soon after his departure, it appeared, that Marius was no stranger to the councils of Sulpicius; and that he hoped, by means of this Tribune, to gratify an ambition which outlived the vigour of his faculties and the strength of his body. His first object was to mortify his rival Sylla, in revoking, by a decree of the People, the appointment of the Senate, and to supersede him in the command of the army against Mithridates. A decree to this purpose was accordingly with ease obtained by Sulpicius, in one of those partial conventions, which took upon them to represent the People of Italy in the streets of Rome; and Marius, now appointed general of the army in Campania, that was destined for the Asiatic war, sent the proper officers to notify his appointment to Sylla, and to receive from him, in behalf of his successor, the charge of the army, and the delivery of the stores. Sylla had the address to make the troops apprehend that this change was equally prejudicial

[1] Plutarch. in Mario, p. 526. edit. Londin. 4to.

OF THE ROMAN REPUBLIC.

prejudicial to them as to himself; that Marius had his favourite legions whom he would naturally employ; and that the same act of violence, by which he had supplanted the general, would bring other officers and other men, to reap the fruits of this lucrative service in Asia. This persuasion, as well as the attachment which the army already bore to their general, produced its effect [1].

CHAP. XIV.

The officers who were charged to make known the appointment of Marius, on declaring their commission, found that violence could take place in the camp as well as in the city. Their orders were received with scorn. A tumult arose among the soldiers; and citizens vested with a public character, formally commissioned to communicate an order of the Roman People, and in the exercise of their duty, were slain in the camp.

In return to this outrage some relations and friends of Sylla were murdered at Rome, and such retaliations were not soon likely to end on either side [2]. Faction is generally blind, and does not see the use that may be made of its own violent precedents against itself. Although Sylla is said to have hesitated, yet he was not a person likely to shrink from the contest, in which his private enemies, and those of the State, had engaged him. Stung with rage, and probably thinking that force would be justified in snatching the republic out of such violent hands, he proposed to the army that they

[1] Appian. de Bell. Civil. lib. i.
[2] Plutarch. in Mario, Edit. Lond. p. 526.

CHAP.
XIV.
they should march to Rome. The proposal was received with joy; and the army, without any of the scruples, or any degree of that hesitation which in adopting this measure is ascribed to their commander, followed where he thought proper to lead them.

On this new and dangerous appearance of things, not only Marius and Sulpicius, with the persons most obnoxious on account of the insults offered to Sylla and to other respectable citizens, were seized with consternation; but even the Senate and the Nobles, seeing questions of state likely to be decided by military force, were justly alarmed.

A faction, it is true, had assumed the authority of the Roman People, to violate the laws, and to overawe the State; but armies, it was thought, are dangerous tools in the quarrels of party; and no good intention on the part of their leaders, no magnanimity or moderation in the execution of their plans, can compensate the ruinous tendency of a precedent which brings force to be employed as an ordinary resource in political contests. Even the present state of the republic did not appear so desperate as to justify such a measure.

The Senate accordingly sent a deputation to Sylla with entreaties, and with commands, that he would not advance to the city. This deputation was received by him within a few miles of the gates. He heard the remonstrance that was made to him with patience, and seemed to be moved: gave orders, in the hearing of the deputies, that the

the army should halt; sent the proper officers to mark out a camp, and suffered the commissioners to return to their employers, full of the persuasion that he was to comply with their request. But in this he only meant to deceive his antagonists; and having lulled them into a state of security, he sent a detachment close on the heels of the deputies of the Senate, with orders to seize the nearest gate; while he himself, with the whole army, speedily followed to support them.

The gate was accordingly seized. The People, in tumult, endeavoured to recover it; Marius secured the Capitol, summoned every person, whether freeman or slave, to repair to his standard; and multitudes assembled, as in a military station, to form on the parade. Sylla, in the mean time, at the head of his army, rushed through the gate, of which his vanguard, though pressed by multitudes by whom they were attacked, were still in possession. He was greatly annoyed from the battlements and windows as he passed, and might have been repulsed by the more numerous army of Roman citizens in the streets, if he had not commanded the city to be set on fire, in order to profit by the confusion into which the People were likely to be thrown in avoiding or in extinguishing the flames. By this expedient he drove Marius from all the stations he had occupied, and obliged his adherents to disperse.

While the army was distributed in different quarters of a city, deformed with recent marks of bloodshed

CHAP. XIV. bloodshed and fire, their general assembled the Senate, and called on them to consider the present state of affairs. Among the measures he suggested on this occasion, was a law by which Marius, with his son, and twelve of his faction, who had secreted themselves, were declared enemies of their country. This sentence was accompanied with a public injunction to seize or to kill them wherever they could be found. The reasons upon which this act of attainder was granted, were, that they had violated the laws, and seduced the slaves to desert from their masters, and to take arms against the republic [1].

While the officers of justice were employed in execution of this decree, and many others were busy in search of their private enemies, thus laid at their mercy, the Tribune Sulpicius, having fled to the marshes on the coast near Laurentum, was dragged from thence and slain. His head, severed from the body, as that of a traitor, who had surpassed every leader of faction in the outrages done to the laws and the government of his country, was exposed on one of the rostra; an example afterwards frequently imitated, and which, though it could not enhance the evil of the times, became an additional expression of the animosity and rancour of parties against each other [2].

Marius,

---

[1] Appian. de Bell. Civil. lib. i. p. 387. The names mentioned in this act of attainder or outlawry, were Sulpicius, Marius' father and son, P. Cethegus, Junius Brutus, Cneius and Pub. Granni, Albinovanus, Marcus Suetonius.

[2] Velleius Paterculus, lib. ii. c. 19.

CHAP. XIV.

Marius, upon his expulsion from Rome, retired to his own villa at Salonium; and being unprovided for a longer flight, sent his son to the farm of one Mutius, a friend in the neighbourhood, to procure what might be necessary for a voyage by sea. The young man was discovered at this place, and narrowly escaped in a waggon loaded with straw, which, the better to deceive his pursuers, he had ordered to take the road to Rome. The father fled to Ostia, and there embarked on board a vessel which was provided for him by Numerius, who had been one of his partizans in the preceding disorders. Having put to sea, he was forced by stress of weather to Circeii, there landed in want of every necessary, and made himself known to some herdsmen, of whom he implored relief. Being informed of the parties that were abroad in pursuit of him, he concealed himself for the night in a neighbouring wood. Afterwards, continuing his flight by the coast, and on his way to the town of Minturnæ, he was alarmed at the sight of some horsemen who seemed to be in search; made for the shore, and, with much difficulty, got on board of a boat which was passing. The persons with whom he thus took refuge resisted the threats and importunities of the pursuers to have him delivered up to them, or thrown into the sea; but having rowed him to a supposed place of safety at the mouth of the L is, they put him on shore, and left him to his fate. Here he first took refuge in a cottage, afterwards under a hollow bank of the river,

CHAP. XIV.

river, and, last of all, on hearing the tread of the horsemen, who still pursued him, he plunged himself to the chin in a marsh; but, though concealed by the reeds and the depth of the water, he was discovered and dragged from thence all covered with mud. He was carried to Minturnæ, and doomed by the magistrates of the place to suffer, in execution of the sentence which had been denounced against himself and his partizans at Rome. He was, however, by some connivance, allowed to escape from hence, again put to sea, and, at the island Ænaria, joined some associates of his flight. Being afterwards obliged to land in Sicily for a supply of water, and being known, he narrowly escaped with the loss of some of the crew that navigated his vessel. From thence he arrived on the coast of Africa; but, being forbid the province by the Prætor Sextilius, continued to shift his abode among the islands or places of retirement on the coast [1].

This adventurer was in his seventieth year when, by means of popular tumults, he made this attempt to overturn the Roman republic, and when he strove to obtain the command of an army in the busiest and most arduous service which the Roman empire had then to offer. Being forced, by his miscarriage in this attempt, into the state of an outlaw, he still amused the world with adventures and escapes, which historians record with the embellishments of a picturesque and even romantic description.

[1] Plutarch. in Mario, edit. Lond. p. 534.

OF THE ROMAN REPUBLIC.

CHAP. XIV.

description. A Gaulish or German soldier, who was employed at Minturnæ to put him to death, it is said, overawed by his aspect, recoiled from the task; and the people of the place, as if moved by this miracle of the terrified soldier, concurred in aiding his escape [1]. The presence of such an exile on the ground where Carthage had stood, was supposed to increase the majesty and the melancholy of the scene. "Go," he said to the Lictor who brought him the orders of the Prætor to depart, "tell him that you have seen Marius sitting on the ruins of Carthage [2]."

The Senate, thus restored to its authority, and, by the suppression of the late sedition, masters of the city, took the proper measures to prevent, for the future, such violations of order from being introduced under pretence of popular government. They resolved that no question of legislation should be agitated in the assembly of the Tribes [3]; and Sylla, before he left the city, thought proper to dispatch the election of consuls for the following year, but did not employ the power, which he now possessed, to make the choice fall on persons who were both of the senatorian party. Together with Octavius, who had the authority of the Senate at heart, he suffered Cinna, though of the opposite faction, to be vested with the powers of Consul, and only exacted a promise from him not to disturb the public tranquillity; nor, in his absence,

---

[1] Velleius Pater. lib. ii. c. 19.   [2] Plutarch in Mario.

[3] Appian, de Bell. Civil. lib. i.

fence, to attempt any thing derogatory of his own honour [1].

Having in this manner restored the city to an appearance of peace, Sylla set out with his army for its destination in Greece. Quintus Rufus, the other Consul of the preceding year, at the same time repaired to his province in the country of the Marsi, where, as has been mentioned, he was to succeed Cn. Strabo in the command of some legions; but being less agreeable to these troops than his predecessor had been, the soldiers mutinied upon his arrival, and put him to death. Cn. Strabo, though suspected of having connived with them in this horrid transaction, was permitted to profit by it in keeping his station. So quick was the succession of crimes which distressed the republic, that one disorder escaped with impunity, under the more atrocious effects of another which followed.

U. C. 666.
L. Corn. Cinna, Cn. Octavius, Coss.

When Sylla was about to depart from the city, Virgilius, one of the Tribunes, moved an impeachment against him for the illegal steps he had lately taken. But the state of the war with Mithridates was urgent, and Sylla took the benefit of the law of Memmius, by which persons named to command had a privilege when going on service to decline answering any charge which should be brought against them, to impede their departure.

The king of Pontus, notwithstanding he had been disappointed in his attempt upon Rhodes, was become master of the Lesser Asia, had fixed his

[1] L. Florus, lib. iii. c. 21. Appian de Bell. Civil. lib. i.

his residence at Pergamus, and employed his officers, with numerous fleets and armies, to continue his operations in different quarters, making rapid acquisitions at once on the side of the Scythian and Thracian Bosphorus, in Macedonia and in Greece. His general, Archelaus, had reduced most of the Greek islands, and was hastening to make himself master of the continent also. Delos had revolted, and had thrown off the yoke of Athens, at the time that it fell into the hands of this general. The king proposed to make use of it as a decoy to bring the Athenians themselves under his power. For this purpose, pretending veneration for the god to whom this island was sacred, he expressed a desire to restore it, with the treasure he had seized there, to its former condition; and sent Aristion, a native of Athens, but now an officer in his own service, with an escort of two thousand men, to deliver this treasure into the hands of the Athenians. Aristion being, under this pretence, received into the Pyræus, took possession of the place, and continued to hold it, with the city of Athens itself, for Mithridates, who, by means of the reinforcements sent into Attica, soon after enabled him to overrun Beotia, Achaia, and Laconia.

To these alarming encroachments on the Roman territory, and to the personal injuries done to such of their generals as had fallen into his hands, Mithridates had joined a barbarous outrage, which roused, in the highest degree, the resentment of the

the Roman People. He had sent orders to all his commanders in every town and station in Asia, on a day fixed, to begin a massacre of the Roman citizens that were any where settled in that country, and to publish a reward for the slaves of any Roman who should succeed in destroying their master. This order was executed with marks of insult, in which the vile instruments of cruelty, for the most part, are apt to exceed their instructions. It is particularly mentioned, that at Ephesus, Pergamus, and other cities of Asia, entire families, without distinction of sex or age, infants with their parents, taking refuge in the temples, and embracing the altars, were dragged from thence and murdered. But the number of persons who perished in this massacre, if ever known, is no where mentioned [1].

The resentment which was natural on this occasion, together with the real danger that threatened the empire, fully justified the contempt with which Sylla treated the impeachment of Virgilius, and the celerity with which he left the city of Rome. Having transported to Dyrachium an army of six legions, he took the route of Thessaly and Ætolia; and having raised in these countries contributions for the pay and subsistence of his army he received the submission of the Beotians, who had lately been obliged to declare for Mithridates, and advanced to Athens, where Aristion in the city, and Archelaus in the Pyræus, were prepared to

[1] Appian. de Bell. Mithrid. p. 585, 586.

to make a vigorous refiftance. Mithridates, who was mafter of the fea, collected together all the troops which he had diftributed in the iflands, and ordered a great reinforcement from Afia to form an army on the fide of Beotia for the relief of Athens.

Sylla, to prevent the enemy, haftened the fiege of this place. He firft made an attempt to force his way into the Pyræus by fcaling the walls; but being repulfed, had recourfe to the ordinary means of attack. He erected towers, and raifing them to the height of the battlements, got upon the fame level with the befieged, and plied his miffiles from thence. He fhook the walls with battering engines, or undermined them with galleries, and made places of arms for his men near to where he expected to open a breach. But the defence of the place was vigorous and obftinate, and fo well conducted, that he was obliged, after many fruitlefs efforts, to turn the fiege into a blockade, or to await the effects of famine, by which the city began already to be preffed, and by which it was in a little time brought to the laft extremity. Thofe who were confined in the place, had confumed all the herbage, and killed all the animals that were to be found within the circuit of the walls; they were reduced to feed on the implements of leather, or other materials that could be turned into fuftenance, and came at laft to prey upon the carcafes of the dead. The garrifon was greatly diminifhed in numbers; and of thofe who
remained,

remained, the greater part was difpirited and weak : but Ariftion, on account of the treacherous manner in which he had feized the place, expecting for himfelf no quarter from the Roman general, ftill withftood the defire of his troops to capitulate ; when Sylla, knowing the weak ftate to which the befieged were reduced, made a vigorous effort, ftormed and forced the walls with great flaughter. Ariftion, who had retired into the Acropolis, was foon afterwards taken and flain.

Archelaus, likewife greatly diftreffed in the Pyræus, found means to efcape by water, and leaving the poft he abandoned to be occupied by Sylla, who razed its fortifications to the ground he haftened to join the army that was forming by order of his mafter on the fide of Theffaly.

The army of Mithridates advanced into Beotia. Every part of it was fumptuoufly provided with all that was neceffary for fubfiftence or parade. There was a numerous cavalry richly caparifoned ; an infantry of every defcription, varioufly armed, fome to ufe miffile weapons, others to engage in clofe fight ; a large train of armed chariots, which, being winged with fcythes, threatened to fweep the plains. The whole army amounted to about an hundred and twenty thoufand men. But their mafter, with all his ability, it appears, in the manner of barbarous nations, relied on the numbers of his hoft, to the neglect of its order, or the proper conduct of its ftrength. Sylla was to oppofe this multitude,

multitude, with no more than thirty thoufand men.

On this inferior enemy, Archelaus continually preffed with all his forces, and endeavoured to bring on a general action, which Sylla cautioufly avoided; waiting for an opportunity that might deprive the enemy of the advantage he had in the fuperiority of his numbers. The armies being both in Beotia, Archelaus inadvertently took poft near Cheronea, on the afcent of a fteep hill that was formed into natural terraces by ledges of rocks, and which terminated at laft in a peak or narrow fummit. On the face of this hill he had crowded his infantry, his cavalry, and his chariots, and trufted that, although the ground was unfavourable to the operations of fuch an army, it was ftill inacceffible, and they could not be attacked.

While the Afiatic general, therefore, believed himfelf fecure in this pofition, the Roman continued to obferve him from the poft he had fortified at a little diftance; and was told by fome natives of the country, that the hill which Archelaus had occupied might be afcended in his rear, and that a body of men might be conducted fafely and unobferved to the fummit. Upon this information Sylla formed his plan to engage the enemy, fent a powerful detachment with proper guides to feize on the heights above their encampment, while he himfelf advanced with his main body in front of their ftation, and by this means diverted their attention from what was paffing on the oppofite

quarter,

quarter, while he himself was prepared to profit by any confusion which might be occasioned by an alarm from thence.

The unexpected appearance of an enemy on the rear, produced the alarm that was intended, in the Asiatic camp. The impetuous descent they were ordered to make from the hill, drove all in confusion before them. The rear fell down on the front. A great uproar and tumult arose in every part. In this critical moment, Sylla, with the main body, began his attack in front, and soon broke into the midst of enemies, who were altogether unprepared to receive him: or who being crowded in a narrow space, and mixed with little distinction of separate bodies, of officers or men; and, under the disadvantage of their ground, could neither resist nor retire. In the centre, numbers were trod under foot by those who pressed upon them from every side, and perished by violence or suffocation; or, while they endeavoured to open a way to escape, employed their swords against one another. Of an hundred and twenty thousand men, scarcely ten thousand could be assembled at Chalcis in Eubœa, the place to which Archelaus directed his flight. Of the Romans, at the end of the action, only fifteen men were missing, and of these, two returned on the following day [1].

Archelaus, even after this rout of his army, being still master at sea, drew supplies from Asia and from the neighbouring islands; and, being secure in his retreat in Eubœa, made frequent descents on the neighbouring

[1] For this particular, Plutarch quotes the Memoirs of Sylla himself.

neighbouring coafts. While Sylla endeavoured to cover the lands of Beotia and Attica from thefe incurfions, Mithridates made great efforts to replace his army in that country; and in a little time had tranfported thither eighty thoufand frefh troops under Dorilaus, to whom Archelaus joined himfelf with thofe he had faved from the late difafter. The new army of Mithridates, confifting chiefly of cavalry, was greatly favoured by the nature of the ground in Beotia, which was flat and abounding in forage. Sylla, though inclined to keep the heights on which he was leaft expofed to the enemy's cavalry, was, in order to cover the country from which he drew his fubfiftence, obliged to defcend to the plains in the neighbourhood of Orchomenos. There he took poft among the marfhes, and endeavoured to fortify himfelf with ditches againft the enemy's horfe. While his works were yet unfinifhed, being attacked by the Afiatic cavalry, not only the labourers, but the troops that were placed under arms to cover the workmen, were feized with a panic, and fled. Sylla, having for fome time in vain endeavoured to rally them, laid hold of an enfign, and rufhed in defpair on the enemy. " To me," he faid, " it is glorious to fall in this place: but for you, if you are " afked where you deferted your leader, you may " fay at Orchomenos." Numbers who heard this reproach, returned to the charge with their general; and wherever they prefented themfelves, ftopped the career of the enemy, and put them to flight.

CHAP. XIV.

flight. The Roman army at length recovered itself in every part of the field; and Sylla, remounting his horse, took the full advantage of the change of his fortune, pursued the enemy to their camp, and forced them to abandon it with great slaughter.

After the loss of this second army, Mithridates appears to have despaired of his affairs in Greece: he suffered Sylla to enter into quiet possession of his winter quarters in Thessaly, and authorised Archelaus to treat of peace.

Both parties were equally inclined to a conference; the king of Pontus urged by his losses, and the Roman Proconsul by the state of affairs in Italy. There, though commanding in Greece by authority from the Roman Senate, Sylla had been degraded, and declared a public enemy, by a formal sentence or resolution of the People at Rome. An officer had been sent from Italy to supersede him; and a Roman army, independent of his orders, was actually employed in the province. Mithridates too, while he had sustained such losses in Greece, was pressed by the other army in Asia, under the command of Fimbria, who, with intentions equally hostile to Sylla as to Mithridates, advanced with a rapid pace, reduced several towns on the coast, and had lately made himself master of Pergamus, where the king himself had narrowly escaped falling into his hands. In these circumstances, a treaty was equally seasonable to both.

Sylla

Sylla had been absent from Rome about two years, during which time, having no supplies from thence, he had supported the war by the contributions which he had raised in Greece, Ætolia, and Thessaly, and with the money he had coined from the plate and treasure of the Grecian temples [1]. The republic, in the mean time, had been in the possession of his personal enemies; and the authority of the Senate was, in a great measure, suppressed. For soon after his departure from Rome, his antagonist Cinna, notwithstanding the engagements he had come under, revived the project of keeping the more respectable citizens in subjection, under pretence of regulations enacted by the collective body of the People.

The designation of a party now in power was the same with that which had distinguished the followers of Tiberius and Caius Gracchus; but the object was changed, and that which was termed the popular faction was itself differently composed. Formerly this faction consisted of the populace of Rome and of the poorer citizens, opposed to the noble and the rich. The objects for which they at that time contended, were the distribution of corn, new settlements, or the division of lands. At present the parties consisted of the inhabitants of the country towns lately admitted, or still claiming to be admitted, on the rolls of the People of one side, and of the Senate and ancient citizens on the other. The object to which the former aspired, was a full and equal participation

[1] Plutarch. in Sylla et Lucullo.

in all the powers that belonged to the Roman People. They were far from being satisfied with the manner of their enrolment into a few particular Tribes, and laid claim to be admitted without diftinction among the ancient citizens, and like them to have confideration and power proportioned to their numbers. In this they were fupported by Cinna, who made a motion in their favour in the affembly of the People, and at the fame time propofed to recal Marius and the other exiles of that party from their banifhment. The Conful Octavius, with the majority of the Senate and ancient citizens, oppofed their defigns; but Cinna was likely to have a powerful fupport in the friends of the exiles, and in the new citizens, who flocked from every town in the country. On the day appointed for the difcuffion of this queftion, his partizans, in great numbers, took poffeffion of the place of affembly, and were obferved to be armed with daggers or fhort fwords. Octavius was attended at his own houfe by a numerous company of the ancient citizens, who were armed in the fame manner, and waited to take fuch meafures as the neceffity of the cafe might require. Being told that the Tribunes who had forbidden the queftion were violently attacked, and likely to be driven from the place. Thefe adherents of the Senate came forth into the ftreets, and drove their antagonifts, with fome bloodfhed, through the gates of the city. Cinna endeavouring to make head againft his colleague, invited the flaves, under a promife of liberty,

to

to his ſtandard. But finding it impoſſible within a city, that was occupied by his opponents, to withſtand their force, he withdrew to the country towns, and folicited ſupplies from thence. He paſſed through Tibur and Præneſte to Nola, and openly implored the inhabitants to aid him againſt their common enemies. On this occaſion he was attended by Sertorius, and by ſome other Senators who had embarked in the ſame ruinous faction. Their ſolicitations at any other time might perhaps have been fruitleſs; but now, to the misfortune of the republic, a number of armies were ſtill kept on foot in Italy, to finiſh the remains of the ſocial war. Cn. Strabo commanded one army in Umbria, Metellus another on the confines of Lucania and Samnium, and Appius Claudius a third in Campania. Theſe armies conſiſted chiefly of indigent citizens, become ſoldiers of fortune, very much at the diſpoſal of the leaders, in whoſe name they had been levied, to whom, as uſual, they had ſworn the military oath, and on whom they depended for the ſettlements and rewards which they were taught to expect at the end of their ſervices. Such men were inclined to take part in the cauſe of any faction that was likely, by the expulſion and forfeiture of any one claſs of the citizens, to make way for preferments and fortunes to thoſe who were employed to expel them.

Cinna diſtruſted Pompey and Metellus; but hoping for a better reception from Appius Claudius, he repaired to the camp of this general, and had the

CHAP. XIV.

Octavius and Merula.

address to gain the troops who were under his command.

Mean time the Senate, without entering into any particular difcuffion of the guilt which Cinna had incurred in the late tumult at Rome, found that, by having deferted his ftation, he had actually divefted himfelf of his office as Conful, and they obtained the election of L. Cornelius Merula, to fupply the vacancy which his defertion had occafioned.

Marius, being informed that one of the armies in Italy, with a Roman Conful at its head, was prepared to fupport him, made hafte from his exile in Africa: he landed in Tufcany, was joined by numbers, and on his approach to Rome had an offer of being vefted with the enfigns of Proconful. But intending to move commiferation or pity, he declined every privilege of a Roman citizen, until the fentence of attainder or banifhment, which had been pronounced againft him, fhould be formally reverfed. He accordingly prefented himfelf to the People as he paffed, in the manner practifed by fuppliants, with a mean habit, and in the ghaftly figure, to which he was reduced by the diftrefs of his exile; but with a countenance, fays his hiftorian, which, being naturally ftern, now rather moved terror than pity [1]. He implored the protection of the country-towns, in whofe caufe he pretended to have fuffered, and whofe interefts were now embarked on the fame bottom with his own. He had many partizans among thofe who had compofed the legions

[1] Plutarch. in Mario.

gions which formerly ferved under his own orders: Had reputation and authority, and foon affembled a confiderable force, with which, in concert with Cinna, Sertorius and Carbo, he advanced towards Rome.

"Thefe adventurers invefted the city in three feparate divifions. Cinna and Carbo lay before it: On the Appian way, Sertorius took poft on the river above, and Marius below it. The laft, to prevent fupplies from the fea, made himfelf mafter of the port of Oftia: Sertorius had fent a detachment to Ariminum, to prevent any relief from the fide of Gaul.

In this extremity the Senate applied to Metellus, requefting that he would make any poffible accommodation with fuch of the Italian allies as were ftill under arms, and haften to the relief of the city. The delays which he made in the execution of thefe orders enabled Cinna and Marius to prevent him in gaining the allies, who at this time had it in their option to accept the privileges they claimed from either party; and, having chofen to join themfelves with the popular faction, they threw their weight into that fcale.

Metellus, however, advanced into Latium ; and, being joined by the Conful Octavius, took poft on the Alban Hill. From thence they found that the troops, being inclined to favour their enemies, deferted apace. The commander himfelf being left with a few attendants, defpaired of the caufe, and
withdrew

CHAP. XIV. withdrew into Africa. Octavius found means to enter the city, and refumed his ftation.

The army lately commanded by Pompeius Strabo was now deprived of its general; he having been killed by lightning in his camp. And the Senate was not inclined to repofe any confidence in the men he had commanded. He himfelf had fome time hefitated between the parties; and the troops, at his death, were ftill fuppofed undecided in their choice. With fo uncertain a profpect of fupport, the Senate thinking it more fafe to capitulate with Cinna and Marius, than to remain expofed to the horrors of a ftorm; offered to reinftate Cinna in the office of Conful, and to reftore Marius, with the other exiles, to their condition of Roman citizens; only ftipulating that they would fpare the blood of their opponents, or proceed in their complaints againft them according to the laws of the commonwealth.

While this treaty was in dependence, Marius, affecting the modefty of a perfon whom the law, according to his late fentence of banifhment, had difqualified to take any part in the ftate, obferved a fullen and obftinate filence. Even when the terms were fettled, and the gates were laid open to himfelf and his followers, he refufed to enter until the attainder under which he lay fhould be taken off, and until he were replaced in his condition as a citizen of Rome. The People were accordingly affembled to repeal their former decree. But Marius, in the character of a

practifed

practised soldier, proposing to take his enemies by surprise, did not wait for the completion of the ceremony he himself had exacted. While the ballots were collecting, he entered the city with a band of armed men, whom he instantly employed in taking vengeance on those who had concurred in the late measures against him. Although the gates, by his orders, were secured, many of the Senators found means to withdraw. The house of Sylla was demolished, such as were reputed his friends were slain, his wife and his children narrowly escaped. Among the signals by which Marius directed the execution of particular persons, it was understood that if he did not return a salute which was offered him, this was to be considered as a warrant for immediate death. In compliance with these instructions, some citizens of note were laid dead at his feet. And as the meanest retainers of his party had their resentments as well as himself, and took this opportunity to indulge their passions, the city resembled a place that was taken by storm, and every quarter resounded with the cries of rage or of terror; a horrid scene, which continued without intermission during five days and five nights. The Consul Octavius was murdered in his robes of office, and in presence of his lictors; two Senators of the name of Cæsar, Caius and Lucius; two of the name of Crassus, the father and the son, attempting to escape, but likely to be taken, fell by their own hands; Attilius Serranus, Publius Lentulus, C. Numitorius, and M. Bæbius, being murdered by persons who bore them a particular hatred, the bodies were fastened on a hook, and dragged by a rope through the streets; Marcus Antonius, one of the first Roman Senators, who had betaken himself entirely or chiefly to the practice of a Pleader at the bar and in the Senate, from which he is known by the name of the Orator, being discovered in a place of concealment, was killed by assassins sent for the purpose. The heads of the others were exposed on the rostra; that of Antonius was placed on the table of Marius, to whom the sight, from peculiar motives of envy or resentment, was singularly gratifying. Catulus, once the colleague of Marius himself in the Consulate, and partner in his last and most decisive victory over the Cimbri, without question one of the most respectable Senators of the age, being included in the warrant for general execution, had numbers to solicit for his life; but Marius, exasperated the more by this appearance of popular regard in his favour, made a short answer, *He must die.* And this victim, choosing to avoid by a voluntary death the insults likely to be offered to his person, having shut himself up in a close chamber, with a brasier of burning charcoal, perished by suffocation. Merula, the Flamen Dialis, or Priest of Jupiter, whose name, without his own knowledge, had been inscribed Consul upon the degradation of Cinna, now likewise, willing to maintain to the last the dignity of his station, opened his own arteries at the shrine of his god, sprinkling the idol with his blood. As he

felt

felt the approach of death, he tore from his head the apex or creſt of the order, which he bore, and with which, by the maxims of his religion, he could not part while in life, but with which on his head it would have been impious, and ominous of evil, to have died. In obſerving this ceremony, he called upon thoſe who were preſent to witneſs the exactneſs with which he performed his duty.

The horrors of this maſſacre are to be imputed chiefly, if not entirely, to the fury of Marius, acting from the original aſperity of his own mind, ſtung with animoſity to every diſtinction of birth, education, or manners, which marked the ſuperior order of citizens, and now wrought up by recent diſappointments of ambition, and by his ſufferings in exile, into a deteſtation and rancour, which nothing ſhort of ſuch a ſcene could aſſuage. In moſt other places, indeed, inſtruments would have been wanting for the execution of ſuch a work: But at Rome were found in ſufficient numbers, fugitive ſlaves, eager to avenge their own ſufferings, in the blood of their maſters; parties in private quarrels; thieves, expecting plunder, in the murder of the wealthy; a populace, ſuch as every where is capable of the wildeſt diſorder, when aſſembled in occaſional tumults; but here peculiarly nurſed in ſcenes of licenſe, with pretenſions to political importance, and even to ſovereignty, deteſting the ſuperior orders of the ſtate, by whom they felt themſelves reſtrained; indigent, but looking for relief, not to their own induſtry or honeſt

honest arts, but to gratuities, obtained by corruption or public profusion. In their very entertainments or sports, whether fights of gladiators, or baiting of wild beasts, trained to a ruthless insensibility and indifference to blood: Such men, having the example and authority of a leader, whom they had long considered as the champion of their cause, and having the several objects of their fury at mercy, burst out into a scene of wild devastation, attended with murders, rapes, and every species of outrage, which could arise from the suspension of Government in a State, where the disorderly were found in such numbers, and the most powerful restraints were necessary.

Cinna himself, though equally bent with his associate on measures to recover his power, and to restore his party, but having fewer resentments to gratify, was shocked with these enormities, and interposed his authority to restrain them. The mandates of office being insufficient for this purpose, he had recourse to military force, and, driving all who were found in the perpetration of such crimes into places inclosed, or into the recess of squares or narrow streets, had them in great numbers, without inquiry or distinction, put to the sword.

Some degree of respite or calm being obtained by these means, it was proposed to resume the appeareance of regular Government, as far as the times could allow. The Consulate of Cinna was accordingly restored; and Marius, though without any form of election, associated in the office. In such a feafon of terror, there could not be any rifk to the party in recurring to the ordinary fuffrage of the People; but an election was deemed unneceffary, and the enfigns of office were affumed without it.

CHAP. XIV.

Marius, though now preceded in form by the Lictors, could not return to the habits of a legal magiftrate. The objects of his refentment were ftill facrificed to his fury, without any trial, and under his own infpection. But, in the midft of cries which were occafioned by thefe executions, the name of Sylla, and the fame of his victories in Greece, gave continual prefage of a retribution, no way likely to fall fhort of the provocation which was now given in the fubverfion of public order at Rome. And although the principal author of thefe wrongs was not deftined to abide the future confequences in his own perfon, the immediate effect to him was fufficiently awful. Even the obdurate foul of Marius, unable to endure fuch a load of guilt and remorfe, paffed from the agitation of fury to that of terror and nocturnal fears, which gave evident figns or indications of a difordered mind. Some one, he imagined, continually founded in his ears the words of a poet, *Horrid is the dying lion's den;* and thefe words being applied to himfelf, feemed to announce his approaching diffolution. He took to the ufe of wine in excefs, contracted a pleurify, and died on the feventh day of his illnefs, in the feventeenth day of his laft or feventh confulate, and in the feventieth year of his age; leaving the tools he had employed in

fubverting

CHAP. XIV.

subverting the government of his country to pay the forfeit of his crimes.

Livy, it appears[1] from the remaining epitome of this part of his work, had made it a question, whether this celebrated personage had been most useful to his country as a soldier, or pernicious as a citizen. It has happened unfortunately for his fame, that he closed the scene of life with examples of the latter kind. In what degree he retained his genius or abilities cannot be known. His insatiable thirst of power, like avarice in the case of the superannuated miser, seemed to grow with age. His hatred of the Nobles, contracted in the obscurity of his early life, remained with him after he himself had laid the amplest foundations of Nobility in his own family. And he died in an attempt to extinguish all just or regular government, in the blood of those who were most eminently qualified or disposed to sustain it.

Upon the death of Marius, the government remained in the hands of Cinna. While many of the Senators, and other citizens, obnoxious to the prevailing party, had taken refuge with Sylla: this general himself was declared a public enemy; his effects were seized; his children, with their mother, having narrowly escaped the pursuit of his enemies, were fled to the father in Greece. In these circumstances he made not any change in his conduct of the war, nor made any concessions to the

[1] Livy, Epitome, lib. viii. Appian. de Bell. Civil. lib. i. Plutarch. in Mario. Florus, lib. iii. c. 21. Velleius Pater. lib. ii. c. 19, &c. Dio. Cass. in Fragmentis.

the enemy againſt whom he was employed. He talked familiarly every day of his intention to ſuppreſs the diſorders at Rome, and to avenge the blood of his friends, but not till he had forced Mithridates to make reparation for the wrongs he had done to the Romans and to their allies in Aſia.

Alarmed by the report of ſuch threats, Cinna took meaſures to ſtrengthen his own party; aſſumed, upon the death of Marius, Valerius Flaccus as his colleague in the office of Conſul; and, having aſſigned him the command in Aſia, with two additional legions, truſted, that with this force he might obtain poſſeſſion of the Province, and furniſh to Sylla ſufficient occupation beyond the limits of Italy.

But Flaccus, upon his arrival in Theſſaly, was deſerted by part of the army he was deſtined to employ; and paſſing through Macedonia in his route to Aſia with the remainder, a diſpute aroſe between himſelf and his lieutenant Fimbria, which ended in the murder of the Conſul, and in the ſucceſſion of Fimbria to the command. So little deference or reſpect did ſoldiers of fortune pay, in the diſorder of thoſe unhappy times, even to the heads of a party they profeſſed to ſerve.

Fimbria, with the troops he had ſeduced to his ſtandard, after he had aſſaſſinated their general, made a rapid progreſs in Aſia, and haſtened, as has been obſerved, the reſolution to which Mithridates was come, of applying for peace. To this ſtately but crafty prince, urged by the neceſſity of his own affairs, the conjuncture appeared to be

favourable,

favourable, when so much distraction took place in the councils of Rome. He had experienced the abilities of Sylla; he knew his eager desire to be gone for Italy, and to be revenged of his enemies; and he expected to gain him by proffering assistance in the war he was about to wage with the opposite party at Rome.

Upon a message from Archelaus, Sylla readily agreed to an interview in the island of Delos; and here being told, in the name of Mithridates, that he should have money, troops, and shipping to make a descent upon Italy, provided he would enter into a confederacy with the king of Pontus, or join him in a war with the Romans, by whom he himself was now proscribed, Sylla, in his turn, proposed to Archelaus to desert Mithridates, to deliver up the fleet and army which was under his command, and to rely for protection and reward on the faith of the Romans. They will speedily seat you, he said, on the throne of Pontus. Archelaus having rejected this proposal with horror, "And you," says Sylla, "the slave, or (if you prefer that title) "the friend of a barbarous tyrant, will not betray "your trust, and yet, to me, have the presump- "tion to propose an act of perfidy. The fields "of Chæronea and Orchomenos should have made "you better acquainted with the character of a "Roman."

Upon this reply Archelaus saw the necessity of purchasing the treaty he was instructed to obtain, and accordingly made the following concessions:

That

That the fleet of Pontus, confisting of seventy Galleys, should be delivered up to the Romans.

That the garrifons should be withdrawn from all places which had been feized in the courfe of this war.

That the Roman province in Afia, together with Paphlagonia, Bithynia, and Cappadocia should be evacuated, and the frontier of Pontus, for the future, be the boundary of Mithridates's territory.

That the Romans should receive two thoufand talents [1], to reimburfe their expence in the war.

That prifoners should be reftored, and all deferters delivered up.

While thefe articles were fent to Mithridates for his ratification, Sylla in no degree relaxed the meafures he had taken to fecure and to facilitate the paffage of his army into Afia. He fent Lucullus [2] round every ftation on the coaft to procure an affemblage of shipping; and he himfelf, after having made fome incurfions into Thrace, to gratify his army with the fpoil of nations who had often plundered the Roman province, continued his route to the Hellefpont, but on his way he was met by the meffengers of Mithridates, who informed him that their mafter agreed to all the articles propofed, except to that which related to the ceffion of Paphlagonia; and at the fame time made a merit of the preference he had given to Sylla in this treaty; as he might have obtained more favourable terms from Fimbria. " That " is a traitor," faid Sylla, " whom I shall fpeedily
" punish

---

[1] About 386,000 l.   [2] Vide Plutarch. in Lucullo.

CHAP. XIV. "punish for his crimes. As for your master, I shall know, upon my descent in Asia, whether he chooses to have peace or war."

Being arrived at the Hellespont, he was joined by Lucullus with a number of vessels, which enabled him to pass the strait. Here he was met by another message from Mithridates, desiring a personal interview; which was accordingly held in the presence of both armies, and at which the king of Pontus, after some expostulations, agreed to all the conditions already mentioned. In this he probably acted from policy, as well as from the necessity he felt in the present state of his affairs. He still hoped, that in consequence of this treaty, he might turn the arms of Sylla against the Romans, and trusted that the peace he obtained for himself in Asia was to be the beginning of a war in Italy, more likely to distress his enemies than any efforts he himself could make against them. With this reasonable prospect he retired into his own kingdom of Pontus; and there, strengthening himself by alliances and the acquisition of territory on the northern coasts of the Euxine, he prepared to take advantage of future emergencies, and to profit by the state of confusion into which the affairs of the Romans were likely to fall.

Sylla having brought the Mithridatic war to an issue so honourable for himself, and having every where gratified his army with the spoils of their enemies, being possessed of a considerable sum of money and a numerous fleet, and being secure of

the

the attachment of the legions, who had experienced his liberality, and rested their hopes in future on the success of his enterprize, prepared to take vengeance on his enemies, and those of the republic in Italy. He proceeded, however, with great deliberation and caution; and, as if the State at Rome were in perfect tranquillity, staid to reduce the army of Fimbria, to resettle the Roman province, and to effect the restoration of the allies, Nicomedes and Ariobarzanes, to their respective kingdoms of Cappadocia and Bithynia.

Fimbria being required by Sylla to resign a command which he had illegally usurped, retorted the charge of usurpation, and treated Sylla himself as an outlaw: but upon the approach of this general, being deserted by his army, he fled to Pergamus, and there had an end put to his life by the hands of a slave, of whom he exacted this service. To punish the province of Asia for its defection to Mithridates, Sylla obliged the inhabitants to pay down a sum equal to five years ordinary tax. He sent Curio to replace on their thrones the kings of Cappadocia and Bithynia, who had persevered in their alliance with Rome, and sent an account of these particulars to the Senate, without taking any notice of the edict by which he himself had been stripped of his command, and declared an enemy [1]. Before he set sail, however, for Italy, he thought proper to transmit a memorial, setting forth his services and his

[1] Appian. in Bell. Mithridat. Plutarch. in Syll.

his wrongs, as well as the injury done to many Senators who had taken refuge in his camp, and concluding with menaces of juſtice againſt his own enemies and thoſe of the republic, but aſſuring the citizens in general of protection and ſecurity. This paper, being read in the Senate, appeared to alarm many of the members, even thoſe who had leaſt to fear from the threats it contained: wiſhed for expedients to reconcile the parties, and to avert the evils which the republic muſt ſuffer from their repeated contentions. A ſoothing anſwer was accordingly ſent to the memorial of Sylla, and earneſt entreaties were made to Cinna, that he would ſuſpend his levies until a reply could be obtained from his antagoniſt.

U. C. 669.
L. Cornelius Cinna 4to. Cn. Papirius Carbo.

But Cinna, in contempt of theſe pacific intentions, took meaſures to ſuſtain the war; divided the faſces with Cn. Papirius Carbo, whom, without any form of election, he aſſumed for his colleague in the Conſulate; and, in the partition of provinces, retained for himſelf the adminiſtration in Italy, while he aſſigned to Carbo the command in the neighbouring Gaul. Theſe titular magiſtrates, with all the adherents of their faction, betook themſelves in haſte to the forming of troops, and ſecuring the fidelity of the towns within the ſeveral diviſions which they had received in charge.

Carbo exacted hoſtages for their good behaviour from all the towns in his diſtrict; but as he had not any regular authority from the Senate for this meaſure, he found himſelf unable to give it effect. To Caſtricius, the chief magiſtrate of Placentia, a perſon

person of great age, who refused to comply with his orders, "Have not I your life in my power?" he said. "And have not I," said the other, "already had life enough¹?"

Cinna, however, having mustered a considerable force, and intending to make head against Sylla in Thessaly, through which he was expected to pass in his way to Italy, was about to transport his army thither; when the troops being averse to embark, he himself, endeavouring to force them, was killed in a mutiny. A general disorder and anarchy pervaded the party. The election of a successor to Cinna was twice interrupted by supposed unfavourable presages, and Carbo remained sole Consul.

At this time an answer was received from Sylla to the proposals made by the Senate towards a reconciliation of parties. In this, he declared, "That he never could return into friendship with persons guilty of so many and such enormous crimes. If the Roman people, however, were pleased to grant an indemnity, he would not interpose, but should venture to affirm, that such of the citizens as chose, in the present disorders, to take refuge in his camp, would find themselves safer than in that of his enemy's." He had embarked his army at Ephesus, and in three days reached the Pyræus, the port of Athens. Here he was taken ill of the gout, and was advised to use the hot baths at Adipsus; at which he accordingly

¹ Val. Max. lib. vi. c. 2.

CHAP. XIV accordingly passed some time, and with singular force of mind, as if divested of all public or private distress, amused himself, in his usual way, with persons of humour, and ordinary company. His fleet, in the mean time, consisting of twelve hundred ships, coasted round the Peloponnesus, and took on board the army which had marched by Thessaly to Dyrachium. Being apprehensive that some part of the legions, upon landing in Italy, and with so near a prospect of returning to their homes, might desert, or, trusting to their consequence in a civil war, might become disorderly and distress the inhabitants, he exacted a special oath, by which every man bound himself, upon his arrival in Italy, to abide by his colours, and to observe the strictest order in his march through the country. The troops, wishing to remove all the remains of a distrust which had suggested this precaution, not only took the oath, but made voluntary offer of a contribution towards the support of the war; and Sylla, without accepting the aid which was proffered to him, set sail with the additional confidence which this proof of attachment in the army inspired.

He had, according to Appian, five Roman legions, with six thousand Italian horse, and considerable levies from Macedonia and Greece, amounting in all to about sixty thousand men. With this force he landed in Italy, in the face of many different armies, each of them equal or superior in number to his own.

Those

Those now at the head of the commonwealth were supposed to have on foot, at different stations, above two hundred thousand men. L. Cornelius Scipio and C. Junius Norbanus, who were leaders of the party, being in possession of the capital and of the place of election, were named for Consuls. Norbanus, as acting for the republic, commanded a great army in Apulia; Scipio, another on the confines of Campania. Sertorius, young Marius, with Carbo, in the quality of Proconsul, and others (as Plutarch quotes from the memoirs of Sylla) to the number of fifteen commanders, had each of them armies, amounting in all to four hundred and fifty cohorts [1]; but of these different bodies none attempted to dispute the landing of Sylla, nor, for some days, to interrupt his march. He accordingly continued to advance as in a friendly country, and in the midst of profound peace. The inhabitants of Italy, considering the superior class of the people at Rome, in whose cause now Sylla appeared, as averse to the claim they had made of being promiscuously enrolled in the Tribes, were likely to oppose him, and to favour the faction which had for some time prevailed in the State. To allay their fears, or to prevent their taking an active part against himself, Sylla summoned the leading men of the country towns as he passed, and gave them assurances that he would confirm the grants which had been made to them, if they did not forfeit these and every other title to favour,

---

[1] About 225,000 men.

favour, by abetting the faction which had subverted the government.

On his march he was joined by Metellus Pius, who, as has been observed, after a fruitless attempt, in conjunction with the Conful Octavius, to cover Rome from the attack of the elder Marius and Cinna, had withdrawn to Africa; and being forced from thence by Fabius, returned into Italy. This officer being in Liguria, where he still retained the enfigns of Proconful, had some forces on foot, and was fustaining the hopes of his party, when so great a change was made in their favour as was produced by the arrival of an army from Greece.

Sylla was likewise, about the same time, joined by Cneius Pompeius, fon to the late Conful Pompeius Strabo, who, though too young for any formal commiffion, had affembled a confiderable body of men, and already made himfelf of importance in the prefent ftruggle. Being now only about nineteen years of age, he was remarked for engaging manners, and a manly afpect, which procured him a general favour and an uncommon degree of refpect [1]. This diftinction being unfought for, was poffibly felt by him as a birth-right, or gave him an early impreffion of that fuperiority to his fellow-citizens, which he continued to bear through the whole of his life. He had ferved in thofe legions with which Cinna intended to have carried the war againft Sylla into Afia or Greece; but, being averfe to the party, had withdrawn

when

[1] Plutarch. in Mario.

when that army was about to embark, and disappearing suddenly, was supposed to have been murdered by the order of Cinna, a suspicion, which, among other circumstances, incited his soldiers to the mutiny in which their general was killed. Sylla appears himself to have been won by the promising aspect of the young Pompey, and received him with distinguishing marks of regard.

Numbers of the Senate and Nobles, who had hitherto remained exposed at Rome to the insults of their enemies, now repaired to the camp of Sylla. The Consul Norbanus, being joined by young Marius, lay at Canusium. Sylla, while he was preparing to attack them, sent an officer with overtures of peace; these they rejected with marks of contempt. This circumstance had an effect which Sylla perhaps foresaw or intended. It roused the indignation of his army, and, in the action which followed, had some effect in obtaining a victory, in which six thousand [1] of the enemy were killed, with the loss of only seventy men to himself.

Norbanus, after this defeat, retreated to Capua; and, being covered by the walls of that place, waited the arrival of Scipio, who intended to join him with the army under his command. Sylla marched to Tianum to prevent their junction; and, on the approach of Scipio, proposed to negotiate. The leaders, with a few attendants, met between the two armies, and were nearly agreed upon terms

---

[1] Plutarch. in Syll. edit. London, p. 83.

terms of peace; but Scipio delayed his final consent until he should consult with Norbanus at Capua. Sertorius was accordingly dispatched to inform Norbanus of what had passed, and hostilities were to be suspended until his return; but this messenger, probably averse to the treaty, broke the truce, by seizing a post at Suessa which had been occupied by Sylla; and the negotiation had no other effect than that of giving the troops of both armies, as well as their leaders, an opportunity of conferring together; a circumstance which, in civil wars, is always dangerous to one or other of the parties. In this case the popularity of Sylla prevailed; and the soldiers of his army, boasting of the wealth which they had acquired under their general, infected his enemies, and seduced them to desert their leader. Scipio was left almost alone in his camp; but Sylla, receiving the troops who deserted to him, made no attempt to seize their commander, suffered him to escape, and, with the accession of strength he had acquired by the junction of this army, continued his march towards Rome. Norbanus at the same time evacuated Capua, and, by forced marches in a different route, arrived at the city before him.

About this time, Sertorius, who, before the war broke out, had, in the distribution of provinces, been appointed Propraetor of Spain, despairing of affairs in Italy, in which probably he was not sufficiently consulted, repaired to his province, and determined to try what the skill of a Roman leader

leader could effect at the head of the warlike natives of that country.

The chiefs of the Marian party, who remained in Italy, made efforts to collect all the forces they could at Rome. Carbo, upon hearing that the army of Scipio had been seduced to desert their leader, said, "We have to do with a lion and a "fox, of which the fox is probably the more dan- "gerous enemy of the two."

Norbanus, soon after his arrival at Rome, procured an edict of the People, by which Metellus, and the others who had joined their forces with Sylla, were declared enemies to their country. About the same time a fire broke out in the Capitol, and the buildings were burnt to the ground. Various suspicions were entertained of the cause; but as no party had any interest in this event, it was probably accidental, and served only to agitate the minds of the People, prone to superstition, and apt to find in every calamity alarming presages, as well as present distress.

The remainder of the season was spent by both parties in collecting their forces from every quarter of Italy; and the term of the Consuls in office being nearly expired, Carbo procured his own nomination to succeed them, and inscribed the name of a young Marius, scarcely twenty years of age, as his colleague. This person is by some said to have been the nephew, by others the adopted son, of the late celebrated C. Marius, whose name had

U.C. 671.
C. Marius,
Cn. Pap.
Carbo.

CHAP XIV. had so long been terrible to the enemies, and at length not lefs fo to the friends, of Rome.

At this time the Senate confented to have the plate and ornaments of the temples coined for the pay of the fuppofed Confular armies. The majority of its members, however, notwithftanding this act of obfequioufnefs, were believed to favour the oppofite party, and not fit to be trufted in cafe the city were attacked. In confequence of this fufpicion, the whole being affembled together by orders of the Prætors, Damafippus and Brutus, numbers were taken afide and put to death; of thofe deftined to die, Quintus Mucius Scævola, Pontifex Maximus, flying to the temple in which he was accuftomed to difcharge his facred office, was killed in the porch.

The military operations of the following fpring began with an obftinate fight between two confiderable armies, one commanded by Metellus, the other by Carinas. The latter being defeated with great lofs, Carbo haftened to the fcene of action, in order to cover the remains of the vanquifhed party.

In the mean time Sylla, being encamped at Setia, and having intelligence that the young Marius was advancing againft him, put his army in motion to meet him, forced him back to Sacriportum, near to Præneste, where an action foon after enfued, in which Marius was defeated.

The routed army having fled in diforder to Præneste, the firft who arrived were received into the place; but as it was apprehended that the enemy alfo

OF THE ROMAN REPUBLIC.

also might enter in the tumult, the gates were shut, and many, being excluded, were flaughtered under the ramparts. Marius himfelf efcaped, by means of a rope which was let down from the battlements, and by which he was enabled to fcale the walls.

In confequence of this victory Sylla invefted Prænefte; and as great numbers were thus fuddenly cooped up in a town, which was not prepared to fubfift them, he had an immediate profpect of feeing them reduced to the neceffity of furrendering at difcretion. Committing the charge of a blockade for this purpofe to Lucretius Offella, he himfelf, with part of the army, proceeded to Rome. Metellus, in a fecond action, had defeated the army of Carbo, and Pompey, another of the fame party near Sena; and thus the forces of Sylla being victorious in every part of Italy, the city was prepared to receive their leader as foon as he fhould appear at the gates. Upon his approach the partizans of the oppofite faction withdrew, and left him mafter of the capital.

Sylla having pofted his army in the field of Mars, he himfelf entered the city, and, calling an affembly of the People, delivered an harrangue, in which he imputed the diforder of the times to the injuftice and cruelty of a few factious men, who had overturned the government, and facrificed the beft blood of the republic to their ambition and to their perfonal refentments. He exhorted the well-difpofed to be of good courage, and affured them that they fhould foon have their freedom reftored.

In

CHAP. XIV.
In the mean time, he gratified his own army with the spoils of the oppofite party, declaring the effects of all thofe to be forfeited who had been acceffary to the crimes lately committed againft the State. After this firft fpecimen of his policy in the city, leaving a fufficient force to execute his orders, he haftened to Clufium, where Carbo, being joined by a confiderable reinforcement from Spain, was preparing to recover the metropolis, or to relieve his colleague Marius, who was reduced to great diftrefs in Præneste.

The events which followed the arrival and operations of Sylla in Tufcany were various, but for the moft part unfavourable to Carbo, whofe force, by defertion and the fword, was declining apace. The iffue of the war feemed to depend on the fate of Præneste, and the whole force of the party was therefore directed to the relief of that place. The Lucanians and Samnites, who had efpoufed the caufe of the late Caius Marius, and who, by his favour, had obtained the promifcuous enrolment to which they afpired, apprehending immediate ruin to themfelves, in the fuppreffion of a party by whom alone they had been favoured, determined to make one great effort for the relief of Præneste.

They were joined in Latium by a large detachment fent by Carbo, under Carinas and Marcius, and made an attempt to force the lines of the befiegers at Præneste, and to open the blockade of that place. But having failed in this defign, they turned, with defperation, on the city of Rome itfelf,
which

which was but flightly guarded by a fmall detachment which had been left for that purpofe. Sylla being informed of their intention, with hafty
marches returned to the city, and found the enemy already in poffeffion of the fuburbs, and preparing to force the gates.

It was about four in the afternoon when he arrived, after a long march. Some of his officers
propofed, that the troops, being fatigued, fhould
have a little time to repofe themfelves; and that,
for this purpofe, they fhould remain under cover
of the walls until the following day. Sylla, however, propofing, rather by his unexpected prefence,
and by coming to action at an unufual hour, to furprife the enemy, gave orders for an immediate attack. The event for fome time was doubtful; the
wing that was led by himfelf was repulfed, or did
not make the impreffion expected; but the other
wing under Craffus had a better fortune, put the
enemy to flight, and drove them to Antemnæ.

The action, though thus various in the different
parts of it, became, in the event, completely decifive. Eighty thoufand of the Marian party were
killed in their flight, and eight thoufand taken.
Carbo, in defpair of the caufe, fled into Sicily.
The troops who were blocked up in Præneste, having no longer any hopes of relief, furrendered
themfelves, and the whole party was difperfed or
cut off. The young Marius attempted to efcape by
the galleries of a mine, of which there were many

under the place¹; and being prevented, killed himself. His head was carried to Sylla, and by his order exposed in the market-place. "That " boy," he said, " should have learnt to row be- " fore he attempted to steer!"

The leader of the victorious party having now removed all impediments from his way, proceeded to retaliate on the authors of the late disorders with a force equal to the violence with which it had been provoked. About six or eight thousand of those who were supposed to have been the busiest instruments of the late usurpations and murders, being taken prisoners in the war, or surprised in the city, were, by his direction, shut up in the circus, and instantly put to death.

While this horrid scene was acting, he had assembled the Senate, at a little distance, in the temple of Bellona; and as many of the members then present had either favoured, or at least tamely submitted to the late usurpation, he made them a speech on the state of the republic, in which he reproached them as accessary to the late disorders, and admonished them, for the future, to respect the legal government and constitution of their country. In the midst of these admonitions, the cries of those who were slaughtered in the circus reaching their ears, the assembly was greatly alarmed, and many of the members started from their seats. Sylla, with a countenance stern, but undisturbed, checked them as for an instance of levity.

¹ Vid. Strabo, lib. v. p. 239.

levity. "Be compofed," he faid, "and attend to the bufinefs for which your are called. What you hear are no more than the cries of a few wretches, who are fuffering the punifhment due to their crimes." From this interruption he refumed his fubject, and continued fpeaking till the maffacre of thefe unhappy victims was completed.

In a harangue which he afterwards delivered to the People, he fpoke of his own fervices to the republic, and of the mifdemeanour of others, in terms that ftruck all who heard him with terror. "The republic," he faid (if his opinion were followed), "fhould be purged; but whether it were fo or no, the injuries done to himfelf and his friends fhould be punifhed." He accordingly ordered military execution againft every perfon who had been acceffary to the late maffacres and ufurpations; and while the fword was yet reeking in his hands, paffed great part of his time, as ufual, in mirth and diffipation with men of humourous and fingular characters. He deigned not even to inquire into the abufes that were committed in the execution of his general plan. Many of the diforders which took place in the former maffacre were accordingly renewed. The perfons who were employed in it, frequently indulged their own private refentment and their avarice in the choice of victims. Among thefe, Cataline, then a young man, had joined the victorious party; and plunged, with a fingular impetuofity, into the midft

of

of a storm which now overwhelmed a part of the city. He is said, among other persons to whom he bore an aversion, or whose effects he intended to seize, to have murdered his own brother, with strange circumstances of cruelty and horror.

While these dreadful murders, though mixed with examples of a just execution, were perpetrated, a young man, C. Metellus, had the courage to address himself to Sylla in the Senate, and desired he would make known the extent of his design, and how far these executions were to be carried? "We intercede not," he said, "for the con-
"demned; we only entreat that you would re-
"lieve out of this dreadful state of uncertainty
"all those whom in reality you mean to spare."

Sylla, without being offended at this freedom, published a list of those he had doomed to destruction, offering a reward of two talents for the head of each, and denouncing severe penalties against every person who should harbour or conceal them. Hence arose the practice of publishing lists of the persons to be massacred, which under the odious name of *Proscription,* was afterwards imitated with such fatal effects in the subsequent convulsions of the State.

The present proscription, although it promised some security to all who were not comprehended in the fatal list, opened a scene, in some respects, more dreadful than that which had been formerly acted in this massacre. By the promised reward, the hands of servants were hired against their masters

ters, and even those of children against their parents. The mercenary of every denomination were encouraged, by a great premium, to commit what before only the executioners of public justice thought themselves entitled to perform; and there followed a scene, in which human nature had full scope to exert all the evil of which it is susceptible, treachery, ingratitude, distrust, malice, and revenge; and would have retained no claim to our esteem or commiseration, if its character had not been redeemed by contrary instances of fidelity, generosity, and courage, displayed by those who, to preserve their friends and benefactors, or even to preserve mere objects of pity, who took refuge under their protection, risked all the dangers with which the proscribed themselves were threatened.

In consequence of these measures, about five thousand persons of consideration were put to death, among whom were reckoned forty Senators, and sixteen hundred of the Equestrian order.

From these beginnings the Romans had reason to apprehend a tyranny, more sanguinary perhaps than any that ever afflicted mankind. " If in the " field you slay all who are found in arms against " you," said Catulus [1], " and in the city you slay " even the unarmed; over whom do you propose " to reign?"

These reproaches were by Sylla received as jests; and the freedom and ease of his manners, as well as the professions he made of regard to

[1] Probably the son of him who perished in the tyranny of Marius.

CHAP.
XIV.
the commonwealth, were imputed to infenfibility, or to a barbarous diffimulation, which rendered his character more odious, and the profpect of his future intentions more terrifying.

In comparing the prefent with the late ufurpation and maffacre, men recollected, that Marius, from his infancy, had been of a fevere and inexorable temper; that his refentments were fanguinary, and even his frowns were deadly; but that his cruelties were the effect of real paffions, and had the apology of not being perpetrated in cold blood; that every perfon on whom he looked with indifference was fafe;, and that even when he ufurped the government of the State, as foon as his perfonal refentments were gratified, the fword in his hand became an innocent pageant, and the mere enfign or badge of his power. But that Sylla directed a maffacre in the midft of compofure and eafe: that as a private man he had been affable and pleafant, even noted for humanity and candour [1]; that the change of his temper having commenced with his exaltation, there were no hopes that the iffues of blood could be ftopped while he was fuffered to retain his power. His daring fpirit, his addrefs, his cunning, and his afcendant over the minds of men, rendered the profpect of a deliverance, if not defperate, extremely remote. The republic feemed to be extinguifhed for ever; and if the rage for blood feemed to abate, after the firft heats of execution were over, it appeared to be ftayed only for
want

[1] Plutarch. in Sylla.

want of victims, not from any principle of moderation, or sentiment of clemency.

Such was the aspect of affairs, and the grounds of terror conceived even by those who were innocent of the late disorders; but to those who had reason to fear the resentment of the victor, the prospect was altogether desperate. Norbanus, having fled to Rhodes, received at that place an account of the proscriptions, and, to avoid being delivered up, killed himself. Carbo, being in Sicily, endeavoured to make his escape from thence, but was apprehended by Pompey, and killed. Thus all the ordinary offices of State were vacated by the desertion or death of those who had filled or usurped them.

Sylla had hitherto acted as master, without any other title than that of the sword; and it was now thought necessary to supply the defect. He retired from the city, that the Senate might assemble with the more appearance of freedom. To name an Interrex was the usual expedient for restoring the constitution; and for proceeding to elections in a legal form after the usual time had elapsed, or when by any accident the ordinary succession to office had been interrupted. Valerius Flaccus was named. To him Sylla gave intimation, that, to resettle the commonwealth, a Dictator, for an indefinite term, should be appointed, and made offer of his own services for this purpose. These intimations were received as commands. And Flaccus, having assembled the People, moved for an act to vest Sylla with the title of Dictator, giving him a discretionary power over the persons, fortunes, and lives of all the citizens.

No example of this kind had taken place for one-hundred and twenty years preceding this date. In the former part of that period, the jealousy of the aristocracy, and in the latter part of it, the negative of the Tribunes, had always prevented a measure from which the parties severally apprehended some danger to themselves. It was now revived in the person of Sylla with unusual solemnity, and ratified by an act of the People, in which they yielded up at once all their own claims to the sovereignty, and submitted to monarchy for an indefinite time. Sylla having named Valerius Flaccus for his lieutenant or commander of the horse, returned to the city, presenting a sight that was then unusual, a single person, preceded by four-and-twenty Lictors, armed with the axe and the rods; and the Dictator being likewise attended by a numerous military guard, it was not doubted that these ensigns of magistracy were to be employed, not for parade, but for serious execution, and were speedily to be stained with the blood of many citizens, whom the sword had spared. Unwilling to be troubled with ordinary affairs, and that the city, in all matters in which it was not necessary for himself to interpose, might still enjoy the benefit of its usual forms, he directed the People to assemble, and to fill up the customary lists of office.

Lucretius

Lucretius Offella, the officer who had commanded in the reduction of Præneste, presuming on his favour with the Dictator, and on his consequence with the army, offered himself for the Consulate. Being commanded by Sylla to desist, he still continued his canvas, and while he solicited votes in the street, was, by order of the Dictator, put to death. A tumult immediately arose; the Centurion, who executed this order against Offella, was seized, and, attended by a great concourse of people, was carried before the Dictator. Sylla heard the complaint with composure, told the multitude who crowded around him, that Offella had been slain by his orders, and that the Centurion must therefore be released. He then dismissed them, with this homely but menacing apologue. " A countryman at his plough, feeling himself " troubled with vermin, once and again made a " halt to pick them off his jacket; but being molested a third time, he threw the jacket, with all " its contents, into the fire. Beware," he said, " of " the fire; provoke me not a third time¹." Such was the tone of a government, which, from this example, was likely to be fatal to many who had concurred in establishing of it, as well as to those of the opposite party.

Sylla, soon after his elevation to the state of Dictator, proceeded to make his arrangements and to new-model the commonwealth. The army ²

U. C. 672.
M. Tullius Decula,
Cn. Corn. Dolabella.

---

¹ Appian. in Bell. Civil. lib. i. Plutarch. in Sylla.

² It appears that Livy reckoned forty-seven legions, Epitom. lib. lxxxix.

CHAP. appeared to have the first or preferable claim to
XIV. his attention. He accordingly proposed to reward
them by a gift of all the lands which had been
forfeited by the adherents of the opposite party.
Spoletum, Interamna, Præneste, Fluentia, Nola,
Sulmo, Volaterra, together with the countries of
Samnium and Lucania, were depopulated to make
way for the legions who had served under himself
in the reduction of his enemies. In these new inhabitants of Italy, whose prosperity depended on
his safety, he had a guard to his person, and a sure
support to his power. By changing their condition from that of soldiers to land-holders and peasants, he dispelled, at the same time, that dangerous cloud of military power, which he himself
or his antagonists had raised over the commonwealth, and provided for the permanency of any
reformations he was to introduce into the civil establishment. The troops, from soldiers of fortune,
became proprietors of land, and interested in the
preservation of peace. In this manner, whatever
may have been his intention in this arbitrary act
of power, so cruel to the innocent sufferers, if there
were any such, the measure had an immediate
tendency to terminate the public confusion. Its
future consequences, in pointing out to new armies, and to their ambitious leaders, a way to supplant their fellow-citizens in their property, and
to practise usurpations more permanent than that
of Sylla, were probably not then foreseen.

The next act of the Dictator appears more entirely

tirely calculated for the security of his own person. A body of ten thousand slaves, lately the property of persons involved in the ruin of the vanquished party, having their freedom and the right of citizens conferred on them, were enrolled promiscuously in all the Tribes; and as the enfranchised slave took the name of the person from whom he received his freedom, these new citizens became an accession to the family of the Cornelii, and in every tumult were likely to be the sure partizans of Sylla, and the abettors of his power. They had received a freedom which was connected with the permanency of his government, and foresaw, that, if the leaders of the opposite party, in whose houses they had served, should be restored, they themselves must return into servitude; and they accordingly became an additional security to the government which their patron was about to establish.

So far the Dictator seemed to intend the security of his own person, and the stability of his government; but in all his subsequent institutions, there appears an intention to restore the constitution in its legislative and judicative departments, to provide a proper supply of officers for conducting the accumulated affairs of the commonwealth, to stop the source of former disorders, and to guard against the growing depravity of the times, by extending and securing the execution of the laws. He began with filling up the rolls of the Senate, which had been greatly reduced by the war, and by

CHAP. XIV.

by the sanguinary policy of the parties who had prevailed in their turns. He augmented the number of this body to five hundred; taking the new members from the Equestrian order, but leaving the choice of them to the People.

Lex de Judiciis.

The legislative power of the Senate, and the judicative power of its members, were restored. The law that was provided for the last of these purposes consisted of different clauses. By the first clause it was enacted, that none but Senators, or those who were entitled to give their opinion in the Senate [1], should be put upon any jury or list of the judges [2]. By the second it was provided, that, of the judges so placed on the roll, the parties should not be allowed to challenge or reject above three.

By a third clause it was allowed, that judgment, in trials at law, should be given either by secret ballot, or openly, at the option of the defendant; and, by a separate regulation, that the nomination of officers to command in the provinces, with the title of Proconsul, should be committed to the Senate.

During the late tribunitian usurpation, the whole legislative and executive power had, under pretence of vesting those prerogatives in the assembly of the Tribes, been seized by the Tribunes. But Sylla restored the ancient form of assembling

---

[1] All the Officers of State, even before they were put upon the rolls, were entitled to speak in the Senate.

[2] Tacit. Annal. lib. xi. Cic. pro Cliento.

fembling the People by Centuries, and reduced the Tribunes to their defenſive privilege of interpoſing by a negative againſt any act of oppreſſion; and he deprived them of their pretended right to propoſe laws, or to harangue the people. He moreover ſubjoined, that none but Senators could be elected into the office of Tribune; and, to the end that no perſon of a factious ambition might chooſe this ſtation, he procured it to be enacted, that no one who had borne the office of Tribune could afterwards be promoted into any other rank of the magiſtracy.

With reſpect to the offices of State, this new founder of the commonwealth revived the obſolete law which prohibited the re-election of any perſon into the Conſulate, till after an interval of ten years; and enacted, that none could be elected Conſul till after he had been Quæſtor, Ædile, and Prætor. He augmented the number of Prætors from ſix to eight; that of Quæſtors to twenty; and, to guard againſt the diſorders which had recently afflicted the republic, declared it to be treaſon for any Roman officer, without the authority of the Senate and People, to go beyond the limits of his own province, whether with or without an army, to make war, or to invade any foreign nation whatever.

He repealed the law of Domitius relating to the election of prieſts, and reſtored to the college the entire choice of their own members.

He made ſeveral additions to the penal code, by

CHAP.
XIV.
by statutes against subornation, forgery, wilful fire, poisoning, rape, assault, extortion, and forcibly entering the house of a citizen; with a statute, declaring it criminal to be found, in places of public resort, with a deadly weapon of any kind. To all these he added a sumptuary law, of which the tenor is not precisely known; but it appears to have regulated the expence at ordinary [1] meals and at funerals, and to have likewise settled the price of provisions.

These laws were promulgated at certain intervals, and intermixed with the measures which were taken to restore the peace of the empire. In order to finish the remains of the civil war, Pompey had been sent into Sicily and Africa, and C. Annius Luscus into Spain. In this province, Sertorius had taken arms for the Marian faction; but being attacked by the forces of Sylla, and ill supported at first by the natives of Spain, he fled into Africa. From thence, hearing that the Lusitanians were disposed to take arms against the reigning party at Rome, he repassed the sea, put himself at their head, and in this situation was able, for some years, to find occupation for the arms of the republic, and for its most experienced commanders.

Soon after the departure of Sylla from Asia, Murena, whom he had left to command in that province, found a pretence to renew the war with Mithridates; and, having ventured to pass the Halys,

[1] Gellius, lib. ii. c. 24.

Halys, was defeated by that prince, and afterwards arraigned as having infringed the late treaty of peace. This accusation was favourably received at Rome, the conduct of Murena censured, and first A. Gabinius, and afterwards Minucius Thermus, were sent to supersede him in the province.

Mean time Sylla, with all his disdain of personal distinction exhibited a triumph on account of his victories in Asia and Greece. Processions were continued for two days. On the first, he deposited in the treasury fifteen thousand pondo of gold [1], and an hundred and fifteen thousand pondo of silver [2]; on the second day, thirteen thousand pondo of gold [3], and seven thousand pondo of silver [4]. There was nothing that had any reference to his victory in the civil war, except a numerous train of Senators, and other citizens of rank, who, having resorted to his camp for protection, had been restored by him to their estates and their dignities, and now followed his chariot, calling him Father, and the Deliverer of his Country.

Upon the return of the elections, Sylla was again chosen Consul, together with Q. Cæcilius Metellus. The latter was destined, at the expiration of his office, to command against Sertorius in Spain. Sylla himself still retained the Dictatorial power, and was employed in promulgating some of the acts of which the chief have been mentioned.

Pompey

[1] Reckoning the pondo at ten ounces, and 4 l. an ounce, this will make about 600,000 l.
[2] About 287,500 l.   [3] About 520,000 l.
[4] About 140,000 l. Plin. lib. xxxiii. initio.

CHAP. XIV.

Pompey having, in the preceding year, by the death of Carbo, and the difperfion of his party, finifhed the remains of the civil war in Sicily, was now ordered by the Senate to tranfport his army into Africa. There Domitius, a leader of the oppofite faction, had erected his ftandard, affembled fome remains of the vanquifhed party, and received all the fugitives who crowded for refuge to his camp. Pompey accordingly being to depart from Sicily, leaving the command of that ifland to Memmius, and embarked his army, confifting of fix legions, in two divifions; of which one landed at Utica, the other in the bay of Carthage. Having foon after come to an engagement with Domitius, who had been joined by Jarbas, an African prince, he obtained a complete victory over their united forces, and purfuing his advantage, penetrated, without any refiftance, into the kingdom of Numidia, which, though dependant on the Romans, had not yet been reduced to the form of a province.

The war being ended in this quarter, Sylla thought proper to fuperfede Pompey in the province, and ordered him to difband his army, referving only one legion, with which he was to wait for his fucceffor. The troops were greatly incenfed at this order; and, thinking themfelves equally entitled to fettlements with the legions who were lately provided for in Italy, refufed to lay down their arms. They earneftly entreated their general to embark for Rome, where they promifed to make him mafter of the government. This young man,

man, with a moderation which he continued to fupport in the height of his ambition, withstood the temptation, and declared to the army, that, if they perfifted in their purpofe, he muft certainly die by his own hands; that he would not do violence to the government of his country, nor be the object or pretence of a civil war. From this conduct we have reafon to conclude that, if in reality he had encouraged the mutiny, it was only that he might thus have the honour of reclaiming the foldiers, and of rejecting their offer. The ambition of this fingular perfon, as will appear from many paffages of his life, led him to aim at confideration more than power.

While Pompey was endeavouring to bring the troops to their duty, a report was carried to Rome, that he had actually revolted, and was preparing, with his army, to make a defeent upon Italy. " It appears to be my fate," faid Sylla, " in my " old age, to fight with boys;" and he was about to recal the veterans to his ftandard, when the truth was made known, and the part which Pompey had acted was properly ¦reprefented. The merit of this young man on that occafion was the greater, that he himfelf was unwilling to difband the army before they fhould return to Italy to attend a triumph, which he hoped to obtain; and that the refolution he took to comply with his orders, proceeded from refpect to the Senate, and deference to the authority of the State.

Sylla,

CHAP. XIV.

Sylla, won by the behaviour of Pompey on this occasion, was inclined to difpenfe with his former commands, and accordingly moved in the affembly of the People, that the legions ferving in Africa might return with their arms into Italy.

This motion was oppofed by C. Herennius, Tribune of the People, who ventured to employ the prerogative of his office, however impaired, againft the power of the Dictator. But Sylla perfifted; obtained a law to authorife Pompey to enter with his army into Italy; and when he drew near the city, went forth with a numerous body of the Senate to receive him. On this occafion, it is faid, that, by calling him the Great Pompey, Sylla fixed a defignation upon him, which, in the Roman way of diftinguifhing perfons by cafual additions, whether of contempt or refpect, continued to furnifh him with a title for life. The times were wretched when armies ftated themfelves in the commonwealth as the partizans of a leader, and when the leader, by not making war on his country, was fuppofed to have laid up a ftore of merit.

Pompey, upon this occafion, laid claim to a triumph. Sylla at firft oppofed it as being contrary to the rule and order of the commonwealth; which referved this honour for perfons who had attained to the rank either of Conful or Prætor; but he afterwards complied, being ftruck, it is faid, with a mutinous faying of this afpiring young man, bidding him recollect, that there were more perfons sons disposed to worship the rising than the setting sun.

In the triumph which Pompey accordingly obtained, he meant to have entered the city on a carriage drawn by elephants; but these animals could not pass abreast through the gates. His donation to the troops falling short of their expectation, and they having murmured, and even threatened to mutiny, he said, the fear of losing his triumph should not affect him; that he would instantly disband the legions, rather than comply with their unreasonable demands. This check, given to the presumption of the army by an officer so young and so aspiring, gave a general satisfaction. P. Servilius, a Senator of advanced age, said, upon this occasion, " That the young man had at last deser-
" ved his triumph and his title."

Pompey, by his vanity in demanding a triumph contrary to the established order of the commonwealth, had impaired the lustre of his former actions; by this last act of magnanimity, in restraining the insolence of the troops, he forfeited the affections of the army; and in both these circumstances together, gave a complete specimen and image of his whole life. With too much respect for the republic to employ violent means for its ruin, he was possessed by a vanity and a jealousy of his own personal consideration, which, in detail, perpetually led him to undermine its foundations.

CHAP. XIV.
U. C. 674.
P. Servilius, Ap. Claudius.

Upon the return of the elections, Sylla was again destined for one of the Consuls; but he declined this piece of flattery, and directed the choice to fall on P. Servilius and Appius Claudius. Soon after these magistrates entered on the discharge of their trust; the Dictator appeared, as usual, in the Forum, attended by twenty-four Lictors; but, instead of proceeding to any exercise of his power, made a formal resignation of it, dismissed his Lictors, and, having declared to the People, that, if any one had matter of charge against him, he was ready to answer it, continued to walk in the streets in the character of a private man, and afterwards retired to his villa near Cumæ, where he exercised himself in hunting [1], and other country amusements.

This resignation, it must be confessed, throws a new light on the character of Sylla, and removes him far from the herd of common usurpers, who sacrifice their fellow-creatures merely to their own lust of dominion. The sacrifices he made, shocking as they were to the feelings of humanity, now appear to have been offered at the shrine of public order, to provide for the future peace to his country. His ruling passion appears to have been disdain of what the vulgar admire, whether distinction or power. When tired of youthful pursuits, he sued for preferment, but with so little animosity or jealousy of competition, that if he had not been hurried by extreme provocation

---

[1] Appian. Bell. Civil. lib. i.

tion into the violent course he pursued; it is probable that he never would have been heard of, but upon the roll of Consuls, or the record of his triumphs, and would have disdained any encroachment on the right of his fellow-citizens as much as he resented the encroachments which were made on his own.

In his first attack of the city with a military force, his whole action showed, that he meant to rescue the Republic from the usurpation of Marius, not to usurp the Government for himself. At his return into Italy from the Mithridatic war, the state of parties already engaged in hostilities, and the violence done to the Republic by those who pretended to govern it, will abundantly justify his having had recourse to arms.

During the short period in which he retained his power of Dictator, without neglecting precautions for the security of his own person in the retirement he was meditating, he took the measures already mentioned, to tear up the roots of future disorder, and effect some reform in the State: but as the past had shown, what are the evils to which an overgrown and corrupted Republic is exposed; so the corrections he attempted, although they served to prolong the struggles of virtuous men for the preservation of their country, yet were not sufficient to prevent its ruin.

For some particulars of his description, which have not entered into the preceding narration, it may be observed, that he was among the few Romans

mans of his time who made any confiderable advance in literary ftudies; and that he wrote memoirs of his own life, continued to within a few days of his death, often quoted by Plutarch. That he neverthelefs appeared fuperior to the reputation of his own moft fplendid performances, and from fimplicity or difdain, mixed perhaps with fuperftition, not from affected modefty, attributed his fuccefs to good fortune or to the favour of the gods; fo much, that while he beftowed on Pompey the title of *Great*, he himfelf was content with that of the *Fortunate* [1].

With refpect to fuch a perfonage, circumftances of a trivial nature become fubjects of attention. His hair and eyes, it is faid, were of a light colour, his complexion fair, and his countenance blotched. He was, by the moft probable accounts, four years old at the time of the fedition of Tiberius Gracchus, and feventeen at the death of Caius, the younger brother of Tiberius; fo that he might have perceived at this date the effect of tribunitian diforders, and taken the impreffions from which he acted againft them. He ferved the office of Quæftor under Marius in Africa at thirty-one; was Conful for the firft time at forty-nine or fifty [2]; was Dictator at fifty-fix; refigned when turned of fifty-eight; and died yet under fixty, in the year which followed that of his refignation.

There remained in the city, at his death, a numerous

[1] Felix.   [2] Vel. Pater. lib. ii. c. 17.

merous body of new citizens, who having been manumised by his order, bore his name: in the country a still more numerous body of veteran officers and soldiers, who held estates by his gift: numbers throughout the empire, who owed their safety to his protection, and who ascribed the existence of the commonwealth itself to the exertions of his great ability and courage: numbers who, although they were offended with the severe and bloody exercise of his power, yet admired the magnanimity of his resignation.

When he was no longer an object of flattery, his corpse was carried in procession through Italy at the public expence. The fasces, and every other ensign of honour, were restored to the dead. Above two thousand golden crowns were fabricated in haste, by order of the towns and provinces he had protected, or of the private persons he had preserved, to testify their veneration for his memory. Roman matrons, whom it might be expected his cruelties would have affected with horror, lost every other sentiment in that of admiration, crowded to his funeral, and heaped the pile with perfumes[1]. His obsequies were performed in the Campus Martius. The tomb was marked by his own directions with a characteristical inscription, to the following effect: " Here lies Sylla, who never " was outdone in good offices by his friend, nor in " acts of hostility by his enemy [2]."

[1] Appian. de Bell. Civ. lib. i. Plutarch. in Sylla.
[2] Plutarch. in Sylla, fine.

CHAP. XV.

State of the Commonwealth and Numbers of the People.—Characters of Persons who began to appear in the Times of Sylla.—Faction of Lepidus.—Sertorius harbours the Marian Party in Spain.—Is attacked by Metellus and Pompey.—His Death, and final Suppression of the Party.—First Appearance of C. Julius Cæsar.—Tribunes begin to trespass on the laws of Sylla.—Progress of the Empire.—Preparations of Mithridates.—War with the Romans.—Irruption into Bithynia.—Siege of Cyzicus.—Raised.—Flight of Mithridates.—Lucullus carries the War into Pontus.—Rout and Dispersion of the Army of Mithridates.—His Flight into Armenia.—Conduct of Lucullus in the Province of Asia.

CHAP.
XV.

THE public was so much occupied with the contest of Sylla and his antagonists, that little else is recorded of the period in which it took place. Writers have not given us any distinct account of the condition of the city, or of the number of citizens. As the State was divided into two principal factions, the office of Censor was become too important for either party to entrust it with their opponents, or even in neutral hands. The leaders of every faction, in their turn, made up the rolls of the People, and disposed, at their pleasure, of the equestrian and senatorian dignities.

At

OF THE ROMAN REPUBLIC.

At a survey of the city, which is mentioned by Livy[1], preceding the admission of the Italians, the number of citizens was three hundred and ninety-four thousand three hundred and thirty-six. At another survey, which followed soon after that event, they amounted, according to Eusebius, to four hundred and sixty-three thousand[2]; and it seems that the whole accession of citizens from the country made no more than sixty-eight thousand six hundred and sixty-four. The great slaughter of Romans and Italians, in which it is said that three hundred thousand men were killed, preceding the last of these musters, and the difficulty of making complete and accurate lists when the citizens were so much dispersed, will account for the seemingly small increase of their numbers.

In this period were born, and began to enter on the scene of public affairs, those persons whose conduct was now to determine the fate of the Republic. Pompey had already distinguished himself, and stood high in the public esteem. He had been educated in the camp of his father, and, by accident, at a very early age, or before he had attained to any of the ordinary civil or political preferments, commanded an army. Cicero, being of the same age, began to be distinguished at the bar. He pleaded, in the second consulate of Sylla, the cause of Roscius Amerinus, and having occasion to censure the actions of Chrysogonus and

[1] Liv. lib. lxiii.   [2] Euseb. in Chronico.

other favourites of the Dictator, by his freedom in that inftance, incurred no refentment from Sylla, and gained much honour to himfelf.

Caius Cæfar, now connected with the family of Cinna, whofe daughter he had married, and being nearly related to the elder Marius, who had married his aunt, narrowly efcaped the fword of the prevailing party. Being commanded to feparate from his wife, he retained her in defiance of this order, and for his contumacy was put in the lift of the profcribed. He was faved, however, by the interceffion of common friends, whofe requeft in his favour Sylla granted, with that memorable faying, "Beware of him: there is many a Ma-"rius in the perfon of that young man." A circumftance which marked at once the penetration of Sylla, and the early appearances of an extraordinary character in Cæfar.

Marcus Porcius, afterwards named Cato of Utica, was about three years younger than Cæfar, and being early an orphan, was educated in the houfe of an uncle, Livius Drufus. While yet a child, liftening to the converfation of the times, he learned that the pretenfions of the Italian allies, then in agitation, were dangerous to the Roman ftate. Pompedius Silo, who managed the claim for the Italians, amufing himfelf with the young Cato, preffed him with careffes to intercede with his uncle in their behalf; and, finding that he was not to be won by flattery, next tried in vain to intimidate by threatening to throw him from the window. "If this were a man," he faid, " I
" believe

"believe we should obtain no such favour." In the height of Sylla's military executions, when his portico was crowded with persons who brought the heads of the proscribed to be exchanged for the reward which had been published, Cato being carried by his tutor to pay his court, asked, "if no one hated this man enough to kill him?" "yes, but they fear him still more than they hate him." "Then give me a sword," said the boy, "and I will kill him." Such were the early indications of characters which afterwards became so conspicuous in the commonwealth.

With the unprecedented degradation of the Tribune Octavius, and the subsequent murder of Tiberius Gracchus, began, among the parties at Rome, a scene of injuries and retaliations, with alternate periods of anarchy and violent usurpation, which must have speedily ended in the ruin of the commonwealth, if the sword had not passed at last into hands which employed it for the restoration of public order, as well as for the avenging of private wrongs.

It is indeed probable, that none of the parties in these horrid scenes had a deliberate intention to subvert the government, but all of them treated the forms of the commonwealth with too little respect; and, to obtain some revenge of the wrongs which they themselves apprehended or endured, did not scruple in their turn to violate the laws of their country. But to those who wished to preserve the commonwealth, the experience of fifty years

CHAP. years was now sufficient to show, that attempts to
XV. restore the laws by illegal methods, and to terminate animosities by retorted injuries and provocations were extremely vain. The excess of the evil had a tendency to exhaust its source, and parties began to nauseate the draught of which they had been made to drink so largely. There were, nevertheless, some dregs in the bottom of the cup, and the supplies of faction which were brought by the rising generation, were of a mixture more dangerous than those of the former age. The example of Sylla, who made himself lord of the commonwealth by means of a military force, and the security with which he held his usurpation during pleasure, had a more powerful effect in exciting the thirst of dominion, than the political uses which he made of his power, or his magnanimity in resigning it, had to restrain or to correct the effects of that dangerous precedent. Adventurers accordingly arose, who, without provocation, and equally indifferent to the interests of party as they were to those of the republic, proceeded, with a cool and deliberate purpose, to gratify their own ambition and avarice, by subverting the government of their country.

U. C. 675.
M. Æm. Lepidus, Q.
Lut. Catulus,
Cofs.

While Sylla was yet alive, Æmilius Lepidus, a man of profligate ambition, but of mean capacity, supported by the remains of the popular faction, stood for the Consulate, and was chosen, together with Q. Lutatius Catulus, the son of him who, with Marius, triumphed for their joint victory over

OF THE ROMAN REPUBLIC. 217

over the Cimbri, and who afterwards perished by the orders of that usurper.

Pompey had openly joined the popular faction in support of Lepidus, and was told upon that occasion by Sylla, that he was stirring the embers of a fire which would in the end consume the Republic. After the death of Sylla, from a mark of disapprobation well known to the Romans, that of not being mentioned in his will, it appeared that Pompey had lost his esteem. In opposition to Lepidus, however, and others, who wished to insult the memory of Sylla, this prudent young man was among the first in recommending and performing the honours that were paid to his remains.

Lepidus, upon his accession to the Consulate, moved for a recal of the proscribed exiles, a restitution of the forfeited lands, and a repeal of all the ordinances of the late Dictator. This motion was formally opposed by Catulus; and there ensued between the two Consuls a debate which divided the city. But the party of the Senate prevailed to have the motion rejected.

In the allotment of provinces the Transalpine Gaul had fallen to Lepidus; and, upon his motion being rejected in the assembly of the People, although it had been some time the practice for Consuls to remain at Rome during their continuance in office, he prepared to leave the city, in order to take possession of his province. This resolution, as it implied great impatience to be at the head of an army, gave some jealousy to the Senate,

nate, who dreaded the defigns of a Conful defirous to join military power with his civil authority. They recollected the progrefs of fedition which began with the Gracchi and Apuleius raifing popular tumults, and ended with Marius and Sylla leading Confular armies into the city, and fighting their battles in the ftreets. And in this point the decifive fpirit of Sylla, although it may have fnatched the commonwealth from the flames by which it began to be confumed, yet fhowed the way to its ruin in the means which he employed to preferve it[1]. The Senators were willing that Lepidus fhould depart from the city; but they had the precaution to exact from him an oath, that he fhould not difturb the public peace. This oath, to avoid the appearance of any particular diftruft of the perfon for whom it was projected, they likewife adminiftered to his colleague[2].

Lepidus, notwithftanding his oath, being arrived in his province, made preparations for war; and, thinking that his faith was pledged only while he was Conful, determined to remain in Gaul at the head of his forces, until his term in office expired. The Senate, in order to remove him from the army he had raifed, appointed him to prefide at the election of his fucceffor. But he neglected the fummons which was fent to him for this purpofe, and the year of the prefent Confuls was

[1] Appian. de Bell. Civ. lib. i.
[2] Ibid.

was by this means suffered to elapse, before any election was made.

The ordinary succession being thus interrupted, the Senate named Appius Claudius, as Interrex, to hold the elections, and at the same time deprived Lepidus of his command in Gaul. Upon this information he hastened to Italy with the troops he had already assembled, and greatly alarmed the republic. The Senate gave to Appius Claudius, and to Catulus, in the quality of Proconsul, the usual charge to watch over the safety of the State. These officers accordingly, without delay, collected a military force, while Lepidus advanced through Etruria, and published a manifesto, in which he invited all the friends of liberty to join him, and made a formal demand of being re-invested with the consular power. In opposition to this treasonable act of Lepidus, the Senate republished the law of Plautius, by which the Prætors were required, in the ordinary course of justice, to take cognizance of all attemps to levy war against the republic, and joined to it an additional clause or resolution of their own, obliging those magistrates to receive accusations of treason on holy-days, as well as on ordinary days of business.

Mean time Lepidus advanced to the very gates of Rome, seized the Janiculum and one of the bridges. But in his farther attempt to force the city, was met by Catulus, repulsed and routed. All his party dispersed; he himself fled to Sardinia, and soon after died. His son, a young man, with part of the

the army, retired to Alba, was there soon after taken, and suffered for a treason in which he had been engaged by his father.

Marcus Brutus, the father of him who, in the continuation of these troubles, afterwards fell at Philippi, having joined with Lepidus in this rash and profligate attempt against the republic, was obliged at Mantua to surrender himself to Pompey, and, by his order, was put to death. But the most considerable part of the army of Lepidus penetrated, under the conduct of Perperna, into Spain, and joined Sertorius, who was now become the refuge of one party in its distress, as Sylla had formerly been of the other. In this province accordingly, while peace began to be restored in Italy, a source of new troubles was opening for the State. The prevailing party in the city was willing to grant an indemnity, and to suffer all prosecution, on account of the late offences, to drop; the extreme to which Sylla had carried the severity of his executions, disposing the minds of men to the opposite course of indulgence and mercy.

Before the arrival of Lepidus with his army in Italy, Mithridates had sent to obtain from the Senate a ratification of the treaty he had concluded with Sylla: but, upon a complaint from Ariobarzanes, that the king of Pontus had not himself performed his part of that treaty by the complete restitution of Cappadocia, he was directed to give full satisfaction on this point before his negotiation

tion at Rome could proceed. He accordingly complied; but by the time his ambaffador had brought the report, the Romans were fo much occupied by the war they had to maintain againſt Lepidus and his adherents, that they had no leiſure for concerns fo remote. This intelligence encouraged Mithridates to think of renewing the war. Senfible that he could not rely on a permanent peace with the Romans, he had already provided an army, not fo confiderable in refpect to numbers as that which he had formerly employed againſt them, but more formidable by the order and difcipline he had endeavoured to introduce on the model of their own legion. He flattered himſelf, that the diſtraction under which the republic now laboured at home, would render it unable to refiſt his forces in Afia, and give him an opportunity to remove the only obſtruction that remained to his own conqueſts. He avoided, however, during the dependence of a negotiation, and without the pretext of a new provocation, to break out into open hoftilities; but he encouraged his fon-in-law Tigranes, king of Armenia, to make war on the Roman allies in his neighbourhood, and thereby laid the foundation of a quarrel which he might either adopt or decline at pleaſure. This prince accordingly, being then building a city, under the name of Tigranocerta, for which he wanted inhabitants, made an incurfion into the kingdom of Cappadocia, and is faid to have carried

ried off from thence three hundred thousand of the people to replenish his new settlement.

Soon after this nfraction of the peace, Mithridates, in order to have the co-operation of some of the parties into which the Roman State was divided, entered into a treaty with Sertorius, and wished, in concert with this adventurer, to execute the project of a march, by the route which was afterwards frequented by the barbarous nations in their succefsful attempts to invade and difmember the Empire of Rome. From the shores of the Euxine it appeared eafy to pafs over land to the Adriatic, and once more to repeat the operations of Pyrrhus and of Hannibal, by making war on the Romans in their own country.

Sertorius, who had erected the standard of the republic in Spain, gave refuge to the Roman exiles from every quarter, and was now at the head of a formidable power, compofed of Italians as well as natives of that country. By his birth and abilities he had pretenfions to the higheft preferments of the State, and had been early diftinguifhed as a foldier, qualified either to plan or to execute. He was attached to Marius in the time of the Cimbric war, and became a party with this leader in his quarrel with Sylla. His animofity to the latter was increafed by the mutual oppofition of their interefts in the purfuit of civil preferments. At the beginning of the civil war, Sertorius took an active part, but fhewed more refpect to the conftitution of his country, and more

mercy

mercy to thofe who were oppofed to him, than either of his affociates Marius or Cinna. When his faction was in poffeffion of the government, he was appointed to command in Spain, and, after the ruin of its affairs in Italy, withdrew into that Province. He was received as a Roman governor; but, foon after, when his enemies had prevailed in Italy, was attacked on their part by Caius Annius, who came with a proper force to diflodge him. He had eftablifhed pofts on the Pyrenees for the fecurity of his province; but the officer to whom they were entrufted being affaffinated, and the ftations deferted, the enemy had free accefs on that fide. Not in condition to maintain himfelf any longer in Spain, he embarked with what forces he could affemble at Carthagena, and continued for fome years, with a fmall fquadron of Cilician galleys, to fubfift by the fpoils of Africa and the contiguous coafts. In this ftate of his fortunes, Sertorius formed a project to vifit the Fortunate Iflands, and if a fettlement could be effected there, to bid farewel for ever to the Roman world, with all its factions, its divifions, and its troubles. But while he was about to fet fail in fearch of this famous retreat in the ocean, he received an invitation from the unfubdued natives of Lufitania to become their leader. At their head his abilities foon made him confpicuous. He affected to confider his new partizans as the Senate and People of Rome, treating the eftablifhment of Sylla in Italy as a mere ufurpation. He

himfelf

himself took the ensigns of a Roman officer of State, selected three hundred of his followers, to whom he gave the title of Senate, and, in all his transactions with foreign nations assumed the name and style of the Roman Republic. In treating with Mithridates, he refused to cede the province of Asia, or to purchase the alliance of that prince by any concessions injurious to the Roman Empire, of which he affected to consider himself and his Senate as the legal head.

While Sertorius was acting this farce, the report of his formidable power, the late accession he had gained by the junction of some of the Marian forces under the command of Perperna, and his supposed preparations to make a descent upon Italy, gave an alarm at Rome. Metellus had been some time employed against him in Spain; but being scarcely able to keep the field, the opposition he gave tended only to augment the reputation of his enemy. The Consuls lately elected were judged unequal to this war, and the thoughts of all men were turned on Pompey, who, though yet in no public character, nor arrived at the legal age of State preferments, had the address on this, as on many other occasions, to make himself be pointed at as the only person who could effectually serve the republic. He was accordingly, with the title of Proconsul, joined to Metellus in the conduct of the war in Spain [1]. It no doubt facilitated the career

U. C. 676.
D. Junius
Brutus,
Mam. Emilianus Livianus.

---

[1] Claudius, in making this motion, alluding to the supposed insignificance of both Consuls, said, that Pompey should be sent not Proconsul, but pro Consulibus.

career of this young man's pretensions, that few men of distinguished abilities were now in the way to sustain the fortunes of the republic. Such persons, of whatever party, had, in their turns, been the first victims of the late violent massacres; and the party of Sylla, which was now the republic, when considered as a nursery of eminent men, had some disadvantage, perhaps in the superiority of its leader, who was himself equal to all its affairs, and taught others to confide and obey, rather than to act for themselves. Pompey was not of an age to have suffered from this influence. He came into the party in its busiest time, and had been entrusted with separate commands. He had already obtained for himself a considerable measure of that artificial consideration which, though it cannot be supported without abilities, often exceeds the degree of merit on which it is founded; and this consideration to the end of his life he continued to augment with much attention and many concerted intrigues. His genius, however, for war was real, and was now about to be exercised and improved in the contest with Sertorius, an excellent master, whose lessons were rough but instructive.

Pompey having made the levies destined for this service, took his departure from Italy by a new route, and was the first Roman general who made his way into Spain by the Alps through Gaul and the Pyrennees[1]. Soon after his arrival, a legion that covered

---

[1] The communication with Spain had hitherto been carried on by sea, and in contradistinction to this communication, Pompey was said to have taken *Hannibal's route.*

covered the foragers of his army was intercepted and cut off by the enemy. Sertorius was engaged in the fiege of Laura. Pompey advanced to relieve it. Sertorius, upon his approach, took poſt on an eminence. Pompey prepared to attack him, and the beſieged had hopes of immediate relief. But Sertorius had made his difpoſition in ſuch a manner, that Pompey could not advance without expoſing his own rear to a party that was placed to attack him. "I will teach this pupil of Sylla," he ſaid, " to look behind as well as before him ;" and Pompey, ſeeing his danger, choſe to withdraw, leaving the town of Laura to fall into the enemy's hands, while he himſelf continued a ſpectator of the ſiege, and of the deſtruction of the place. After this unſucceſsful beginning of the war, he was obliged to retire into Gaul for the winter [1].

U. C. 677.
Cn. Octavius C.
Scribonius Curio.

The following year, Cn. Octavius and C. Scribonius Curio being Conſuls, Pompey ſtill retained his command; and, having repaſſed the Pyrennees, directed his march to join Metellus. Sertorius lay on the Sucro [2], and wiſhed to engage one or other of theſe parties before their junction; and Pompey, on his part, being deſirous to reap the glory of a ſeparate victory, an action enſued, in which the wing on which Pompey fought was defeated by Sertorius; but the other wing had the victory over Perperna. As Sertorious was about to renew the action on the following day, he

---

[1] Plutarch. in Pompeio et Sertorio. Appian. Liv. Obſequens. Frontinus Stratagim. lib. ii. c. 5.

[2] The Xucar, which falls into the Bay of Valentia.

he was prevented by the arrival of Metellus. "If
" the old woman had not interpofed," he faid,
" I fhould have whipt the boy, and fent him back
" to his fchools at Rome."

This war continued about two years longer with various fuccefs, but without any memorable event, until it ended by the death of Sertorius, who, at the inftigation of his affociate Perperna, was betrayed and affaffinated by a few of his own attendants. Perperna, having removed Sertorius by this bafe action, put himfelf at the head of both their adherents, and endeavoured to keep them united, at leaft until he fhould be able to purchafe his peace at Rome. He was, however, deferted by numbers of thofe who had been attached to Sertorius, and at laft furprifed by Pompey, and flain. He had made offers to difclofe the fecrets of the party, and to produce the correfpondence which many of the principal citizens at Rome held with Sertorius, inviting him to return into Italy, and promifing to join him with a confiderable force. The letters which had paffed in this correfpondence were fecured by Pompey, and, without being opened, were burned. So mafterly an act of prudence, in a perfon who was yet confidered as a young man, has been defervedly admired. It ferved to extinguifh remains of the Marian faction, and reconciled men, otherwife difaffected, to a fituation in which they were now affured of impunity and even of concealment.

CHAP.
XV.
While Pompey was thus gathering laurels in the field, C. Julius Cæsar, being about seven years younger, that is, twenty-three years of age, was returned from Asia; and, to make some trial of his parts, lodged a complaint against Dolabella, late Proconsul of Macedonia, for oppression and extortion in his province. Cotta and Hortensius, appearing for the defendant, procured his acquittal. Cicero says, that he himself was then returned from a journey he had made into Asia, and was present at this trial. The following year Cæsar left Rome, with intention to pass some time under a celebrated master of rhetoric at Rhodes. In his way he was taken by pirates, and remained their prisoner about forty days, until he found means to procure from Metellus a sum of fifty talents [1], which was paid for his ransom. He had frequently warned the pirates, while yet in their hands, that he should punish their insolence; and at parting, he told them to expect the performance of his promise. Upon being set on shore, he assembled and armed some vessels on the coast, pursued his late captors, took and brought them into port. From thence he hastened to Junius Silanus, the Proconsul of Bythinia, and applied for an order to have them executed; but being refused by this officer, he made his way back with still greater dispatch, and, before any instructions could arrive to the contrary, had his prisoners nailed to the cross. Such lawless banditti had long infested the seas of Asia

---

[1] Near to L. 10,000.

Asia and of Greece, and furnished at times no inconsiderable employment to the arms of the republic. Servilius Vatia, who afterwards bore the title of Isauricus, had lately been employed against them; and, after clearing the seas, endeavoured likewise to destroy or to secure their sea-ports and strong-holds on shore. They, nevertheless, recovered from this blow they had received from Isauricus, and continued to appear at intervals in new swarms, to the great interruption of commerce and of all the communications by sea, in the empire.

Under the reformations of Sylla, which, by disarming the tribunitian power, in a great measure shut up the source of former disorders, the republic was now restored to some degree of tranquillity, and resumed its attention to the ordinary affairs of peace. The bridge on the Tiber, which had been erected of wood, was taken down and rebuilt with stone; bearing the name of Æmilius, one of the Quæstors under whose inspection the fabric had been reared; and as a public concern of still greater importance, it is mentioned, that a treatise on agriculture, the production of Mago a Carthaginian, and in the language of Carthage, was, by the express orders of the Senate, now translated into Latin. At the reduction of Carthage, the Romans were yet governed by husbandmen, and, amidst the literary spoils of that city, this book alone, consisting of twenty-eight rolls or volumes, was supposed to merit so much of the public

blic attention, as to be secured for the State. A number of persons, skilled in the Punic language, together with Silanus, who had principal charge of the business, were now employed in translating it [1].

The calm, however, which the republic enjoyed under this period of regular government and pacific pursuits, was not altogether undisturbed. In the Consulate of Cn. Octavius and C. Scribonius Curio, the Tribune Licinius made an attempt to recover the former powers of the office. He ventured, in presence of both the Consuls, to harangue the People, and exhorted them to reassume their ancient rights. As a circumstance which serves to mark the petulant boldness of these men, it is mentioned that the Consul Octavius, on this occasion, being ill, was muffled up, and covered with a dressing which brought flies in great numbers about him. The Consuls being placed together, Curio made a vehement speech, at the close of which, the Tribune called out to Octavius, " You never can repay your colleague's service of " this day; if he had not been near you, while he " spoke, and beat the air so much with his gesti- " culations, the flies must by this time have eaten " you up [2]." The sequel is imperfectly known; but the dispute appears to have been carried to a great height, and to have ended in a tumult, in which the Tribune Licinius was killed.

Upon a review of Sylla's acts intended to restore the authority of the Senate, it may be questioned,

[1] Plin. lib. xviii. c. 3.
[2] Cicero de Claris Oratoribus.

tioned, whether that claufe in the law relating to the Tribunes, by which all perfons having accepted of this office were excluded from any further preferment in the State, may not have had an ill effect, and required correction. It rendered the Tribunate an object only to the meaneft of the Senators, who, upon their acceptance of it, ceafing to have any pretenfions to the higher offices of State, were, by this means, deprived of any intereft in the government, and exafperated of courfe againft the higher dignities of the commonwealth from which they were themfelves excluded. Aurelius Cotta, one of the Confuls that fucceeded Cn. Octavius and Curio, moved perhaps by this confideration, propofed to have that claufe repealed, and was warmly fupported by the Tribune Opimius, who, contrary to the prohibition lately enacted, ventured to harangue the People; and for this offence, at the expiration of his office, was tried and condemned [1].

*By the defects which the People began to apprehend in their prefent inftitutions, or by the part which their demagogues began to take againft the ariftocracy, the Roman State, after a very fhort refpite, began to relapfe into its former troubles, and was again to exhibit the curious fpectacle of a nation divided againft itfelf, broken and diftracted in its councils at home, but victorious in all its operations abroad, and gaining continual acceffions of empire, under the effect of convulfions which fhook

U.C. 678. L. Octavius, C. Aurelius Cotta.

[1] Cicero, 3tio, in Verrem, & Pædianus, ibid.

shook the commonwealth itself to its base; and, what is still less to be paralleled in the history of mankind, exhibiting the spectacle of a nation, which continued from the earliest ages to proceed in its affairs abroad with a success that may be imputed in a great measure to its divisions at home.

War, in the detail of its operations, if not even in the formation of its plans, is more likely to succeed under single men than under numerous councils. The Roman constitution, though far from an arrangement proper to preserve domestic peace and tranquillity, was an excellent nursery of statesmen and warriors. To individuals trained in this school, all foreign affairs were committed with little responsibility and less controul. The ruling passion, even of the least virtuous citizens, during some ages, was the ambition of being considerable, and of rising to the highest dignities of the State at home. In the provinces they enjoyed the condition of monarchs; but they valued this condition only as it furnished them with the occasion of triumphs, and contributed to their importance at Rome. They were factious and turbulent in their competition for preferment and honours in the capital; but, in order the better to support that very contest at home, were faithful and inflexible in maintaining all the pretensions of the State abroad. Thus Sylla, though deprived of his command by an act of the opposite faction at Rome, and with many of his friends, who escaped from the bloody hands of their persecutors,

tors, condemned and outlawed, ſtill maintained the part of a Roman officer of ſtate, and preſcribed to Mithridates, in the terms which might have been expected from a Roman Magiſtrate in the moſt undiſturbed exerciſe of his truſt. Sertorius, in the ſame manner, acting for the oppoſite faction, in ſome meaſure preſerved a ſimilar dignity of character, and on the propoſals which were made to him by the ſame Prince, refuſed to make conceſſions unworthy of the Roman republic. Contrary to the fate of other nations, where the State is weak, while the conduct of individuals is regular; here the State was in vigour, while the conduct of individuals was in the higheſt degree irregular and wild.

The reputation of the Romans, even in the intervals of war, procured them acceſſions of territory without labour, and without expence. Thus, kingdoms were bequeathed to them by will; as that of Pergamus formerly by the teſtament of Attalus; that of Cyrene, at the bequeſt of Ptolomy Appion; and that of Bithynia, about this time, by the will of Nicomedes. To the ſame effect, princes and ſtates, where they did not make any formal ceſſion of their ſovereignty, did ſomewhat equivalent, by ſubmitting their rights to diſcuſſion at Rome, and by ſoliciting from the Romans, grants of which the world now ſeemed to acknowledge the validity, by having recourſe to them as the baſis of tenures by which they were to hold their poſſeſſons. To the ſame effect alſo, the ſons of the laſt Antiochus,

Antiochus, king of Syria, having passed two years at Rome, waiting decisions of the Senate, and soliciting a grant of the kingdom of Egypt, on which they formed their opposite pretensions, thus stated themselves as subjects or dependents on the republic of Rome.

In Asia, by these means, the Roman empire advanced on the ruin of those who had formerly opposed its progress. The Macedonian line, in the monarchy of Syria, was now broken off, or extinct. The monarchy itself was no more. For on the defeat of Antiochus at Sipylus, followed by the defection of provincial governors and tributary princes, who, no longer awed by the power of their former master, entered into a correspondence with the Romans, and were by them acknowledged as sovereigns, the empire of Syria, once so entire, was split and dismembered. In this manner also the states of Armenia, long subject to the Persians, and afterwards to the Macedonians, now became the seat of a new monarchy under Tigranes. And, to complete these revolutions of empire, the natives of the last district to which the name of Syria was affixed, weary of the degeneracy and weakness of their own court, of the irregularity of the succession to the throne of their own kingdom; weary of the frequent competitions which involved them in blood, invited Tigranes the king of Armenia to wield a sceptre which the descendants of Seleucus were no longer in condition to hold. This prince, accordingly, extended his kingdom to

both

both sides of the Euphrates, and held the remains of Assyria itself as one of its divisions[1].

In these circumstances, the Romans were left undisturbed to re-establish their province in the Lesser Asia: and under the auspices of Servilius, who, from his principal acquisition in those parts, had the name of Isauricus, were extending their limits on the side of Cilicia, and were hastening to the sovereignty of that coast, when their progress was suddenly checked by the re-appearance of an enemy, who had already given them much trouble in the eastern part of the empire.

Mithridates, king of Pontus, who appears to have revived in his own breast the animosities of Pyrrhus and of Hannibal against the Romans, had never ceased, since the date of his last mortifying treaty with Sylla, to devise the means of renewing the war. Having attempted in vain to engage Sylla in a league with himself against the Romans, he made a similar attempt on Sertorius, to which we have already referred. Affecting to consider this fugitive, with his little Senate, as head of the republic, he pressed for a cession of the Roman province in Asia in his own favour, and in return offered to assist the followers of Sertorius with all his forces in the recovery of Italy. In this negotiation, however, he found, as has been already remarked, that whoever assumed the character of a Roman officer of state, supported it with a like inflexible dignity. Sertorius refused to dismember the empire, but accepted of the proffered aid from Mithridates,

[1] Strabo, lib. xi. fine.

CHAP. Mithridates, and agreed to fupply him with of-
XV. ficers of the Roman eftablifhment to affift in the
formation and difcipline of his troops.

The king of Pontus, now bent on correcting the error which is common in extenfive and barbarous monarchies, of relying entirely on numbers, with lefs attention to difcipline or military fkill, propofed to form a more regular army than that which he had affembled in the former war; and, however little fuccefsful in his attempts, he endeavoured to rival his enemy in every particular of their difcipline, in the choice and ufe of their weapons, and in the form of their legion. With troops beginning to make thefe reformations, and amounting to one hundred and twenty thoufand foot, and fixteen thoufand horfe, he made an open declaration of war, and, without refiftance, took poffeffion of Cappadocia and Phrygia, beyond the bounds which the Romans had prefcribed to his kingdom. As he was to act both by fea and by land, he began with cuftomary oblations to Neptune and to Mars. To the firft he made an offering of a fplendid carriage, drawn by white horfes, which he precipitated from a cliff, and funk in the fea; to the other he made a facrifice, which, as defcribed by the hiftorian [1], filled the imagination more than any of the rites ufually practifed by ancient nations. The king, with his army, afcended the higheft mountain on their route, formed on its fummit a great pile of wood, of which he himfelf laid

[1] Appian.

laid the first materials, and ordered the fabric to be raised in a pyramidical form to a great height. The top was loaded with offerings of honey, milk, oil, wine, and perfumes. As soon as it was finished, the army around it began the solemnity with a feast, at the end of which the pile was set on fire, and in proportion as the heat increased, the host extended its circle, and came down from the mountain. The smoke and the flames continued to ascend for many days, and were seen, it is said, at the distance of a thousand stadia, or above an hundred miles [1].

After this solemnity was over, Mithridates endeavoured to animate and to unite in a common zeal for his cause the different nations which, in forming his army, had been collected from the most distant parts of the empire. For this purpose he enumerated the successes by which he himself had raised his kingdom to its present pitch of greatness, and represented the numerous vices or defects of the enemy with whom he was now to contend, reciting their divisions at home, their oppression abroad, their avarice, and their insatiable lust of dominion.

The Romans were some time undetermined in the choice of a person to be employed against this formidable enemy. Pompey, being still in Spain, saw with regret a service of this importance likely to fall to the share of another; and he had his partizans at Rome who would have gladly put off the

[1] Appian. de Bell. Mithridat.

the nomination of any general to this command, until he himself could arrive with his army to receive it. He had about this time, impatient of his absence from Rome, wrote a letter to the Senate, complaining, in petulant terms, of their neglect, and of the straits to which the troops under his command were reduced for want of pay and provisions, and threatening, if not speedily supplied, to fall back upon Italy. The Consul Lucullus, apprehending what might be the consequence of Pompey's arrival, with a military force, and wishing not to furnish him with any pretence for leaving his province, had the army in Spain completely supplied, and, at the same time, took proper measures to support his own pretensions to the command in Asia. From his rank as Consul in office, he had a natural claim to this station; and from his knowledge of the country, and of the war [1] with this very enemy, in which he had already borne some part under Sylla [2], he was well

---

[1] Vide Ciceronis in Lucullo, c. 1 et 2.

[2] Plutarch. in Lucull. initio. Edit. Lond. 4to, vol. iii. p. 137.

Cicero is often quoted to prove, that Lucullus, at this time, was a mere novice in war, and owed the knowledge by which he came to be distinguished, to speculation and study, not to experience. It is observed by Lord Bolingbroke, that Cicero, who, among his other pretensions to fame, aspired to that of a military commander, had an interest in having it believed, that great officers might be formed in this manner: But as he could not be ignorant that Lucullus had acted under Sylla, it is probable, that he affected to consider the part which was assigned to him by Sylla, as a mere civil employment. He is indeed mentioned as having charge of the coinage with which Sylla paid his army, and of the fleet with which he transported them into Asia: but it is not to be supposed, that these were the only operations confided by Sylla to a lieutenant of so much ability.

well entitled to plead his qualifications and his merits.

When the provinces came to be diftributed, the difficulties which prefented themfelves in Afia were thought to require the prefence of both the Confuls. The kingdom of Bythinia, which had been lately bequeathed to the Romans, was in danger of being invaded before they could obtain a formal poffeffion of this inheritance; at the fame time that the enemy, by whom they were threatened, was not likely to limit his operations to the attack of that country. Of the Confuls, Cotta was appointed to feize on the kingdom of Bythinia, and Lucullus to lead the army againft Mithridates wherever elfe he fhould carry the war. Cotta fet out immediately for his province. Lucullus, being detained in making the neceffary levies, followed fome time afterwards; but before his arrival in Afia, Cotta had been obliged to evacuate Bythinia, and to take refuge in Chalcedonia. The king of Pontus, being fuperior both by fea and by land, had over-run the country in the neighbourhood of this place; and, having broke the chain which fhut up the mouth of the harbour, entered and burnt fome Roman gallies, which were ftationed there. Not thinking it advifable to attack the town of Chalcedonia, he turned his forces againft Cyzicus, a port on the Propontis, and blocked up the place both by fea and by land; being well-provided with battering engines, and the other neceffaries of a fiege, he had hopes of being foon able

CHAP.
XV.
able to reduce it by ſtorm. The inhabitants, nevertheleſs, were prepared to reſiſt, and were in expectation of being ſpeedily relieved by the Romans.

Such was the ſtate of affairs when Lucullus arrived in Aſia; and having joined his new levies to the legions which had ſerved under Fimbria, and to the other troops already in the province, he aſſembled an army of about thirty thouſand men, with which he advanced to re-eſtabliſh Cotta in his province, and to relieve the town of Cyzicus.

Mithridates being elated by his own ſucceſſes, and by the ſuperiority of his numbers, did not ſufficiently attend to the motions of Lucullus, ſuffered him to get poſſeſſion of the heights in his rear, and to cut off his principal ſupplies of proviſions and forage. Truſting, however, that his magazines would not be exhauſted before he ſhould have forced the town of Cyzicus to ſurrender, he continued the ſiege. But his engines not being well ſerved, and the defence being obſtinate, his army began to be diſtreſſed for want of proviſions, and it became neceſſary to leſſen his conſumption. For this purpoſe he ſecretly detached ſome part of his cavalry, which being intercepted by the Romans on their march, were cut off or diſperſed; and the king, now ſeeing the remainder of his troops unable to ſubſiſt any longer in their preſent ſituation, embarked on board one of his gallies, ordered the army to force their way to Lampſacus, while he himſelf endeavoured to eſcape with his fleet. In this retreat, being harraſſed by Lucullus, the great-

er

er part of the late besigers of Cyzicus perished in passing the Asopus and the Grannicus. The king himself, having put into Nicomedia, and from thence continuing his voyage through the Bosphorus to the Euxine, was overtaken on that sea by a storm, and lost the greatest part of his shipping. His own galley being sunk, he himself narrowly escaped in a barge.

The whole force with which the king of Pontus had invaded Bythinia, being thus dispelled like a cloud, Lucullus employed some time in reducing the towns into which any of the troops of Mithridates had been received; and having effectually destroyed the remains of the vanquished army, took his route by Bythinia and Galatia towards Pontus. At the entrance into this kingdom was situate the town of Amysus, a considerable fortress on the coast of the Euxine, into which had been thrown a sufficient force to retard the progress of an enemy. Mithridates, under favour of the delays obtained by the defence of this place, assembled a new army at Cabira, near the frontier of Armenia. Here he mustered about forty thousand foot, and a considerable body of horse, and was soliciting the Scythians, Armenians, and all the nations of that continent to his aid.

Lucullus, in order to prevent, if possible, any further reinforcements to the enemy, committed the siege of Amysus to Murena, and advanced with his army into the plains of Cabira. On this ground the Roman horse received repeated checks from those of the enemy, and were kept in continual

CHAP.
XV.
alarm until their general, having time to obferve the country, avoided the plains on which the king of Pontus, by means of his cavalry, was greatly fuperior. In purfuit of this plan, though very much ftraitened for provifions, Lucullus kept his pofition on the heights, until the enemy could be attacked with advantage. The fkirmifhes which happened between the foraging parties, brought into action confiderable numbers from the refpective armies; and the troops of Mithridates, having been routed in one of thefe partial encounters, the king took a refolution to decamp in the night, and remove to a greater diftance from his enemy. As foon as it was dark, the equipage and the attendants of the leading men in the camp, to whom he had communicated this refolution, began to withdraw; and the army, greatly alarmed with that appearance, was feized with a panic, and could not be reftrained from flight. Horfe and foot, and bodies of every defcription crowded in diforder into the outlets from the camp, and were trod under foot, or in great numbers perifhed by each other's hands. Mithridates himfelf, endeavouring to ftop and to undeceive them, was carried off as by the torrent, which could not be withftood.

The noife of this tumult being heard to a great diftance, and the occafion being known in the Roman camp, Lucullus advanced with his army to profit by the confufion into which the enemy were fallen, and by a vigorous attack, having

ving put many to the sword, hastened their total rout and dispersion.

The king himself was, by one of his servants, with difficulty mounted on horseback; and must have been taken, if the pursuing party had not been amused in seizing some plunder, which he had ordered on purpose to be left in their way. A mule, loaded with some part of the royal treasure, turned the attention of his pursuers, while he himself made his escape.

In his flight the king appeared to be most affected with the fate of his women. The greatest number of them were left at the palace of Pharnacea, a place that must soon fall into the hands of the enemy. He therefore dispatched a faithful eunuch with orders to put them to death, leaving the choice of the manner to themselves. A few are particularly mentioned. Of two, who were his own sisters, Roxana and Statira, one died uttering execrations against her brother's cruelty, the other extolling, in that extremity of his own fortune, the generous care he took of their honour. Monimé, a Greek of Miletus, celebrated for her beauty, whom the king had long wooed in vain with proffers of great riches, and whom he won at last only by the participation of his crown, and the earnest of the nuptial rites, had ever lamented her fortune, which, instead of a royal husband and a palace, had given her a prison, and a barbarous keeper. Being now told, that she must die, but that the manner of her death was left to her own choice,

choice, she unbound the royal fillet from her hair, and, using it as a bandage, endeavoured to strangle herself. It broke in the attempt: "Bauble," she said, "it is not fit even for this!" then stretching out her neck to the eunuch, bid him fulfil his master's purpose. Berenice of Chios, another Græcian beauty, had likewise been honoured with the nuptial crown, and, having been attended in her state of melancholy elevation by her mother, who, on this occasion, likewise resolved to partake of her daughter's fate; they chose to die by poison. The mother intreated that she might have the first draught; and died before her daughter. The remainder of the dose not being sufficient for the queen, she put herself likewise into the hands of the executioner, and was strangled. By these deaths, the barbarous jealousy of the king was gratified, and the future triumph of the Roman general deprived of its principal ornaments.

Lucullus, after his victory, having no enemy in the field to oppose him, overran the country, and passed without interruption through most of the towns in the kingdom of Pontus. He found many palaces enriched with treasure, and adorned with barbarous magnificence; and, as might be expected under such a violent and distrustful government, every where places of confinement crowded with prisoners of state, whom the jealousy of the king had secured, and whom his supercilious neglect had suffered to remain in custody, even after his jealousy was allayed.

Mithridates,

Mithridates, from his late defeat, fled into Armenia, and claimed the protection of Tigranes, who, being married to his daughter, had already favoured him in his defigns againft the Romans.

This powerful prince, now become fovereign of Syria as well as Armenia, ftill continued his refidence in the laft of thefe kingdoms at Tigranocerta, a city he himfelf had built, ftocked with inhabitants, and diftinguifhed by his own name. On the arrival of Mithridates to fue for his protection, Tigranes declined to fee him, but ordered him a princely reception in one of the palaces.

Lucullus continued his purfuit of this flying enemy only to the frontier of Armenia; and from thence, fending Publius Clodius, who was his brother-in-law, to the court of Tigranes, with inftructions to require that Mithridates fhould be delivered up as a lawful prey, he himfelf fell back into the kingdom of Pontus, and foon after reduced Amyfus, together with Sinope, and other places of ftrength, which were held by the troops of the king.

The inhabitants of thefe places had been originally colonies from Greece, and having been fubdued by the Perfians, were, on the arrival of Alexander the Great, from refpect to their origin, reftored to their freedom. In imitation of this example, and agreeably to the profeffion which the Romans ever made of protecting the liberties of Greece, Lucullus once more declared thofe cities to be free.

CHAP. XV.

In his quality of Proconful having now fufficient leifure to attend to the general ftate of the Roman affairs that were committed to his government, found the following particulars from which we may collect the meafure of abufe to which the conquered provinces were expofed. The collectors of revenue, under pretext of levying the tax impofed by Sylla, had been guilty of the greateft oppreffions. The inhabitants, in order to pay this tax, borrowed money of the Roman officers and merchants at exorbitant intereft; and, when they no longer had any credit, their effects were diftrained for payment, or themfelves threatened with imprifonment and tortures: private perfons were reduced to the neceffity of expofing their children to fale, and corporations of felling the pictures, images, and other ornaments of their temples, in order to fatisfy thefe inhuman creditors. Willing to reftrain, or to correct thefe abufes, Lucullus ordained, that where the fum exacted for ufury was equal to the capital, the debt fhould be cancelled; and in other cafes, fixed the intereft at a moderate rate. Thefe acts of beneficence or juftice to the provinces were, by the farmers of the revenue, reprefented as acts of oppreffion and cruelty to themfelves, and were, among their connections, and the fharers of their profits at Rome, ftated againft Lucullus as fubjects of complaint and reproach.

CHAP.

CHAP. XVI.

*Escape and Revolt of the Gladiators at Capua.
—Spartacus.—Action and Defeat of Lentulus
the Roman Conful.—And of Caffius the Prætor of
Gaul.—Appointment of M. Craffus for this Ser-
vice.—Destruction of the Gladiators.—Triumph
of Metellus and Pompey.—Confulship of Pompey
and Craffus.—Tribunes restored to their former
Powers.—Confulate of Metellus and Hortenfius.
War in Crete.—Renewal of the War in Pontus
and Armenia.—Defeat of Tigranes.—Negotia-
tion with the King of Parthia.—Mutiny of the
Roman Army.—Complaints of Piracies commit-
ted in the Roman Seas.—Commiffion propofed to
Pompey.—His Conduct againft the Pirates.—His
Commiffion extended to Pontus.—Operations againft
Mithridates.—Defeat and Flight of that Prince.
—Operations of Pompey in Syria.—Siege and
Reduction of Jerufalem.—Death of Mithridates.*

SOON after the war, of which we have thus ftated the event, had commenced in Afia, Italy was thrown into great confufion by the accidental efcape of a few gladiators from the place of their confinement at Capua. Thefe were flaves trained up to furnifh their mafters with a fpectacle, which, though cruel and barbarous, drew numerous crowds of beholders. It was at firft introduced as a fpecies of human facrifice at funerals, and fuch victims were now kept by the weal-

CHAP.
XVI.

U. C. 680.
M. Teren.
Varro, C.
Caff. Va-
rus.

thy in great numbers for the entertainment of the public, and even for private amusement. The handsomest, the most active, and the boldest of the slaves or captives were selected for this purpose. They were sworn to decline no combat, and to shun no hardship, to which they were exposed by their masters; they were of different denominations, and accustomed to fight in different ways; but those from whom the whole received their designation, employed the sword and buckler, or target; and they commonly fought naked, that the place and nature of the wounds they received might the more plainly appear.

Even in this prostitution of valour, refinements of honour were introduced. There were certain graces of attitude which the gladiator was not permitted to quit, even to avoid a wound. There was a manner which he studied to preserve in his fall, in his bleeding posture, and even in his death. He was applauded, or hissed, according as he succeeded or failed in any of these particulars. When, after a tedious struggle, he was spent with labour and with the loss of blood, he still endeavoured to preserve the dignity of his character, dropt or resumed the sword at his master's pleasure, and looked round to the spectators for marks of their satisfaction and applause [1].

Persons of every age, condition, and sex, attended at these exhibitions; and when the pair who were engaged began to strain and to bleed, the spectators,

[1] Cicer. Tusculanarum, lib. ii. c. 17.

spectators, being divided in their inclinations, endeavoured to excite, by their cries and acclamations, the party they favoured; and when the contest was ended, called to the victor to strike, or to spare, according as the vanquished was supposed to have forfeited or to have deserved his life[1]. With spectacles of this sort, which must create so much disgust and horror in the recital, the Romans were more intoxicated than any populace in modern Europe now are with the baiting of bulls, or the running of horses, probably because they were more deeply affected, and more intensely moved by the scene.

Spartacus, a Thracian captive, who, on account of his strength and activity, had been destined for this barbarous profession, with about seventy or eighty of his companions, having escaped from their place of confinement, armed themselves with such weapons as accident presented to them, and retiring to some fastness on the ascents of Vesuvius, from thence harassed the country with robberies and murders. "If we are to fight," said the leader of this desperate band, " let us fight against our " oppressors, and in behalf of our own liberties, " not to make sport for this petulant and cruel " race of men." Multitudes of slaves from every quarter flocked to his standard. The Præfect of Capua turned out the inhabitants of his district against them, but was defeated.

This feeble and unsuccessful attempt to quell
the

[1] Cicero pro Sexto, c. 27. Tufcul. Quæft. Spartacus, lib. ii. c. 27.

CHAP.
XVI.
the infurrection, furnifhed the rebels with arms, and raifed their reputation and their courage. Their leader, by his generofity in rejecting his own fhare of any booty he made by his conduct and his valour, acquired the authority of a legal commander; and, having named Crixus and Oenomaus, two other gladiators, for his fubordinate officers, he formed the multitudes that reforted to him into regular bodies, employed a certain number to fabricate arms, and to procure the neceffary accommodations of a camp, till at length he collected an army of feventy thoufand men, with which he commanded the country to a great extent. He had already fucceffively defeated the Prætors Clodius, Varinus, and Coffinius, who had been fent againft him with confiderable forces, fo that it became neceffary to order proper levies, and to give to the Confuls the charge of repreffing this formidable enemy.

Spartacus had too much prudence to think himfelf fit to contend with the force of the Roman State, which he perceived muft foon be affembled againft him. He contented himfelf, therefore, with a more rational fcheme of conducting his army by the ridge of the Appenines, till he fhould gain the Alps, from whence his followers, whether Gauls, Germans, or Thracians, might feparate, each into the country of which he was a native, or from which he had been brought into the ftate of bondage, from which they now endeavoured to extricate themfelves.

While

While he began his progress by the mountains, in order to execute this project, the Consuls, Gellius and Lentulus, had already taken the field against him. They at first surprised and cut off a considerable body under Crixus, who had fallen down from the heights in order to pillage the country. But Lentulus afterwards pressing hard upon Spartacus, who led the main body of the rebels, brought on an action, in which the consular army was defeated with considerable loss. Cassius too, the Prætor of Cisalpine Gaul, having advanced upon him with an army of ten thousand men, was repulsed with great slaughter.

In consequence of these advantages, Spartacus might no doubt have effected his retreat to the Alps; but his army being elated with victory, and considering themselves as masters of Italy, were unwilling to abandon their conquest. He himself formed a new project of marching to Rome; and for this purpose destroyed all his superfluous baggage and cattle, put his captives to death, and refused to receive any more of the slaves, who were still in multitudes resorting to his standard. He probably expected to elude or to pass the Roman armies without a battle, and to force the city of Rome itself by an unexpected assault. In this he was disappointed by the Consuls, with whom he was obliged to fight in the Picenum; and, though victorious in the action, he lost hopes of surprising the city. But still thinking himself in condition to keep his ground

CHAP.
XVI.

U. C. 681.
L. Gell. Poplicola, Cn. Corn. Lent. Clodianus.

in Italy, he only altered his route, and directed his march towards Lucania.

The Romans, greatly embarrassed, and thrown into some degree of consternation, by the unexpected continuance of an insurrection which had given them much trouble, and which exposed their armies to much danger, with little prospect of honour; not being courted, as usual, for the command in this service, they imposed rather than conferred it on Marcus Crassus, then in the rank of Prætor, and considered as a person of consequence, more on account of his wealth than of his abilities; though in this service, after others had failed, he laid the foundation of a more favourable judgment. They at the same time sent orders to Pompey, who had finished the war in Spain, to hasten into Italy with his army; and to the Proconsul of Macedonia, to embark with what forces could be spared from his province.

Crassus assembled no less than six legions, with which he joined the army which had been already so unsuccessful against the revolt. Of the troops who had miscarried, he is said to have executed, perhaps only decimated, four thousand, as an example to the new levies, and as a warning of the severities they were to expect for any failure in the remaining part of the service.

Upon his arrival in Lucania he cut off ten thousand of the rebels, who were stationed at a distance from the main body of their army, and he endeavoured to shut up Spartacus in the peninsula

of

of Brutium, or head of land which extends to the Straits of Meffina. The gladiators defired to pafs into Sicily, where their fellow-fufferers, the flaves of that ifland, were not yet entirely fubdued, and where great numbers at all times were prepared to revolt: but they were prevented by the want of fhipping. Craffus at the fame time undertook a work of great labour, that of intrenching the land from fea to fea with a ditch fifteen feet wide, and as many deep, extending, according to Plutarch, three hundred ftadia, or above thirty miles. Spartacus endeavouring to interrupt the execution of this work, was frequently repulfed; and his followers beginning to defpond, entertained thoughts of furrender. But in order to fupply by defpair what they loft in courage, he put them in mind that they fought not upon equal terms with their enemies; that they muft either conquer or be treated as fugitive flaves; and, to enforce his admonitions, he ordered one of his captives to be nailed to the crofs in fight of both armies. "This," he faid to his own people, "is "an example of what you are to fuffer if you "fall into the enemy's hands."

Whilft Craffus was bufy completing his line of countervallation, Spartacus prepared to force it; and, having provided faggots and other materials for this purpofe, filled up the ditch at a convenient place, and paffed it in the night with the whole body of his followers. Directing his flight to

Apulia,

CHAP. Apulia, he was purfued, and greatly haraffed in
XVI. his march.

Accounts being received at once in the camp of
Craffus and in that of Spartacus, that frefh troops
were landed at Brundufium from Macedonia, and
that Pompey was arrived in Italy, and on his
march to join Craffus, both armies were equally
difpofed to hazard a battle; the gladiators, that
they might not be attacked at once by fo many enemies as were collecting againft them; and the Romans under Craffus, that Pompey might not arrive
to fnatch out of their hands the glory of terminating
the war. Under the influence of thefe different
motives, both leaders drew forth their armies;
and when they were ready to engage, Spartacus,
with the valour rather of a gladiator than of a general, alighting from his horfe, and faying aloud,
in the hearing of his followers, " If I conquer to-
" day, I fhall be better mounted; if not, I fhall
" not have occafion for a horfe," he plunged his
fword into the body of the animal. With this
earneft of a refolution to conquer or to die, he advanced towards the enemy; directing the divifion
in which he himfelf commanded to, make their
attack where he underftood the Roman general
was pofted. He intended to decide the action by
forcing the Romans in that quarter; but after
much bloodfhed, being mangled with wounds, and
ftill almoft alone in the midft of his enemies, he
continued to fight till he was killed; and the victory of courfe declared for his enemy. About a

thoufand

thousand of the Romans were slain; of the vanquished the greatest slaughter, as usual in ancient battles, took place after the flight began. The dead were not numbered; about six thousand were taken, and, in the manner of executing the sentence of death on slaves, they were nailed to the cross in rows, that almost lined the way from Capua to Rome. Such as escaped from the field of battle, being about five thousand, fell into the hands of Pompey, and furnished a pretence to his flatterers for ascribing to him the honour of terminating the war.

The mean quality of the enemy however, in the present case, precluded even Crassus from the honour of a triumph; he could have only an ovation or military procession on foot. But instead of the myrtle wreath, usual on such occasions, he had credit enough with the Senate to obtain the laurel crown [1].

Pompey too arrived at the same time in the city with new and uncommon pretensions, requiring a dispensation from the law and established forms of the commonwealth. The service he had conducted in Spain being of the nature of a civil war of Roman citizens against one another, or against subjects of the empire, with a Roman general at their head, did not give a regular claim to a triumph: The victor himself was yet under the legal age, and had not passed through any of the previous steps of Questor, Ædile and Prætor; yet on the present

[1] Ad. Gellius, lib. v.

CHAP. XVI.

present occasion he not only insisted on a triumph, but put in his claim likewise to an immediate nomination to the office of Consul.

It now became extremely evident, that the established honours of the State, conferred in the usual way, were not adequate to the pretensions of this young man: that he must have new and singular appointments, or those already known bestowed on him in some new and singular manner. His enemies observed, that he avoided every occasion of fair competition with his fellow citizens; that he took a rank of importance to himself, which he did not submit to have examined; and that he ever aspired to an eminence in which he might stand alone, or in the first place of public consideration and honour. His partizans, on the contrary, stated the extraordinary favours bestowed on him, as the foundation of still farther distinctions [1]. In enumerating his services upon his return from Spain, they reckoned up, according to Pliny, eight hundred and seventy-one towns, from the Pyrennees to the extremities of that country, which he had reduced; observed that he had surpassed the glory of all the officers who had gone before him in that service; and, in consequence of these representations, though still in a private station, he was admitted to a triumph, or partook with Metellus in this honour.

Pompey had hitherto, in all the late disputes, taken part with the aristocracy; but not without suspicion

[1] Vid. Cicer. pro Lege Manilia.

fufpicion of aiming too high for republican go- CHAP.
vernment of any fort. While he fupported the XVI.
Senate, he affected a kind of diftinction fuperior to thofe who compofed it, and was not content with equality, even among the firft ranks of
his country. He acquiefced, neverthelefs, in the
mere fhew of importance, and did not infift on
prerogatives which might have engaged him in
contefts, and expofed his pretenfions to too near
an infpection. Upon his approach at the head of
an army from Spain, the Senate was greatly alarmed; but he gave the moft unfeigned affurances
of his intention to difband his army as foon as they
fhould have attended his triumph. The Senate
accordingly gave way to this irregular pretenfion,
and afterwards to the pretenfion, ftill more dangerous, which, without any of the previous conditions which the law required, he made to the Con- U. C. 683.
fulate. Craffus, who having been Prætor in the M Licin.
preceding year, now ftood for the fame office, en- Cn. Pomp
tered into a concert with Pompey, by which not- Magnus.
withftanding their mutual jealoufy of each other,
they joined their interefts, and were elected together.

Under the adminiftration of thefe officers fome
important laws are faid to have paffed, although
moft of the particulars have efcaped the notice
of thofe from whom our accounts are taken. It
appears that Pompey now began to pay his court to
the popular faction; and, though he profeffed to
fupport the authority of the Senate, wifhed to have

Vol. II.   R   it

it in his power, on occasion, to take the sense of what was called the assembly of the People against them, or, in other words, to counteract them by means of the popular tumults which bore this name.

The Tribunes, Quinctius and Palicanus, had for two years successively laboured to remove the bars which had, by the constitution of Sylla, been opposed to the abuses of the tribunitian power. They had been strenuously resisted by Lucullus and others, who held the office of Consul, during the dependence of the questions which had arisen on that subject. By the favour of Pompey and Crassus, however, the Tribunes obtained a restitution of the privileges which their predecessors, in former times of the republic, had so often abused; and, together with the security of their sacred and inviolable character, and their negative in all proceedings of the State, they were again permitted to propose laws, and to harangue the people; a dangerous measure, by which Pompey at once rendered fruitless that reformation which was the only apology for the blood so lavishly shed, not only by Sylla, but likewise by himself. Caius Julius Cæsar, at the same time, having the rank of Legionary Tribune conferred upon him by the public choice, was extremely active in procuring those popular acts; a policy in which he was more consistent with himself than Pompey, and only pursued the course of that party with which he had been associated in his earliest years [1].

Under

---

[1] Suetonius in C. Jul. Cæsar. lib. i.

Under this Confulate, and probably with the encouragement of Pompey, the law of Sylla, refpecting the judicatures, was, upon the motion of the Prætor, Aurelius Cotta, likewife repealed; and it was permitted to the Prætors to draught the judges in equal numbers from the Senate, the Knights, and a certain clafs of the People ¹, whofe defcription is not clearly afcertained. This was, perhaps, a juft correction of Sylla's partiality to the Nobles; and, if it had not been accompanied by the former act, which reftored to the Tribunes powers which they had fo often abufed, might have merited applaufe.

In the mean time, corruption fpread with a hafty pace; among the lower ranks, in contempt of government; among the higher, in covetoufnefs and prodigality, with an ardour for lucrative appointments, and the opportunity of extortion in the provinces. As the offices of State at Rome began to be coveted with a view to the employments abroad, to which they conducted, Pompey, in order to difplay his own difintereftednefs, with an oblique reproof to the Nobility who afpired to magiftracy with fuch mercenary views, took a formal oath in entering on his Confulate, that he would not, at the expiration of his office, accept of any government in the provinces; by this example of generofity in himfelf, and by the cenfure it implied of others, he obtained great credit with the People, and furnifhed his emiffaries, who were ever

CHAP. XVI.

Lex Aurelia, Judiciaria.

¹ Tribuni Erarii.

CHAP. XVI. ever bùfy in founding his praife, with a pretence for enhancing his merit. It may, however, from his cháracter and policy in other inftances, be fufpected, that he remained at Rome with intention to watch opportunities of raifing his own confideration; and of obtaining, by the ftrength of his party, any extraordinary truft or commiffion of which the occafion fhould arife.

This adventurer, in the adminiftration of his Confulate, had procured the revival of the Cenfors functions. Thefe had been intermitted about fixteen years, during great part of which time the republic had been in a ftate of civil war; and the prevailing parties, in their turns, mutually had recourfe to acts of banifhment, confifcations, and military executions againft each other. In fuch times, even after the fword was fheathed, the power of Cenfor, in the firft heat of party-refentment, could not be fafely entrufted with any of the citizens; and the attempts which were now made to revive it, though in appearance fuccefsful, could not give it a permanent footing in the commonwealth. The public was arrived at a ftate in which men complain of evils, but cannot endure their remedies.

L. Gellius Poplicola and Cn. Cornelius Lentulus, being entrufted, in the character of Cenfors, with the making up of the rolls of the People, muftered four hundred and fifty thoufand citizens. They purged the Senate with great feverity, having expunged fixty-four from the number, and among thefe C. Antonius, afterwards Conful, affigning

ing as their reason, that he, having the command on the coasts of Asia and Greece, had pillaged the allies, and mortgaged and squandered his own estate. But what most distinguished this Censorship was an incident, for the sake of which, it is likely, the solemnity of the Census had been now revived.

It was customary on such occasions for the Knights to pass in review, each leading his horse before the Censors. They were questioned respecting their age, the number of their campaigns, and the persons under whose command they had served; and if they had been already on the military list the ten years prescribed by law, they received an exemption for the future, and were vested with the privileges which were annexed to this circumstance. At this part of the ceremony the People were surprised to see their Consul, Pompey the Great, descending into the market-place, leading his horse in quality of a simple Knight, but dressed in his consular robes, and preceded by the Lictors. Being questioned by the Censor, whether he had served the stated number of years, he answered that he had, and all of them in armies commanded by himself. This farce was received with loud acclamations of the People; and the Censors having granted the customary exemption, rose from their seats, and, followed by a great multitude of the People, attended this equestrian Consul to his own house [1].

[1] Plutarch. in Pompeio. Pompey, it is probable, was still no more than a Knight, having a seat in the Senate as magistrate without being yet placed on the rolls.

CHAP. XVI.

It is obferved that Craffus and Pompey, although they entered on office in concert, yet differed in the courfe of their adminiftration on fubjects which are not particularly mentioned. As Craffus was in poffeffion of great wealth, he endeavoured, by his liberalities, to vie with the impofing ftate and popular arts of his colleague. In this view he gave a public entertainment at ten thoufand tables, and diftributed three months provifion of corn to the more indigent citizens. To account for his being able to court the People in fo fumptuous a manner, it is faid, that having inherited from his father a fortune of three hundred talents, or near fixty thoufand pounds; he increafed it, by purchafing at a low price the eftates of thofe who were profcribed in the late troubles, and by letting for hire the labour of a numerous family of flaves, inftructed in various arts and callings; and by thefe means was become fo rich, that when, fome time after this date, he was about to depart for Afia, and confecrated the tenth part of his eftate to Herculus, he was found to poffefs feven thoufand one hundred talents, or about one million three hundred and feventy thoufand and three hundred pounds Sterling [2].

Pompey, at the expiration of his year in the Confulfhip, agreeably to the oath he had taken, remained at Rome in a private ftation; but, ftill unchanged in his manner, maintained the referve and

---

[2] Plutarch. in Craffo. As the intereft of money was prohibited at Rome, under the denomination of ufury being clandeftine, was in fact unlimited, the annual returns from fuch a capital muft have been immenfe.

and statelinefs of a person raised above the condition of a mere citizen, or even above that of the first Senators of consular rank. Other candidates for consideration and public honours endeavoured, by their talents and eloquence, to make themselves necessary to those who had affairs to solicit with the public, or even to make themselves feared by those who were obnoxious to the law. They laboured to distinguish themselves as able advocates or formidable accusers at the bar, and to strengthen their interest by procuring the support of those to whom their talents either were or might become of importance. Pompey, on the contrary, stating himself as an exception to common rules, avoided the courts of justice and other places of ordinary resort, did not commit his talents to the public judgment, nor present his person to the public view; took the respect that was paid to him as a right; seldom went abroad, and never without a numerous train of attendants[1]. He was formed for the state of a prince, and might have stolen into that high station even at Rome, if men, born to equality, could have suffered an elevation which no measure of personal merit could at once have procured; or had been willing, when troubled with faction, to forego their own importance, in order to obtain peace and the comforts of a moderate government. The pretensions of Pompey, however, were extremely disagreeable to the Senate, and not otherwise acceptable, even

to

[1] Plutarch. in Vit. Pomp.

CHAP. XVI.

U.C. 684.
Q. Hortenfius, Q. Cæcil. Metellus Creticus.

to the People, than as they tended to mortify the pride of that order of men.

The Confulate of Craffus and Pompey was fucceeded by that of Q. Hortenfius and Q. Cæcilius Metellus. In the diftribution of provinces, Crete, with the command of an armament to be fent into that ifland, fell to the lot of Hortenfius; but this citizen, having acquired his confideration by his eloquence in pleading the caufes of his friends, and being accuftomed to the bar, perhaps in a degree that interfered with the ordinary military character of a Roman officer of State, declined to accept of this government; leaving it, together with the command of the army that was to be employed in the reduction of the ifland, to his colleague Metellus, who afterwards received the appellation of Creticus, from the diftinction he acquired in this fervice.

The Cretans, and moft of the other feafaring people on the confines of Afia and Europe, had in the late war taken an active part againft the Romans. They had, by the influence of Mithridates, and by their own difpofition to rapine and piracy, been led to prey upon the traders, and upon the carriers of revenue who were frequently paffing to Rome from the provinces. The defire of fharing in the profits that were made by this fpecies of war, had filled the fea with pirates and freebooters, againft whom the Senate had employed a fucceffion of officers, with extenfive commands, on the coafts both of Afia and Europe. Among

Among others, M. Antonius had been sent on this service, and was accused of abusing his power, by oppressing the Sicilians, and the people of other maritime provinces, who were innocent of the crimes he was charged to repress. In a descent on the island of Crete he was defeated and killed[1], and left the Romans engaged with the people of that island in a war which was thought to require the presence of one of the Consuls. And the lot, as has been observed, having fallen on Hortensius, was transferred to his colleague Metellus.

Such was the state of affairs, and such the destination of the Roman officers, when Lucullus received from Tigranes a return to the demand which he made of having Mithridates delivered up as his prisoner. This prince, at the arrival of Clodius, who bore the message, had made a progress to the coasts of Phœnicia, and to the farther extremities of his empire. To verify the state and title which he assumed of King of Kings, he affected, when he mounted on horseback, to have four captive sovereigns to walk by his stirrup, and obliged them, on other occasions, to perform every office of menial duty and servile attendance on his person. Lucullus, instead of the stile which was affected by this prince, had accosted him in his letter only with the simple title of king. His messenger, however, was admitted to an audience, and made his demand that Mithridates, a vanquished enemy, whose territories were already in the possession of the

---

[1] Pædianus in Orat. in Verrem.

CHAP. XVI.

the Romans, should be delivered up to adorn the victor's triumph. This, if refused, said the bearer of the message, the Roman general would be entitled to extort by force, and would not fail, with a mighty army for that purpose, to pursue his fugitive wherever he was received and protected. The king of Armenia, unused even to a plain address, much less to insult and threats, heard this demand with real indignation; and though, with an appearance of temper, he made offer of the customary presents and honours to the person who delivered the message, he took his resolution against those from whom it came, and from having barely permitted Mithridates to take refuge in his kingdom, determined to espouse his cause. He gave for answer to Clodius, that he would not deliver up the unfortunate king, and that, if the Romans invaded his territories, he knew how to defend them. He soon afterwards admitted Mithridates into his presence, and determined to support him with the necessary force against his enemies.

Upon receiving this answer from Tigranes, Lucullus resolved without delay to march into Armenia. He chose for this expedition two legions and a body of horse, on whom he prevailed, though with some difficulty, to enter on a new war at a time when they flattered themselves that their labours were ended, and that the rewards they expected were within their reach. With hasty marches he arrived on the Euphrates, and passed that river before the enemy were aware of his approach.

Tigranes

Tigranes treated the firſt reports of his coming with contempt, and ordered the perſon who preſumed to bring ſuch accounts to be puniſhed. But being aſſured, beyond a poſſibility of doubt, that an enemy was actually on his territories, he ſent Metrodorus, one of his generals, at the head of a conſiderable force, with orders to take alive the perſon of Lucullus, whom he was deſirous to ſee, but not to ſpare a man of the whole army beſides.

With theſe orders, the Armenian general ſet out on the road by which the Romans were known to advance, and haſtened to meet them. Both armies, on the march, had intelligence of each other. Lucullus, upon the approach of the enemy, halted, began to intrench, and, in order to gain time, detached Sextilius, with about three thouſand men, to obſerve the Armenians, and, if poſſible, without riſking an action, to amuſe them till his works were completed. But ſuch was the incapacity and preſumption of the enemy, that Sextilius, being attacked by them, gained an entire victory with but a part of the Roman army; Metrodorus himſelf being killed, his army was put to the rout with great ſlaughter.

After this victory Lucullus, in order the more effectually to alarm and to diſtract the Armenians, ſeparated his army into three diviſions. With one he intercepted and diſperſed a body of Arabs, who were marching to join the king; with another he ſurpriſed Tigranes himſelf, in a diſadvantageous ſituation, and obliged him to fly with the loſs of
his

his attendants, equipage, and the baggage of his army. At the head of the third division he himself advanced to Tigranocerta, and invested that place.

After these disasters Tigranes made an effort to assemble the force of his kingdom; and bringing into the field all the troops of his allies, as well as his own, mustered an army of one hundred and fifty thousand heavy-armed foot, fifty-five thousand horse, and twenty thousand archers and slingers. He was advised by Mithridates not to risk a battle, but to lay waste the country from which the Romans were supplied with provisions, and thereby oblige them to raise the siege of Triganocerta, and repass the Euphrates, with the disadvantage of having an enemy still in force to hang on their rear. This counsel of Mithridates, founded in the experience he had so dearly bought, was ill suited to the presumption of the king. He therefore advanced towards the Romans, impatient to relieve his capital, and the principal seat of his magnificence. Lucullus, trusting to the specimens he had already seen of the Armenian armies, ventured to divide his force, and, without raising the siege, marched with one division to meet this numerous enemy. In the action that followed, the Armenian horse being in the van, were defeated, and driven back on the foot of their own army, threw them into confusion, and gave the Romans an easy victory, in which, with very inconsiderable loss to themselves, they made a great slaughter of the

the enemy. The king himfelf, to avoid being known in his flight, unbound the royal diadem from his head, and left it to become a part in the fpoils of the day.

Mariæus, who commanded in Tigranocerta, hearing of his mafter's defeat, and fearing a revolt of the Greeks and other foreigners, who had been affembled by force in that fettlement, ordered them to be fearched and difarmed. This order they looked on as the prelude to a maffacre, and crowding together, defended themfelves with the clubs and other weapons they could feize. They furrounded a party that was fent to difperfe them, and having by that means got a fupply of arms, they took poffeffion of a tower which commanded one of the principal gates, and from thence invited the Romans to enter the place. Lucullus accordingly feized the opportunity, and became mafter of the city. The fpoil was great; Tigranes having collected here, as at the principal feat of his vanity, the wealth and magnificence of his court.

Mithridates, who had been prefent in the late action, met the king of Armenia in his flight; and, having endeavoured to re-eftablifh his equipage and his retinue by a participation of his own, exhorted him not to defpair, but to affemble his army anew, and to perfift in the war. They agreed, at the fame time, on an embaffy to the king of Parthia, with offers of reconciliation on the part of Tigranes, who, at this time, was at war with

that

CHAP. XVI. that prince, and of satisfaction on the subjects in contest between them, provided the Parthians would join in the confederacy against the Romans. They endeavoured to persuade the king of Parthia, that he was by no means an unconcerned spectator in the present contest; that the quarrel which the Romans now had with the kings of Armenia and Pontus, was the same with that which they formerly had with Philip and with Antiochus; and which, if not prevented, they would soon have with Arsaces, and was no other than his being possessed of a rich territory, which tempted their ambition and avarice. Those republicans, they said, originally had not any possessions of their own, and were grown rich and great only by the spoils of their neighbours. From their strong-hold in Italy, they had extended their empire on the West to the coast of the ocean; and, if not interrupted by the powerful monarchies which lay in their way, were hastening to reach a similar boundary on the East. The king of Parthia, they added, might expect to be invaded by these insatiable conquerors, and must now determine whether he would engage in a war joined with such powerful allies, of whom one by his experience, the other by his resources, might enable him to keep the danger at a distance from his own kingdom[1], or wait until these powers being overthrown, and become an accession to the Roman force, he should have the contest to maintain in his own territory singly and

[1] Letter of Mithridates in the Fragments of Sallust.

and unsupported from abroad. To these representations Arsaces seemed to give a favourable ear, agreed to the proposed confederacy, on condition that Mesopotamia, which he had formerly claimed, was now delivered up to him. At the same time he endeavoured to amuse Lucullus with offers of alliance against the king of Armenia.

In this conjuncture, it probably was, that Lucullus, in the apprehension of being superseded and deprived of the honour of terminating the war, made his report that the kingdom of Mithridates was now in his possession, and that the kingdom of Tigranes was also in his power; and therefore, that the Senate should, instead of a successor, send the usual commission to settle the form of the province, and to make a proper establishment to preserve the territories which he had already subdued. But after these representations were dispatched by Lucullus, it became apparent that the king of Parthia had deceived him with false professions, while he actually made great progress in a treaty with his enemies the kings of Armenia and Pontus, and meant to support them with all his force. In resentment of this act of treachery, or to prevent the effects of it, Lucullus proposed to carry the war into Parthia; and, for this purpose, ordered the legions that were stationed in Pontus to march without delay into Armenia.

These troops, however, already tired of the service, and suspecting that they were intended for some distant and hazardous enterprise, broke out

into

CHAP.
XVI.
into open mutiny, and refused to obey their officers. This example was soon afterwards followed by other parts of the army; and the general was obliged to confine his operations to the kingdom of Armenia. He endeavoured, by passing the mountains near to the sources of the Euphrates and the Tigris, to penetrate as far as Artaxata, the capital of the kingdom. By this march he forced Tigranes once more to hazard a battle, and obtained a victory; but his own army, notwithstanding their success, were so much discouraged with the change of climate, which they experienced in ascending the mountains of Armenia, and with the early and severe approach of winter in those high lands, that they again mutinied, and obliged their general to change his plan of the war. He accordingly turned his march to the southward, fell down on Mesopotamia, and, after a short siege, made himself master of Nisibis, a rich city in that territory, where, with other captives, he took Guras, brother to the king, who commanded in the place.

Here, however, the mutinous spirit still continuing to operate in the Roman army, it began to appear, that the general, who had so often overcome the kings of Pontus and Armenia, was better qualified to contend with an enemy, than to win or to preserve the good-will of his own troops. A report being spread that he was soon to be recalled, he, from that moment, lost the small remains of his authority; the legions deserted their colours,

lours, and treated, with scorn or indifference, all the attempts which he made to retain them.

This mutiny began in that part of the army, which, having been transported into Asia, with the Consul Valerius Flaccus at their head, had murdered this general, to put themselves under the command of Fimbria, and afterwards deserted their new leader to join with Sylla. Such crimes, under the late unhappy divisions of the republic, either remained unpunished, or were stated as merits with the party in whose favour the crime was committed. These legions, however, were, by Sylla, who was not willing to employ such instruments, or to intrust his own fate, or that of the commonwealth, in such hands, left in Asia, under pretence of securing the province; and they accordingly made a considerable part in the armies successively commanded by Murena and by Lucullus. The disposition which they now exhibited, and that of the army in general, to disorder and mutiny, was greatly excited by the factious spirit of Publius Clodius, the relation of Lucullus, who, having himself taken offence at the general, gave this earnest of his future conduct in the State, by endeavouring to stir up rebellion among the troops. "We, who "have already undergone so many hardships," he said, "are still kept on foot to escort the camels "which carry the treasures of our general, and are "made to pursue, without end, a couple of bar- "barous fugitives over barren desarts, and unculti- "vated

"vated wastes, while the soldiers of Pompey, after a few campaigns in Spain, or in Italy, are enjoying the fruits of their labour in comfortable settlements, procured by the favour of their leader."

Lucullus was so much aware of the decline of his authority, that he did not venture to hazard an affront by attempting to effect even a mere change of position. He hoped, that while he did not issue any orders of moment, the resolution of his army not to obey him might remain a secret to the enemy. This state of his affairs, however, soon became known to Mithridates, and encouraged him to hope he might be able to recover his kingdom. That he might not suffer the opportunity to escape him, he fell back into Pontus, with what troops he had then under his command, and, by his authority and influence over his own subjects, soon augmented his force, penetrated among the scattered quarters of the Romans, who were left to occupy the country, and separately surprised or destroyed considerable bodies of their troops. Among these, he attacked and defeated Fabius, the officer who was entrusted with the general command; and this king, though now turned of seventy, exposing his own person in the action, received a wound which stopped him in the pursuit of his victory, and by that means prevented its full effect.

Lucullus, being informed of what had passed in Pontus, had influence enough with the army, now anxious for their own safety, to put them in motion towards that kingdom; but before his arrival, Mithridates had shut up Fabius in Cabira, and defeated Triarius with considerable slaughter. Here again the veteran monarch was wounded; and, to satisfy the troops that he was not dead, was raised up on a platform, where he remained in sight of the army while his wound was dressed. In this last defeat the Romans lost twenty-four legionary Tribunes, one hundred and fifty Centurions, and seven thousand men.

It was not doubted, however, that Lucullus, on his arrival, if the men had been disposed to act under his command, would have been able soon to retrieve his affairs: but he was at this time superseded; and it was known in the army, that Acilius Glabrio was set out from Rome on his way to succeed him. The legions, therefore, under pretence that Lucullus was no longer their general, or that they themselves, by a decree of the People, had received their dismission, refused to obey him; and numbers, in fact, began to disband, taking the route of Cappadocia on their return to Italy.

This was the state of affairs when the commissioners, who, upon the report of Lullucus, had been sent by the Senate to settle the kingdom of Pontus in the form of a province, actually arrived. They found the Proconsul destitute of power in his own camp, and Mithridates, whom they believed to be vanquished, again in possession of his kingdom,

dom, and joining to the experience of old age all the ardour and enterprise of youth [1].

The Roman army in Asia, as a prelude to their present defection, had been taught to contrast the parsimony of Lucullus with the liberality and munificence of Pompey, and from the comparison they made, were impatient to change their leader, a disposition, which, it is not doubted, Pompey, by his intrigues, and with the aid of his agents, greatly encouraged. He could in reality ill brook the private station to which, by his late oath, in entering on the Consulate, he had bound himself. As he ever studied to support the public opinion of his own importance, he wished for occasions to derive some advantage from that opinion; but nothing had occurred for two years that was worthy of the high distinction to which he aspired. The command in Asia he coveted the more, that it seemed to be secured to Lucullus by the splendor of his successes, and by the unanimous judgment of the Senate and Nobles, who knew his faithful attachment to their order, and his fidelity to the aristocratical part of the constitution. The difficulties in that service were over, and nothing but the glory of terminating the war remained. Pompey, either from envy to Lucullus, or from a design to open a way to this glory for himself, contributed to the appointment of Glabrio, and to the nomination of the Prætors, who were sent with separate commands into the provinces of Asia and Bythinia.

[1] Appian. Bell. Mithridat. Plutarch. in Lucullo. Dio Cassius.

nia. If, upon the change he had thus produced, the war should become unsuccefsful, or languish, he had hopes to be called for by the general voice of the People, as the only perfon fit to bring it to a happy conclufion. Meanwhile a project was ftarted, which was to place him near to this fcene of action, and, if judged expedient, was likely to facilitate his farther removal, to the command of the army in Pontus.

The pirates ftill continued to infeft the feas, and were daily rifing in their prefumption, and increafing in their ftrength. They were receiving continual acceffion of numbers from thofe, who, by the unfettled ftate of Afia, were forced to join them for fubfiftence. The impunity which they enjoyed during the diftraction of councils at Rome, and the profits they made by their depredations, encouraged many who frequented the feas to engage in the fame way of life. They had been chaced, and numbers of them taken by M. Antonius the orator, by Servilius Ifauricus, and, laft of all, by C. Antonius, the father of him who, in the quality of Triumvir, is to become fo confpicuous in the fequel of this hiftory. But they had their retreats; and, upon the leaft remiffion of vigilance in the Roman officers, they again multiplied apace, put to fea in formidable fquadrons, and embarked fuch numbers of men, as not only enabled them to fcour the feas, but likewife to make defcents on the coafts, to enter harbours, deftroy fhipping, and pillage the maritime towns. They even

CHAP. XVI. even ventured to appear off the mouth of the Tiber, and to plunder the town of Oſtia itſelf. All the coaſts of the empire were open to their depredations. Roman magiſtrates were made priſoners in paſſing to and from their provinces; and citizens of every denomination, when taken by them, were forced to pay ranſom, kept in captivity, or put to death. The ſupply of proviſions to Italy was intercepted, or rendered precarious and difficult, and the price in proportion enhanced. Every report on theſe ſubjects was exaggerated by the intrigues of Pompey, who perceived, in this occaſion of public diſtreſs, the object of a new and extraordinary commiſſion to himſelf.

Frequent complaints having been made, and frequent deliberations held on this ſubject in the Senate, Gabinius, one of the Tribunes, at laſt propoſed, that ſome officer of Conſular rank ſhould be veſted, during three years, with abſolute powers, in order to put an effectual ſtop to theſe outrages, and to eradicate the cauſe of them, ſo as to ſecure for the future the inhabitants of the coaſt, as well as to protect the navigation of the ſeas. As Gabinius was known to be in concert with Pompey, the deſign of the propoſition was manifeſt; and it was received in the Senate with a general averſion. "For this," it was ſaid, " has Pompey declined "the ordinary turn of Conſular duty upon the " expiration of his office, that he might lie in " wait for extraordinary and illegal appointments." Gabinius being threatened with violence if he

ſhould

should perſiſt in his motion, thought proper to withdraw from the aſſembly.

A report was immediately ſpread in the city, that the perſon of the Tribune Gabinius had been actually violated; multitudes aſſembled at the doors of the Senate-houſe, and great diſorders were likely to follow; it was judged prudent for the Senate to adjourn; and the members, dreading ſome inſult from the populace, retired by ſeparate ways to their own houſes. Gabinius, without farther regard to the diſſent of the Senate, prepared to carry his motion to the People; but the other nine Tribunes were inclined to oppoſe him. Trebellius and Roſcius, in particular, were engaged to put a ſtop by their negative, to any further proceedings on that buſineſs. Pompey, in the mean time, with a diſſimulation which conſtituted part of his character, affected to diſapprove the motion of Gabinius, and to decline the commiſſion with which it was propoſed to inveſt him. He had recourſe to this affectation, not merely as the fitteſt means on the preſent occaſion to diſarm the envy of the Nobles, and to confirm the People in their choice; but ſtill more as a manner of proceeding which ſuited his own diſpoſition, being no leſs deſirous to appear forced and courted into high ſituations, than ſolicitous to gain and to hold them. He thus provoked the citizens of his own rank, no leſs by the ſhallow arts which he practiſed to impoſe on the public, than by the ſtate which he aſſumed. He could ſcarcely expect to find a ſupport in the or-

CHAP. XVI. der of Nobles, and least of all among those who were likely to become the personal rivals of his fortune in the commonwealth: and yet it is mentioned, that Julius Cæsar, now about two-and-thirty years of age, and old enough to distinguish his natural antagonists in the career of ambition, took part with the creatures of Pompey on this occasion. He was disposed to court the popular faction, and to oppose the aristocracy; either of which principles may explain his conduct in this instance. He had himself already incurred the displeasure of the Senate, but more as a libertine than as a disturber of the State, in which he had not hitherto taken any material part. In common with the youth of his time, he disliked the Senators, on account of the remaining austerity of their manners, no less than the inferior people disliked them on account of their aristocratical claims to authority and power. But whatever we may suppose to have been his motives, Cæsar, even before he seemed to have formed any ambitious designs of his own, was ever ready to abet those of any desperate adventurer who counteracted the Senate, or set the orders of government at nought; and seemed to be actuated by a species of instinct, which set him at variance with every form of a civil or political nature, if it checked the licence of faction, or bore hard on disorderly citizens of any sort [1].

On the day in which the question respecting the motion of Gabinius was to be put to the People, Pompey

[1] Zonaras, Ar. lib. x. c. 3.

Pompey appeared in the Comitium; and, if we may judge from the speech which is ascribed to him, employed a dissimulation and artifice somewhat too gross even for the audience to which it was addressed. He took occasion to thank the People for the honours he had received; but complained, that, having already toiled so much in the public service, he still should be destined for new labours. "You
"have forgotten," he said, "the dangers I en-
"countered, and the fatigues I underwent, while
"yet almost a boy, in the war with Cinna, in the
"wars in Sicily and in Africa, and what I suffer-
"ed in Spain, before I was honoured with any
"magistracy, or was of age to have a place in the
"Senate. But I mean not to accuse you of in-
"gratitude; on the contrary, I have been fully
"repaid. Your nomination of me to conduct the
"war with Sertorius, when every one else declin-
"ed the danger, I consider as a favour; and the
"extraordinary triumph you bestowed in conse-
"quence of it, as a very great honour. But I
"must entreat you to consider, that continued
"application and labour exhaust the powers of
"the mind as well as those of the body. Trust
"not to my line of life alone, nor imagine that I
"am still a young man, merely because my number
"of years is short of what others have attained.
"Reckon my services and the dangers to which
"I have been exposed; they will exceed the
"number of my years, and satisfy you, that I
"cannot much longer endure the labours and
"cares

"cares which are now propoſed for me. But if this be not granted me, I muſt beg of you to conſider what loads of envy ſuch appointments are likely to draw upon me from men, whoſe diſpleaſure, I know, you neither do, nor ought to regard, although to me their envy might be fatal: and I confeſs, that, of all the difficulties and dangers of war, I fear nothing ſo much as this. To live with envious perſons; to be called to account for miſcarriage, if one fails in the public ſervice; and to be envied, if one ſucceeds; who would chooſe to be employed on ſuch conditions? For theſe, and many other reaſons, I pray you to leave me at reſt; leave me to the care of my family, and of my private affairs. As for the preſent ſervice, I pray you to chooſe, among thoſe who deſire the employment, ſome perſon more proper; among ſo many, you cannot ſurely be at a loſs. I am not the only perſon that loves you, or that has experience in military affairs. There are many, whoſe names, to avoid the imputation of flattery, I will not mention."

To this ſpeech Gabinius replied; and, affecting to believe the ſincerity of Pompey's declarations, obſerved, that it was agreeable to the character of this great man, neither to deſire command, nor raſhly to accept of what was preſſed upon him. "They who are beſt able to ſurmount difficulties," he ſaid, "are likewiſe leaſt inclined to engage in them. But it is your buſineſs, fellow-citizens,

"citizens, to confider, not what is agreeable to
"Pompey, but what is neceffary to your own af-
"fairs; not to accept of thofe who court you for
"offices, but of thofe who are fit to difcharge the
"duties of them. I wifh we had many perfons
"of this defcription, befides the man I have propo-
"fed to your choice. Did we not all wifh for
"fuch perfons likewife, when we fearched among
"the young and the old for fome one to be oppo-
"fed to Sertorius, and found none but bimfelf?
"But wifhes cannot avail us; we muft take men
"as they are; we cannot create them. If there
"be but one man formed for our purpofe, with
"knowledge, experience, and good fortune, we
"muft lay hold of him, and feize him, if neceffary,
"even by force. Compulfion here is expedient
"and honourable for both parties; for thofe who
"employ it, becaufe it is to find them a perfon
"who can conduct their affairs; for him who
"fuffers it, becaufe he is to have an opportunity
"of ferving his country, an object for which no
"good citizen will refufe to expofe his perfon, or
"to facrifice his life.

"Do you think that Pompey, while yet a boy,
"was fit to command armies, to protect your al-
"lies, to reduce your enemies, to extend your
"empire; but that now in the prime of life, ripe
"in wifdom and experience, he can ferve you no
"longer? You employed the boy, you fuffer the
"man to be idle. When a private citizen of
"Equeftrian rank, he was fit for war and affairs of
"State;

"State; now he is a Senator, forsooth, he is fit for
"nothing! Before you had any trial of him, you
"made choice of him for the most important trust;
"now that you have experience of his ability, of
"his conduct, and of his success, you hesitate. Is
"the present occasion less pressing than the for-
"mer? Is the antagonist of Sertorius not fit to
"contend with pirates? But such absurdities can-
"not be received by the Roman People. As for
"you Pompey, submit to the will of your fellow-
"citizens. For this you was born, for this you
"was educated. I call upon you as the property
"of your country; I call upon you as its safe-
"guard and its defence. I call upon you to lay
"down your life, if necessary. This I know, if
"your country require it, you will not, you can-
"not refuse.

"But it is ridiculous to accost you in this man-
"ner; you who have proved your courage and
"your love to your country in so many and such
"arduous trials. Be ruled by this great assembly.
"Despise the envy of a few, or study the more to
"deserve the general favour. Let the envious
"pine when they hear of your actions, it is what
"they deserve. Let us be delivered from the
"evils by which we are surrounded, while you
"proceed to end your life as you began it, with
"success and with glory."

When Gabinius had finished his speech, Trebellius another of the Tribunes, attempted to reply; but such a clamour was immediately raised
by

by the multitude, that he could not be heard. He then, by the authority of his office, forbad the question; and Gabinius instantly proposed to have the sense of the Tribes, Whether Trebellius had not forfeited the character of Tribune? Seventeen Tribes were of this opinion, and the eighteenth would have made the majority, when Trebellius thought proper to withdraw his negative. Roscius, another of the Tribunes, intimated by signs (for he could not be heard) that a second should be joined with Pompey in this commission. But the clamour was renewed, and the meeting likely to end in riot and violence. Then all opposition to the motion was dropt. And, in this state of the business, Gabinius, trusting that, in the present humour of the People, no man would dare to oppose the measure, or wishing to increase the honour of Pompey's nomination, by the seeming concurrence of some of the more respectable citizens, called upon Catulus, who was then first on the roll of the Senate, to deliver his opinion, and led him up into the rostra for this purpose.

This citizen, by the equability of his conduct, and by his moderation, though in support of the aristocracy, had great authority even with the opposite party. He began his speech to the People with professions of public zeal, which obliged him to deliver with plainness what he thought was conducive to their good, and which entitled him to a deliberate hearing, before they should pronounce on the merits of what he was about to deliver. " If you " listen,"

"listen," he said, "something may still be offered to inform your judgment; if you break forth again into disorders and tumults, your capacity and good understanding will avail you nothing. I must begin with declaring my opinion, that powers so great, and for so long a time as are now proposed for Pompey, should not be committed to any single citizen whatever.

"The precedent is contrary to law, and in itself, in the highest degree, dangerous to the State. Whence came the usurpations of Marius, but from the habit of continual command; from his being put at the head of every army, intrusted with every war, and no less than six times re-elected Consul in the space of a few years? What inflamed to such a degree the arrogant spirit of Sylla, but the continual command of armies, and the exorbitant power of Dictator? Such is human nature, that in age, as well as in youth, we are debauched with power; and if inured for any time to act as superiors, we cannot submit afterwards to the equal and moderate station of citizens.

"I speak not with any particular reference to Pompey; I speak what the law requires, and what I am sure is for your good. If high office and public trust be an honour, every one who has pretensions should enjoy them in his turn; if they be a load or a burden, every one ought to bear his part. These are the laws of justice and of republican government. By observing them,

"republics

"republics have an advantage over moſt other
" ſtates. By employing many men in their turns,
" they educate and train many citizens for every
" department, and have numbers amongſt whom
" they may chooſe the fitteſt to ſerve on every par-
" ticular emergence. But if we ſuffer one or a
" few to engroſs every office or ſervice of mo-
" ment, the liſt of thoſe who are qualified for
" any ſuch truſt will decreaſe in proportion. If
" we always recur to the ſame perſon in every try-
" ing occaſion, we ſhall ſoon have no other per-
" ſon to employ. Why were we ſo much at a
" loſs for experienced commanders, when Serto-
" rius appeared to threaten Italy with an inva-
" ſion? Becauſe command, for a conſiderable time
" before that period, had been engroſſed by a few,
" and thoſe few alone had any experience. Al-
" though, therefore, I have the higheſt opinion
" of Pompey's abilities and qualification for this
" ſervice, I muſt prefer to his pretenſions the
" public utility and the expreſs declaration of the
" laws.

" You annually elect Conſuls and Prætors: to
" what purpoſe? to ſerve the State; or to carry
" for a few months the enſigns of power? If to
" ſerve the State, why name private perſons with
" unprecedented commiſſions, to perform what
" your magiſtrates are either fit to perform, or are
" not fit to have been elected?

" If there bè any uncommon emergency that
" requires more than the ordinary exertions of go-
" vernment,

"vernment, the conſtitution has provided an ex-
"pedient. You may name a Dictator. The
"power of this officer has no bounds, but in re-
"ſpect to the place in which it is to be exer-
"ciſed, and to the time during which it is to laſt.
"It is to be exerciſed within the limits of Italy,
"where alone the vitals of the State can be ex-
"poſed to any great or preſſing attack; it is li-
"mited to ſix months, a ſufficient period in which
"to remove the cauſe of any ſudden alarm. But
"this unlimited power, which is now propoſed for
"ſo long a time, and over the whole empire, muſt
"end in calamities, ſuch as this and other nations
"have ſuffered from the ambition and uſurpation
"of arbitrary and preſumptuous men.

"If you beſtow unlimited power by ſea and by
"land on a ſingle man, in what manner is he to
"exerciſe his power? Not by himſelf in perſon,
"for he cannot be every where preſent; he muſt
"have lieutenants or ſubſtitutes who act under his
"orders. He cannot even attend to what is paſ-
"ſing at once in Egypt and in Spain, in Africa, in
"Syria, and in Greece. If ſo, then why may not
"thoſe who are to act be officers named by you,
"and not by any intermediate perſon; account-
"able to you, and not to another; and in the
"dangers they run, animated with the proſpect of
"honour to themſelves, not to a perſon who is un-
"neceſſarily interpoſed between them and their
"country? Gabinius propoſes to inveſt this officer
"with authority to name many lieutenants; I

"pray

"pray you to confider, whether thefe officers
"fhould depend upon any intermediate perfon, or
"upon yourfelves alone? and whether there be fuf-
"ficient caufe to fufpend all the legal powers, and
"to fuperfede all the magiftrates in the common-
"wealth, and all the governors of provinces in
"every part of your empire, in order to make war
"on pirates?"

So much of what Catulus is fuppofed to have delivered on this occafion is preferved among the fragments of Dion. Caffius [1]. It is mentioned by others, that the audience expreffed their good-will and refpect for this Senator in a compliment which they paid to him, probably near the clofe of his fpeech, when urging fome of his former arguments, he afked, " If this man to whom alone, by "thus employing him in every fervice, you give "an opportunity of acquiring the fkill and habits "of a ftatefman or foldier, fhould fall, to whom "will you next have recourfe?" The People anfwered, with a general acclamation, *To yourfelf* [2]. They revered, for a moment, the candour and ability of this eminent citizen, but could not withftand the arts of Pompey, and the tide of popularity, which then ran fo high in his favour.

This day being far fpent in debate, another day was appointed in which to collect the votes, when a decree paffed to veft Pompey with the fupreme command over all the fleets and armies of the republic, in every fea without diftinction or limit, and

[1] For thefe fpeeches fee Fragments of Dio. Caffius, lib. 36.
[2] Cicero pro Lege Manilia.

CHAP. XVI.

and on every coast within four hundred stadia, or fifty miles of the shore. This commission took place in Italy, and extended throughout every province, during three years from the time of the act being passed.

As Pompey owed these extraordinary powers to the Tribune Gabinius, he intended to have employed him next in command to himself; but the law which excluded the Tribunes from succeeding to any public employment, in the first year after the expiration of their office, stood in the way of this choice; and Pompey did not persist in it.

Upon the publication of an edict investing an officer of so much renown with such mighty powers for restoring the navigation of the seas, corn and every other article of importation at Rome considerably fell in their price. The friends of Pompey already triumphed in the success of their measure, and he himself soon after, notwithstanding the meanness of the enemy opposed to him, gained much credit by the rapid, decisive and effectual measures he took to obtain the end of his appointment. Although it was the middle of winter, a season too rough, even in the Mediterranean, for such shipping as was then in use, he gave orders to arm and put to sea as many vessels as could be collected or fitted out in every maratime station. In a little time he had returns of two hundred and seventy gallies fit for service, one hundred and twenty thousand foot, and four thousand horse embodied within the limits to which his
commission

commiffion extended. That the pirates might be every where attacked at once, and find no refuge by changing their ufual places of retreat, he divided the coafts of the empire into feparate diftricts, appointed lieutenants with full powers in each, affigned their ftations, and allotted their quotas of fhipping and troops. He himfelf, with a fquadron of fixty fhips, propofed to infpect the whole, or to give his prefence where it fhould be required. He began with vifiting the ports of Spain and Gaul, and the feas of Sardinia and Corfica; and in paffing from thence, he himfelf went on fhore, and travelled by land, while his fquadron, coafting round the peninfula of Italy, had orders to join him at Brundifium. In this journey, upon his approach to Rome, he enjoyed, in all refpects, the ftate of a great monarch, was received with acclamations by the People, and was courted by multitudes of every condition who went forth to receive him. All his complaints and reprefentations were received as commands. The Conful Pifo, being fuppofed not to forward his levies with fufficient alacrity, would have been degraded, if Pompey himfelf had not interpofed to prevent a motion which the Tribune Gabinius intended to make for this purpofe.

The fleet being arrived at Brundifium, Pompey haftened to reimbark, and from thence paffed by the ftations of his feveral lieutenants in the fea-ports of Macedonia and Greece, to thofe of Pamphylia and Cilicia, which were the principal refort of the pirates. Such of thefe banditti, as he captured in his way,

way, were treated with mildnefs; and this circumftance, together with the great preparations which were reported from every quarter to be making againft them, with the fmall hopes they had of being able to efcape, induced them, in great numbers, to furrender themfelves. In the bay of Cilicia he found a fquadron of their fhips affembled, and ready to cover the harbours at which they had been accuftomed to collect their naval ftores, and to lodge their booty. They feparated, however, upon his appearance, took refuge in different creeks of that mountainous fhore, and afterwards furrendered at difcretion, delivering up all the forts they had erected, with all their ftores of timber, cordage, and fails, of which they had made a confiderable provifion.

By thefe means the war was finifhed about the middle of fummer, fix months after the nomination of Pompey to this command. In that time feventy-two gallies were funk, three hundred and fix were taken, and a hundred and twenty piratical harbours or ftrong-holds on fhore were deftroyed. Ten thoufand of the pirates were killed in action, and twenty thoufand, who had furrendered themfelves, remained prifoners at the end of the war. Thefe Pompey, having fufficiently deprived of the means of returning to their former way of life, tranfplanted to different parts of the continent, where the late or prefent troubles, by thinning the inhabitants, had made room for their fettlement. Upon this occafion he repeopled the city of of Soli in Cilicia, which had been lately laid waste, and forcibly emptied of its inhabitants by Tigranes, to replenish his newly established capital of Tigranocerta in Armenia. After this re-establishment of Soli, the place, in honour of its restorer, came to be known by the name of Pompeiopolis [1].

Whilst this succesful commissioner was thus employed in disposing of the pirates on the coast of Cilicia, he received a message from Lappa in the island of Crete, then besieged by Metellus, intimating that the people of this place, although they held out against Metellus, were willing to surrender to Pompey. This sort of preference implying estimation and popular regard, was one of the temptations which Pompey was supposed unable to resist; he accordingly, without consulting with Metellus, sent an officer to receive the surrender of Lappa.

Metellus had commanded about two years in Crete, had almost reduced the island, and had a near prospect of that triumph, which he afterwards, with the title of Creticus, actually obtained, on account of this conquest. Pompey's commission, as commander in chief of all the sea and land forces of Rome within fifty miles of the coast, no doubt, extended to Lappa; but it was justly reckoned invidious to interfere in the province of a Proconsul, whose appointment preceded his own. And this step revived all the former imputations against him, that he considered himself as every one's superior, strove to suppress every grow-

[1] Dion. Cassius, lib. xxxvi. c. 20.

ing fame, and threw his perfonal confideration as a bar in the way of every rifing merit. Metellus, ftung with refentment, and trufting to the fupport of the Senate, ventured to contemn his orders; even after Octavius, who had been fent by Pompey to take the inhabitants of Lappa under his protection, had entered the town, and in his name commanded Metellus to defift from the attack of a place already in poffeffion of the Romans. He neverthelefs continued the fiege, forced the town to furrender, and threatening to treat Octavius himfelf as a rebel, obliged him to be gone from the ifland. The Senate, without otherwife deciding the controverfy which was likely to arife on this fubject, afterwards acknowledged Metellus as the conqueror of Crete, and decreed him a triumph in that capacity [1].

The difpute, however, at this time, might have led to difagreeable confequences, if Pompey, while he was preparing to pafs into Crete againft Metellus, had not found another object of more importance to his plan of greatnefs [2]. Lucullus had always appeared to him a rival in power and confideration more formidable than Metellus, and the war in Pontus and Armenia, likely to furnifh a more ample field of glory than the deftruction of pirates.

Mithridates, though once nearly vanquifhed, was, by means of the diftractions which, commu-
nicating

[1] Liv. Epit. Plutarch in Pompeio. Dion. Caff. lib. xxxv.
[2] Dion. Caff. lib. xxxvi. c. 28.

nicating from the popular factions at Rome, had infected the army of Lucullus, enabled to renew the war with fresh vigour. Knowing that the Roman general was no longer obeyed, he not only obtained possession, as has been mentioned, of his own kingdom, but, together with Tigranes, began to act on the offensive, and made excursions even into Cilicia. Acilius Glabrio, the Proconsul appointed to succeed in the command of the Roman army, hearing the bad state of affairs in Pontus, stopped short in Bithynia, and even refused to furnish Lucullus with the reinforcements he had brought from Italy. In these circumstances the province of Asia, likely to become a principal source of revenue to the commonwealth, was in imminent danger of being wrested from their hands; and the friends of Pompey seized this opportunity to propose a farther enlargement of his powers. Manilius, one of the Tribunes, in concert with Gabinius, moved the People to extend his commission to the provinces of Phrygia, Bithynia, Cappadocia, and Pontus; and of course to commit the war in Armenia and Pontus to his direction. This motion was strenuously opposed by Catulus, Hortensius, and all the principal members of the Senate. It was supported by Marcus Tullius Cicero and by Caius Julius Cæsar, who both intended, on this occasion, to court the popular party, by espousing the cause of a person so much in favour with the People.

Cicero was one of the first of the Romans who rested his consideration entirely on civil accomplishments,

ments, and who became great by the services he was qualified to render his friends in a civil capacity, without any pretensions to the merit of a soldier. The character of a pleader was become one of the most powerful recommendations to public notice, and one of the surest roads to consequence and civil preferment. Cicero, with a fine genius and great application, was supposed to excel all who had gone before him in this line of pursuit. His talents were powerful instruments in his own hands; they rendered him necessary to others, and procured him the courtship of every party in its turn. He was understood to favour the aristocracy, and was inclined to support the Senate, as the great bulwark of the State, against the licence of the populace, and the violence of factious leaders. But being now Prætor, with a near prospect of the Consulate, he sacrificed much to his ambition in the pursuit of preferments, which were new in his family, and which the antient nobility were disposed to envy. His speech, upon the motion of Manilius, was the first he had ever made in a political character: it is still extant, and does more honour to his talents as a pleader, than to his steadiness in support of the constitution and government of his country[1]. He turned aside, by artful evasions, the wise counsels of Hortensius and Catulus; and, under pretence of setting forth the merits of Pompey, and of stating precedents in his favour, dazzled his audience, by enumerating the irregular honours

---

[1] Cicer. Orat. pro Lege Manilia.

honours which they themselves had already conferred on this object of their favour.

With such able advocates, in a cause to which the People were already so well disposed, the interest of Pompey could not miscarry; and an addition was accordingly made to his former commission, by which he became in reality sovereign of the fairest part of the empire. Upon the arrival of this news in Cilicia, where he then was, he affected surprise and displeasure. "Are my enemies," he said, " never to give me any respite " from war and trouble?" He had talents, undoubtedly, sufficient to support him in the use of means less indirect; but a disposition to artifice, like every other ruling passion, will stifle the plainest suggestions of reason, and seems to have made him forget, on the present occasion, that his own attendants at least had common penetration. They turned away from the farce which he acted with shame and disgust [1]; and he himself made no delay in showing the avidity with which he received what he thus affected to dislike; laid aside all thoughts of other business; immediately dispatched his orders to all the provinces that were now subjected to his power; and, without passing his mandates through the hands of Lucullus, summoned Mithridates, then with an army of between thirty and forty thousand men on the frontier of Pontus, to surrender himself at discretion. This prince, being then in treaty with Phraates, who had

---

[1] Plutarch. in Pompeio.

had lately succeeded his father Arsaces in the kingdom of Parthia, and being in expectation of a powerful support from that quarter, refused to listen to this imperious message: and being disappointed in his hopes of assistance from the Parthians, and finding that Phraates had joined in a league with his enemies, he endeavoured to pacify the Roman general; and finding that his advances for this purpose had no effect, he prepared for a vigorous resistance.

Pompey set out for Pontus, and in his way had an interview with Lucullus, who was then in Galatia. They accosted each other at first with laboured expressions of respect and of compliment on their respective services, but ended with disputes and sharp altercations. Pompey accused Lucullus of precipitation, in stating the kingdom of Pontus as a Roman province, while the king himself was alive and at liberty. Lucullus suspected that the late mutiny had been fomented by the emissaries of Pompey, to make way for his own succession to the command. He persisted in maintaining the propriety of the report which he had made to the Senate, and in which he had represented the kingdom of Pontus as conquered; and in which he had desired that commissioners should be sent as usual to secure the possession; observed that no province could be kept, if the troops stationed to preserve it refused to obey their general; that if such disorders were made the engine of politics in the competition of candidates

for

for office, the republic had worſe conſequences to fear than the loſs of any diſtant province; that although the fugitive king had taken advantage of the factions at Rome and in the army, to put himſelf again at the head of ſome forces, he had not recovered any conſiderable portion of his kingdom, nor at the arrival of the commiſſioners of the Senate, been able to diſturb them in ſettling the province; that there was then nothing left for a ſucceſſor, but the invidious taſk of ſnatching at the glory which had been won by another.

From this conference Pompey entered on the command with many indications of animoſity to Lucullus; he ſuſpended the execution of his orders; changed the plan of his operations; remitted the puniſhments, and recalled the rewards he had decreed to particular perſons, and in a manner which ſeemed to juſtify the ſuſpicion of his having encouraged the late diſorders, ſuffered them to paſs with impunity; and treated with the uſual confidence even the legions which had refuſed to obey the orders of their general. His own authority, in the outſet, ſeemed to be ſecured by the animoſity of the army to their late commander, and by their deſire to contraſt their own conduct, and the ſucceſs of the war under their preſent leader, with that which had taken place under his predeceſſor. Finding himſelf, therefore, at the head of numerous and well-affected forces, both by ſea and by land, he covered the coaſts of the Egean and Euxine Seas with his galleys, and, at at the head of a great army, advanced in search of the enemy.

Mithridates, upon the approach of Pompey, continued retiring before him towards the Lesser Armenia, laid waste the country through which the Roman army was to pass, endeavouring to distress them by the want of provisions and forage.

For several days successively the armies encamped in sight of each other. Mithridates took his posts in such a manner, that he could not be safely attacked; and as his object was to pass the Euphrates without being forced to a battle, he generally decamped in the night, and, by his superior knowledge of the country, passed through ways in which the Roman army could not hastily follow without manifest danger of surprise. Pompey, sensible that, upon this plan of operation, the king of Pontus must effect his retreat, took a resolution to pass him by a forced march, not in the night but in the heat of the day, when the troops of Asia were most inclined to repose. If he should succeed in this design, and get between their army and the Euphrates, he hoped to force them to a battle, or oblige them to change their route. Accordingly, on the day he had chosen for this attempt, he doubled his march, passed the enemy's camp at noon-day unobserved, and was actually posted on their route, when they began to decamp, as usual, on the following night. In the encounter which followed, having all the advantages of a surprise, and in the dark, against an army on its march, and

little

little accustomed to order, he gained a decisive victory, in which he cut off or dispersed all the forces on which the king of Pontus had relied for the defence of his kingdom [1].

Mithridates escaped with a few attendants; and, in this extremity, proposed to throw himself again into the arms of Tigranes; but was refused by this prince, who was himself then attacked by a rebellion of his own son. Upon this disappointment he fled to the northward, passing by the sources of the Euphrates to the kingdom of Colchis, and from thence, by the eastern coasts of the Euxine, to the Scythian Bosphorus, now the Straits of Coffa, in order to take refuge in the Cherfonesus, or Crim Tartary, at Panticapæa, the capital of a kingdom which he himself had acquired, and which he had bestowed on Machares, one of his sons. Upon his presenting himself at this place, he found that Machares had long since abandoned his father's fortunes; and, upon hearing of the ill state of his affairs on his first flight from Lucullus into Armenia, had sent, as an offering of peace, a golden crown to that general, and sued for the protection of the Romans. The father, highly provoked with this act of pusillanimity or treachery, assembled a force among his Scythian allies, and, deaf to all offers of submission or entreaties of this undutiful son, dragged him from the throne, and either ordered him to be put to death, or made his situation so painful, that he thought proper to put an end to his own life.

In

[1] Dio. Cass. lib. xxxvi. c. 31.

CHAP.
XVI.
In this manner Mithridates entered anew on the poffeffion of a kingdom, in which he had not only a fafe retreat, but likewife the means of executing new projects of war againſt his enemies. By the maxims of the Romans, which Pompey himſelf had urged in his late difpute with Lucullus, no kingdom was fuppofed to be conquered, till the king was either killed, taken, or forced to furrender; and the Roman general, by this flight of the king of Pontus, found himſelf under a neceffity either of purfuing him into his prefent retreat, or of doing what he himſelf had blamed in his predeceffor, by making his report of a conqueſt before it was fully accomplifhed. While he was deliberating on the meaſures to be taken in thefe circumftances, he was invited by the younger Tigranes, fon to the king of Armenia, then in rebellion againſt his father, to enter with his army into that kingdom, and to give judgment on the differences fubfifting between the father and the fon.

In confequence of this invitation, Pompey marched into Armenia, joined the rebel prince, and, under pretence of fupporting the fon, was about to ftrip the father of his kingdom, when this monarch, as ufual, with a meannefs proportioned to the prefumption with which he had enjoyed his profperity, now refolved to caſt himſelf entirely upon the victor's mercy. For this purpoſe he defired to be admitted into Pompey's prefence, and, with a few attendants, prefented himſelf for this purpoſe. Being told, at the entrance

of

of the camp, that no stranger could pass on horse-back, he dismounted, and was conducted on foot to the general's presence. In entering the tent, he uncovered his head, and having the diadem in his hand, offered to lay it on the ground at Pompey's feet; but was told with great courtesy, that he might resume it; that, by submitting himself to the generosity of the Romans, he had not lost a kingdom, but gained a faithful ally [1]. At the same time, under pretence of reimbursing the expence of the war, a sum of six thousand talents, or about one million one hundred and twenty-eight thousand pounds sterling was exacted from him; and he himself, to this great sum which was paid to the State, added a gratuity to the army of a talent [2] to each of the Tribunes, ten minæ [3] to each of the Centurions, and half a mina [4] to each private man.

Pompey, in disposing of the two Armenias, which were now in his power, allotted Sophene, or the Lesser Armenia, on the right of the Euphrates, to Tigranes the son, reserving Syria and Phœnicia, to which Antiochus, the last representative of the Macedonian line, had been restored by Lucullus, together with Cilicia and Galatia, to the disposal of the Romans.

Tigranes the father with great submission acquiesced in this partition; but the son, who probably

[1] Dio. Cass. lib. xxxvi. c. 35. Plutarch. in Pompeio.
[2] 93 l. 15 s.
[3] 32 l. 5 s. 10 d.
[4] 1 l. 12 s. 3½ d. Vid. Arbuthnot of Ancient Coins.

bably expected to have been put in possession of the whole of his father's kingdom, was greatly discontented, and, while Pompey was yet in Armenia, entered into a correspondence with the king of Parthia, and solicited his assistance to overturn the settlement which was now made. On account of these practices, whether real or supposed, this undutiful son of Tigranes was taken into custody, carried into Italy, and made a part in the ornaments of the victor's triumph [1].

The Roman general, having in this manner disposed of the kingdom of Armenia, or retained it still farther at the disposal of the Romans, by the confinement of the rebel prince, resumed the thoughts of pursuing Mithridates into his present retreat. For this purpose he left Afranius in Armenia, with a force sufficient to secure his rear, and to prevent any disturbance on this side of the Euphrates. He himself passed the Araxes, and wintered on the Cyrus, or the Cyrnus, on the confines of Albania and Iberia. In the following summer, having defeated the natives of those countries in repeated encounters, he advanced to the mouth of the Phasis, where he was joined by his fleet, then plying in the Euxine Sea, under the command of Servilius. Here he appears to have deliberated, whether he should attempt to pursue Mithridates any farther; but upon considering the difficulties of the voyage, and of the march along a coast and a country entirely unknown, unfurnished with any safe harbour

---

[1] Plutarch. in Pompeio. ad p. 458.

OF THE ROMAN REPUBLIC.

CHAP. XVI.

harbour for his ships, or even with any means of subsistence to his army by land, he took his resolution to return, and to avail himself, in the best manner he was able, of the dominions which had been abandoned to him by the flight of their king[1]. With this resolution he directed his march, by the coast, back into the kingdom of Pontus; and, finding no resistance, took all his measures as in a conquered province. At one place he found a considerable treasure, which was disclosed to him by Stratonice, one of the concubines of the king, by whom she had a son named Xiphares. This woman made the discovery on condition that, if her son were taken by the Romans, his life should be spared. But this unhappy son was exposed to other dangers besides those now apprehended by the mother. Mithridates, upon hearing of the price which was paid for the life of Xiphares, ordered him to be slain. "That woman," he said, "should have likewise bargained with me in fa-"vour of her son." At other places the Roman army found the vestiges of great magnificence, joined to monuments of superstition and of cruelty. They found some productions of an art, in which the king was supposed to be master, relating to the composition of poisons, and of their antidotes, and some records of dreams, together with the interpretations[2], which had been given by his women.

From Pontus, Pompey, having made a proper disposition of the fleet in the Euxine, to defend the coast

[1] Dio. Cass. lib. 37. c. 3. Plutarch. in Pompeio. Appian. in Mithridat.
[2] Plutarch. in Pomp. p. 462.

CHAP. XVI.

coast against attempts of invasion from Mithridates, whose forces were still formidable on the Bosphorus and the opposite shores, set out for the kingdom of Syria, which he now determined to seize in behalf of the Romans. Lucullus had already, agreeably to the policy of his country, or under pretence of setting the Syrians free, separated their kingdom from the other possessions of Tigranes: but the pretence upon which he acted in this matter being sufficient to prevent his seizing upon Syria as a Roman province, he was content, in the mean time, with restoring it to Antiochus, the last pretender of the Macedonian line, who had lived eighteen years in the greatest obscurity in Cilicia. But Pompey now proposed to complete the transaction, by seizing for the Romans themselves, what the other affected only to restore to the lawful owner [1]; and this owner now pleaded in vain against the sentence of Pompey that right of descent from the Macedonian line, which Lucullus had employed to supplant Tigranes [2].

On the march into Syria, the Roman general, either in person or by his lieutenants, received the submission of all the principalities or districts in his way, and made the following arrangements. The Lesser Armenia, once intended for the younger Tigranes, he gave to Dejotarus, king of Galatia [3], who remained on the frontier of the empire a faithful dependent, and whose possessions served as a barrier against hostile invasions

[1] Justin. lib. xl. c. 1. & 2.
[2] Appian. in Mithridat. p. 244.
[3] Eutropius, lib. vi.

sions from that quarter. Paphlagonia was given to Attalus and Pylæmenus, who were liberal triubtaries to the Roman officers, and vigilant guards on the frontiers of the empire. Upon his arrival at Damascus, he had many applications from the late subjects or dependents of the Syrian monarchy; among others, from Hyrcanus and Ariftobulus, two brothers contending for the fovereignty of Judea, who now repaired to his tribunal for judgment, and requested the interpofition of his power in behalf of the party he should be pleafed to favour.

Of thefe rivals, who were the fons of Alexander, late high-prieft of the Jews, Hyrcanus the elder had fucceeded to his mother Alexandra, whom the father had left his immediate fucceffor in the kingdom; but was difpoffeffed by his younger brother Ariftobulus, who, being of a more active fpirit, had formed a powerful faction againft him among the people.

Hyrcanus took refuge among the Arabs, and prevailed upon Aretas, the chieftain of fome powerful tribe of that people, to affift him in recovering the fovereignty of his country. In conjunction with this ally, Hyrcanus accordingly laid fiege to Jerufalem, but was difappointed of his object by Scaurus, one of Pompey's lieutenants, who being then in Syria, interpofed at the requeft of Ariftobulus, from whom he received a prefent of three hundred talents [1], and obliged the Arabs to

---

[1] About L. 57,500.

CHAP.
XVI.
to defift from their enterprize. Upon the arrival of Gabinius, whom Pompey had sent before him into Syria, Ariftobulus thought proper to make him likewife a prefent of fifty talents, and by thefe means remained in poffeffion of Jerufalem at the arrival of Pompey.

It is alleged that each of the contending parties made their prefents alfo to the Proconful himfelf; Hyrcanus in particular, that of a beautiful piece of plate, admired for its workmanfhip and weight, being the model of a fpreading vine, with its leaves and fruit in maffy gold [1]; and fuch prefents merit attention, as they furnifh fome inftances of the manner in which great riches, now in fo much requeft at Rome, were amaffed by Roman officers in the courfe of their fervices. Befides what they obtained in this manner, it is likely that every conqueft they effected, every revolution they brought about, and every protection they granted, was extremely profitable.

Pompey, on hearing the merits of the queftion between the two brothers, notwithftanding what his lieutenants had done for Ariftobulus, declared for Hyrcanus, and advanced towards the city of Jerufalem, to execute the decree he had paffed. Upon his approach he was again met by Ariftobulus, who made frefh offers of fubmiffion, and of a public contribution in money; and Gabinius was detached, to take poffeffion of the city, in terms of this fubmiffion. But upon a report that the friends

[1] Jofeph. Antiq. lib. xiv. c. 2.

OF THE ROMAN REPUBLIC.

friends of Ariftobulus, though himfelf ftill in the hands of Pompey, refufed to admit the Roman detachment, this prince was put in arreft, and the whole army advanced to the walls.

The citizens being divided, thofe who efpoufed the caufe of Hyrcanus prepared to open the gates of the city, while the others, who were attached to Ariftobulus, retired into the temple, and broke down the bridge by which this edifice was joined to the ftreets, and made every other preparation in that retreat to defend themfelves to the laft extremity.

The Romans, upon the arrival of Pompey, being joined by the friends of Hyrcanus, took poffeffion of all the principal ftations within the walls, and prepared to attack the temple, into which their antagonifts had retired. This building had all the advantages of a citadel or fortefs, built on a height, furrounded with natural precipices, or with a deep ditch overhung with lofty battlements and towers. To reduce it, Pompey fent for battering engines to Tyre, and cut down all the woods in the neighbourhood to furnifh materials for the works he was about to erect. All his attempts being, with great obftinacy, refifted by thofe who had taken refuge in the Temple. He obferved, in the courfe of his operations, that the people within, although they at all times defended their own perfons, when attacked, yet on the Sabbathday they did no work, either in repairing any of
their

their own defences, in obstructing or attempting to demolish what the besiegers were erecting. He accordingly took advantage of this circumstance, made no assaults on that day, but continued his labour in filling up the ditch, and erected such works as were required to cover his approach. In this manner his towers, without interruption, were raised to the level of the battlements, and his engines playing from thence, made great havock among the besieged. These devotees, however, animated with zeal in defence of their Temple, even under the discharge of the enemy's missiles, still continued at the altar to perform their usual rites; and took so little precaution against the dangers to which they were exposed, that numbers perished in offering up the sacrifices, and mingled their blood with that of the victims.

In the third month after the siege began, one of the towers of the Temple was brought in ruin to the ground; and Faustus, the son of Sylla, with two Centurions at the head of the divisions they commanded, entered the breach, and putting all whom they met to the sword, made way for more numerous parties to follow them, and covered the avenues and porches of the Temple with the slain. The priests, who were even then employed in the sacrifices, waited for the enemy with the utmost composure, and, without discontinuing their duties, were slain at the altars. Numbers of the people threw themselves from the precipices; and others, setting fire to the booths in which they had lodged under the walls of the Temple, were consumed in

the

the flames. About twelve or thirteen thousand perished on this occasion, without any proportional loss to the besiegers, or to those who conducted the storm.

Pompey, being master of the Temple, and struck with the obstinate valour with which it had been defended, had much curiosity to visit the interior recess, for the sake of which he was told that so much blood had been shed, and all his efforts withstood with so much desperation. This place, into which no one was ever admitted, besides the highpriest, he supposed to contain the sacred emblems of that power who inspired his votaries with so ardent and so unconquerable a zeal. And he ventured, to the equal consternation and horror of his own party among the Jews, as of those who opposed him, to enter with his usual attendance into the Holy of Holies. He found it adorned with lamps, candlesticks, cups, vessels of incense, with their supports, all of solid gold, containing a mass of the richest perfumes, and a sacred treasure of two thousand talents [1].

Having satisfied his curiosity, it is mentioned that he respected the religion of the place so much as to have left every part of this treasure untouched, and to have given directions that the Temple itself should be purified, in order to expiate the profanation of which he himself had been guilty. He restored Hyrcanus to the priesthood or sovereignty of Judea, but charged him with a considerable

[1] About L. 386,000.

considerable tribute to the Romans, and at the same time stript the nation of all those possessions or dependencies in Palestine and Celesyria, which had been acquired or held in subjection by their ancestors. Such were Gadara, Scythopolis, Hyppus, Pella, Samaria, Marissa, Azotus, Jamana, Arethusa, Gaza, Joppa, and Dora, with what was then called Strato's Tower, and afterwards Cæsarea. Under pretence of restoring these several places to their liberties, they were released from their subjection to the Jews, but in reality annexed to the Roman province of Syria [1].

Pompey now recollecting that he had formerly carried his arms to the shores of the Atlantic, and to the boundaries of Numidia and of Spain; that he had recently penetrated to the coasts of the Euxine, and to the neighbourhood of the Caspian Sea; in order that he might not leave any part of the known world unexplored by his arms, now formed a project to finish this round of exploits, by visiting the shores of the Asiatic or Eastern Ocean: a circumstance which was to complete the glory of his approaching triumph, and raise him, as his flatterers were pleased to observe, to a rank above every conqueror of the present or any preceding age [2].

But while the Roman Proconsul was employed in the settlement of Syria, in the reduction of Jerusalem, and meditating these farther conquests, Mithridates

---

[1] Joseph. de Bell. Jud. lib. i. & vii. & Ant. lib. xiv. c. 6.
[2] Plutarch. in Pom. p. 463.

OF THE ROMAN REPUBLIC.

CHAP. XVI

thridates was bufy in making preparations to renew the war. Having heard of the extremities to which the citizens of Rome had been frequently reduced by invafions from Gaul and Africa, and by the infurrections of their own fubjects and flaves, he concluded that they were weakeft at home, or might be attacked with the greateft advantage in Italy. He again, therefore, refumed the project of marching an army of Scythians by the Danube and the Alps. He vifited all the princes in his neighbourhood, made alliances with many, which he confirmed by giving to fome of them, his daughters in marriage, and perfuaded them, by the hopes of a plentiful fpoil, to join with him in the project of invading Europe. He even difpatched his agents into Gaul, to fecure the co-operation of nations on that fide of the world, and trufted that, on his appearance in Italy, many of the difcontented inhabitants would become of his party, in the fame manner as they had declared for Hannibal; and that the flaves, fo lately at open war with their mafters, would likewife be a plentiful fupply of recruits to his army.

Thefe projects, however, appeared to his own nation too hazardous and vaft. They were fuited to the ftate of a king who wifhed to perifh with fplendor; but not to that of fubjects and followers who had humbler hopes, and who chofe to be governed by more reafonable profpects of fortune. The king himfelf, while he meditated fuch extenfive defigns, being confined by an ulcer in his face,

had

had been for a considerable time concealed from public view, and had not admitted any person to his presence besides some favourite Eunuchs. The minds of his subjects, and of his own family in particular, were much alienated from him by the late acts of barbarous severity against Machares and Xiphares, two of his own children, who, with some others, as we have mentioned, had incurred his resentment.

Pharnaces, another son, still attended the father; and, though disposed to betray him, was much in his confidence. The people of Phanagoria, a town on the shore of the Bosphorus, opposite to the fortress at which the king now resided, together with the inhabitants of the country, pretending a variety of provocations, revolted and the army, during his confinement, losing the usual awe of his person, mutinied, and acknowledged Pharnaces for king. They assembled round the fortress in which Mithridates was lodged, and which he had garrisoned with a chosen body of men. When he appeared on the battlements, and desired to know their demands: " To exchange " you," they said, " for Pharnaces ; an old king " for a young one." Even while he received this answer, and while many of his guards deserted him, he still hoped that, if he were at liberty, he might retrieve his affairs. He desired, therefore, by repeated messages, to know whether he might have leave to depart in safety? But none of the messengers he sent with this question being suffered to return,

turn, he apprehended that there was a defign to deliver him up into the hands of the Romans. Under this apprehenfion he had recourfe to his laft refort, a dofe of poifon, which, it is faid, he always carried for ufe in the fcabbard of his fword. Being to apply this fovereign remedy for all his evils, he difmiffed, with expreffions of kindnefs and gratitude, fuch of his attendants as ftill continued faithful to him; and being left with two of his daughters, who earneftly defired to die with their father, he allowed them to fhare in the draught, he had prepared and faw them expire. But the portion which remained for himfelf not being likely to overcome the vigour of his conftitution, or, as was believed in thofe credulous times, being too powerfully counteracted by the effect of fo many antidotes as he had taken againft poifon, he ordered a faithful flave who attended him, to perform with his fword what was in thofe times accounted the higheft proof, as it was the laft act, of fidelity in a fervant to his mafter.

Accounts of this event were brought to Pompey, while his army was encamped at the diftance of fome days march from the capital of Judea, in his way to Arabia. The meffengers appeared carrying wreaths of laurel on the points of their fpears; and the army, crowding around their general to learn the tidings, were informed of the death of Mithridates. This they received with acclamations, and immediately proceeded to make all the ordinary demonftrations of joy. Pompey

CHAP. XVI.

pey himself, having now accomplished the principal object of the war, dropped his design on Arabia, and directed the march of his army towards Pontus. Here he received the submission of Pharnaces, and, with many other gifts, was presented with the embalmed corpse of the king. The whole army crowded to see it, examined the features and the scars, testifying, by these last effects of their curiosity, the respect which they entertained for this extraordinary man. He had, with short intervals, occupied the arms of the Romans during forty years; and, though he could not bring the natives of Asia to match the legions of Rome, yet he frequently, by the superiority of his own genius, being firm in distress, rose from misfortune with new and unexpected resources. He was tall, and of a vigorous constitution, addicted to women, and, though superior to every other sort of seduction, to this his ardent and impetuous spirit made him a frequent and an easy prey. He appears to have loved and trusted many of that sex with a boundless passion. By some of them he was followed in the field; others he distributed in his different palaces; had many children, and although, even towards his own sons, as well as towards every one else, on occasions which alarmed the jealousy of his crown, he was sanguinary and inexorable, yet in general he appears to have entertained more parental affection than commonly attends the polygamy of Asiatic princes.

Pompey

Pompey proceeded to settle the remainder of his conquests; and, besides the arrangements already mentioned, annexed the kingdom of Pontus to the province of Bithynia, gave the Bosphorus to Pharnaces, and put the province of Syria, extending to the frontier of Egypt, under the government of Scaurus. He had now, from the time of his appointment to succeed Lucullus, for about three years, had the sole direction of the affairs of the Romans in Asia [1]; and had exchanged with the king of Parthia provoking messages, which, in a different conjuncture, might have led to immediate hostilities. But the circumstances were not yet ripe for such a measure, and Pompey had provided sufficient materials for a triumph, without attempting to break through those boundaries on which so many Roman generals were doomed to disappointment, and on which the progress of the empire itself was destined to stop.

Without entertaining any farther projects for the present, he set out with two legions on the route of Cilicia towards Europe, having Tigranes, son to the king of Armenia, together with Aristobulus, late usurper of the Jewish throne, with his family, two sons and two daughters, as captives to adorn his triumph [2].

---

[1] Dion. Cass. lib. xxxvii. c. 6.
[2] Joseph. de Bell. Jud. lib. i. c. 7.

CHAP. XVII.

Growing Corruption of the Roman Officers of State.—The love of Consideration changed for Avarice, Rapacity, and Prodigality.—Laws against extortion.—Cataline a candidate for the Consulship.—Conspiracy with Autronius.—Competition for the Consulate.—Election of Cicero and Antonius.—Condition of the Times.—Agrarian Law of Rullus.—Trial of Rabirius.—Cabals of the Tribunes.—Of Cataline.—His Flight from the City.—Discovery of his Accomplices.—Their Execution.

CHAP. XVII.
U. C. 686.
C. Calpurnius Piso,
M. Aul. Glabrio.

ABOUT the time that Pompey obtained his commission to command with so extensive a power in the suppression of the pirates, the tide began to run high against the aristocratical party at Rome. The populace, led by some of the Tribunes, were ever ready to insult the authority of the Senate; and the vices of particular men gave frequent advantages against the whole order of nobles. Corruption and dangerous faction prevailed at elections, and the preferments of State were generally coveted, as steps to the government of provinces, where fortunes were amassed by every species of abuse, oppression, and violence. Envy and indignation together concurred in rousing the People against these abuses. Cornelius, one of the Tribunes, proposed a severe law against bribery, by which persons convicted of this crime should be disqualified for any office whatever in the commonwealth

lex Cornelia de ambitu.

monwealth. The Senate wifhed to foften the rigour of this law, by limiting the penalty to a pecuniary fine; and the Conful, Calpurnius Pifo, moved for an edict to this purpofe, in order to anticipate and to preclude the more violent law of Cornelius. But the Tribune prevailed, and obtained an act impofing the feverer penalty. He likewife, by another decree of the People, attacked the difcretionary jurifdiction of the Prætors[1], obliged them to be more explicit in the edicts they publifhed, and to obferve them more exactly.

The crime of extortion in the provinces, however, was the great difgrace of the Romans. To have found an effectual remedy for this evil, would have done more honour to the People than they had derived from all their conquefts. Severe laws were accordingly enacted, complaints were willingly received, and profecutions encouraged. Candidates for popularity and public favour, generally began with endeavouring to bring fome offender under this title to public juftice; but the example of this State, after all, has left only this piece of inftruction to mankind; That juft government over conquered provinces is fcarcely to be hoped for, and leaft of all where republics are the conquerors.

Manilius, one of the Tribunes of the People, in order to ftrengthen the inferior clafs of his conftituents, had obtained by furprife an act[2], by which the citizens of flavifh extraction were to be promifcuoufly

[1] Dio. Caff. lib. xxxvi. c. 23.   [2] Ibid. lib. xxxvi.

CHAP. XVII.

Lex Manilia.

miscuously inrolled in all the Tribes. This act, having drawn upon him the resentment of the Senate, compelled him to seek for security under the protection of Gabinius and Pompey. With this view it was that he moved his famous act, in which Cicero concurred, to vest Pompey with the command in Asia. This motion had procured him a powerful support, and on some occasions, raised the general voice of the People in his favour. Insomuch that soon after this transaction, being prosecuted for some offence at the tribunal of Cicero, who was then Prætor, and being refused the usual delays, the Prætor was obliged to explain this step in a speech to the People; in which he told them, that he actually meant to favour Manilius, and that, his own term in office being about to expire, he could not serve him more effectually, than by hastening his trial, and by not leaving him in the power of a successor, who might not be equally disposed to acquit him. Such were the loose and popular notions of justice then prevailing, and the sacrifices made to party at Rome¹.

At the election of Consuls for the following year, there occurred an opportunity to apply the law against bribery. Of four candidates, Publius Autronius Pætus, Publius Cornelius Sylla, L. Aurelius Cotta, and L. Manlius Torquatus, the majority had declared for the former two; but these being convicted of bribery, were set aside, and their competitors declared duly elected.

About

---

¹ Plutarch. in Vit. Cicer.

OF THE ROMAN REPUBLIC.

CHAP. XVII.

About the same time L. Sergius Catalina, who has been already branded as the murderer of his own brother, under pretence of Sylla's proscriptions, having returned from Africa, where he had served in the quality of Prætor, and intending to stand for the Consulate, was accused of extortion in the province, and stopped in his canvas by a prosecution raised on this account. In his rage for this disappointment, he was ripe for any project of horror; and, being readily joined by Autronius and Piso, the late disappointed candidates, formed a conspiracy to assassinate their rivals [1], to massacre the Senate, to seize the ensigns of power, and, with the aid of their faction, to lay hold of the government [2]. Marcus Crassus and Caius Cæsar, are mentioned by Suetonius as accessory to this plot. Crassus was to have been named Dictator, and Cæsar his general of the horse [3]. Cæsar was to have made a signal for beginning the massacre, by uncovering his shoulders of his gown; but Crassus having wavered, absented himself from the Senate, and Cæsar, though present, having made no signal, the occasion passed without the projected attempt.

This is the conspiracy for which Publius Sylla came to be tried as an accomplice, and was defended by Cicero, in a pleading which is still extant; whether Crassus and Cæsar, being, according to Seutonius, implicated in the first steps, afterwards broke off the connection, may be questioned. But it is certain, that the plot was carried

[1] Cic. in P. Sylla & in Catal. i. c. 6. [2] Dion. lib. xxxvi. &c.
[3] Sueton. in Cæsar.

CHAP. XVII.

ried on by the others to its full detection, in the manner which remains to be told. The times indeed were pregnant with the feeds of extreme evil; many of those who, from their outset and prospects, were destined to run the political course, overwhelmed with the effects of prodigality and immoderate expence in their suit to the People, incurred a ruin, which, if successful in their pretensions to office, was to be repaired by odious expedients abroad, or, if disappointed, led them to projects of desperation and rage at home[1].

The State appears to have apprehended an increase of these evils from the number of foreigners, who, from every quarter, crowded to Rome as to the general resort of persons who wished to indulge their own extravagance, or to prey upon that of others. Under this apprehension, an edict was obtained, upon the motion of C. Papius, Tribune of the People, to oblige all strangers to leave the city: but it is likely, that the State was in greater danger from natives than foreigners. Cataline, having prevailed upon Clodius, by the consideration of a sum of money, to drop the prosecution, which had been commenced against him, was left to offer himself a candidate for the Consulate of the following year[2].

Lex Papia de Perigrinis.

The office of Censor had been revived in the persons of Catulus and Crassus; but these officers found that its authority, so powerful in former times, was now greatly reduced. They scarcely ventured to give it a trial within the city; and, having differed about the enrolment of citizens residing

[1] Plutarch. in Vit. Ciceronis.   [2] Cicero de Aurufpicum Responsis.

siding beyond the Po, and about some other particulars, they resigned their power¹. Censors were again named in the following year, but with no greater effect; some of the Tribunes, fearing to be themselves degraded from the Senate, put a negative on the usual function of these officers in revising the rolls ²;

In the next Consulate, that of Lucius Julius Cæsar, and C. Marcius Figulus, Caius Cæsar, accused by Suetonius, as above, of hidden designs, but of whom we are from this time scarcely ever to lose sight, being now thirty-five years of age, entered on his career of popularity and ambition. It is remarked, that in his present Edileship, together with Marcus Bibulus, not satisfied with the joint exhibition of public shews which were given to the People, at a common expence with his colleague, he gave separate entertainments on his own account. And destined, it should seem, to be a thorn in the side of those who were solicitous of public order, the gladiators he had assembled on this occasion gave an alarm to the magistracy, and he was ordered not to exceed a certain number. In his present office, or in that of Prætor, to which he was afterwards in course advanced, it is observed, that he took some steps that were likely to revive the animosity of the late parties of Marius and Sylla; and, notwithstanding the act of indemnity which had passed, raised prosecutions, on a charge of assassination, against all those who had put any citizen to death in execution of Sylla's proscrip-

¹ Dion. lib. xxxvi. Plutarch. in Crasso. ² Ibid.

CHAP.
XVII.
proscription [1]. From this time Suetonius observes, that Cicero, though it may be thought premature, dated the beginning of his project to subvert the republic, and to make himself master of the State [2].

What has most distinguished the present Consulate of Lucius Cæsar, and Marcius Figulus, however, is the competition of candidates for the succession to that office on the following year, and the consequences of the election which followed. The candidates were M. Tullius Cicero, C. Antonius, son of the late celebrated orator, L. Sergius Catalina, P. Sulpitius Galba, and L. Cassius Longinus, Quintus Cornificius, and Licinius Sacerdos.

Cicero was the first of his family who had ever resided, or enjoyed any honours, at Rome. He was a native of Arpinum, a country-town of Italy, and was considered as an obscure person by those who were descended of antient families, but had great consideration on account of his eloquence and the consequences of it, to all such as had any interests at stake before the tribunals of justice. Being solicited by Cataline to undertake his defence on a trial for malversation in Sicily, he did not at once reject the request, nor always deny his aid to the factious Tribunes in support of their measures. He was undoubtedly, like other ambitious men at Rome, disposed to court every party, or to gain individuals [3]; and had of late, in particular,

---

[1] Sueton. in Vit. C. J. Cæsaris.

[2] Ibid. c. ix. Suetonius supposes, that Cicero alluded to the conspiracy of Autronius and Sylla, in which Crassus, as well as Cæsar, was said to be engaged.

[3] Ep. ad Atticum, lib. i. ep. 2.

ticular, confiderably ftrengthened his intereft with the People, by having fupported the pretenfions of their favourite Pompey, in having joined the popular Tribunes, in what they propofed in behalf of this afpiring citizen. He was, notwithftanding, probably by his averfion to appear for fo bad a client as Cataline, faved from the reproach of having efpoufed his caufe; and by his known inclination in general to fupport the authority of the Senate, he difpofed the ariftocratical party to forgive the occafional part which he took with the Tribunes in particular queftions, not immediately fuppofed to affect their afcendant in the State.

In the courfe of this competition for the Conful(hip, Antonius and Cataline joined interefts together, and fpared no kind or degree of corruption. Cicero complained of their practices in the Senate, and moved to revive the law of Calpurnius againft bribery, with an additional penalty of ten years banifhment [1]. Cataline confidered this meafure as levelled againft himfelf; and incited by this provocation, as well as by the animofity of a rival, was then fuppofed to have formed a defign againft Cicero's life, and to have expreffed himfelf to this purpofe, in terms that gave a general alarm to the electors, and determined great numbers againft himfelf. He had drawn to his interefts many perfons of infamous character and defperate fortune, many youths of good family, whom he debauched or encouraged in their profligacy. His language, at their meetings, was all indignation

[1] Dio. lib. xxxvii. c. 39.

dignation at the unequal and supposed unjust distribution of fortune and power. "Riches, authority and honour," he said, "are engrossed by a few, while others of more merit are kept in poverty and obscurity, or oppressed with debts." He professed his intention, when in office, to remove these grievances, to cancel the debts of his friends, to enrich them by plentiful divisions of land, and to place them in the stations of honour to which they were entitled.

These declarations, being made to numerous companies assembled together, could not be concealed. Curius, one of the faction, boasted to Fulvia, a woman of rank, with whom he had a criminal intrigue, that a revolution must soon take place, and specified the particular hopes and designs of their party. This woman mentioned the subject to her own confidents, but concealed the author of her information. In the mean time, Cataline was considered as a person of the most dangerous designs, and was opposed in his election by all who had any regard to public order, or to the safety of the commonwealth. Cicero, at the same time, being supported by the Senate, was elected, together with Caius Antonius. The latter indeed stood candidate upon the same interest with Cataline, and was preferred to him only by a small majority.

U. C. 690. M. Tullius Cicero, C. Antonius.

By this event the designs of Cataline were supposed to be frustrated; but the Consuls were not likely to enter on a quiet administration. The Tribunitian power, from the time of its restoration,

OF THE ROMAN REPUBLIC.

CHAP. XVII.

was gradually recovering its force, and extending its operations. Every perfon that could give any public difturbance, that could annoy the Senate, or mortify any of its leading members; every one that had views of ambition adverfe to the laws, or who wifhed to take part in fcenes of confufion and tumult; every perfon oppreffed with debt, who wifhed to defraud his creditors; every perfon who, by his profligacy or crimes, was at variance with the tribunals of juftice, was comprehended under the general denomination of the popular party. The Roman People had once been divided into Patrician and Plebeian, next into Noblemen and Commoners; but now individuals took their fide with little regard to former diftinctions againft or for the prefervation of public order. In the affembly of the Centuries, as well as in that of the Tribes, the diforderly and the profligate began to prevail; and as it was impoffible that the collective body of the People could meet in any fingle affembly, the comitia, for the moft part, was but another name for fuch riotous tumults, as were made up of the perfons who haunted the ftreets of Rome. The minds of fober men were full of fear and diftruft, alarmed with furmifes of plots, and various combinations of defperate perfons, who united their influence, not to carry elections or obtain preferments, but to overturn the government, or to fhare in its fpoils [1].

One of the Tribunes of the prefent year, Servilius Rullus, foon after his admiffion into office, un-

Lex Servilia Agraria.

[1] Cicero de Lege Agraria.

CHAP. XVII.

der pretence of providing settlements for many of the citizens, promulgated the heads of an Agrarian Law, which he carried to the Senate and the People. The subject of former grants was now in a great measure exhausted, and all Italy was inhabited by the citizens of Rome. This Tribune proposed a new expedient to provide for the indigent, not by conquest, but by purchase. It was proposed, that all estates, territories, or possessions of any sort, which belonged to the republic, should be sold; that all acquisitions of territory recently made, and the spoils taken from any enemy, should be disposed of in the same manner; that the money arising from such sales should be employed in purchasing arable and cultivable lands, to be assigned in lots to the necessitous citizens; and that, to carry this law into execution, ten commissioners should be named in the same manner in which the Pontiffs were named, not by the whole People, but by seventeen of the Tribes selected by lot: that these commissioners should be judges, without appeal, of what was or was not public property; of what was to be sold, of what was to be bought, and at what price; that they were to receive and to judge of the accounts of every Consul, or other officer, except Pompey, commanding in any province, where any capture had been made, or new territory acquired: and in short, that they should, during five years, which was the intended term of their commission, be the sole masters of all property

perty within the empire, whether public or private.

On the day that the new Confuls entered on their office, when they returned in proceffion from the Capitol, and gave the firft meeting to the Senate, Rullus had the prefumption to propofe this law, and to move the Confcript Fathers, that they would be pleafed to give it the fanction of their approbation and authority in being carried to the People. Upon this occafion, Cicero made his firft fpeech in the character of Conful. The former part of it is loft; the remainder may be reckoned among the higheft fpecimens of his eloquence. In this and the two fpeeches he delivered to the People, on the fame fubject, he endeavoured to demonftrate, (if we may venture to imitate the profufion of his own expreffions) that, from the firft claufe of this law to the laft, there was nothing thought of, nothing propofed, nothing done, but the erecting in ten perfons, under the pretence of an Agrarian Law, an abfolute fovereignty over the treafury, the revenue, the provinces, the empire, the neighbouring kingdoms and ftates; and, in fhort, over all the world as far as it was known to the Romans. He painted in fuch lively colours the abufes which might be committed by Rullus, and by his affociates, in judging what was private and what public property, in making fales, in making purchafes, in planting the colonies; and fo expofed the impudence of the cheat, by which it was propofed to furprife the People into the granting

of

of such powers, the absurdity and the ruinous tendency of the whole measure, that it was instantly rejected, and its author hissed from the assembly, and treated as an object of ridicule and scorn.

The splendour of the Consul's eloquence, on this occasion, appeared with great distinction, and the spirit of the times continued to furnish him with opportunities to display it [1]. Roscius Amerinus, having been Tribune of the People a few years before, had, by the authority of his office, set apart some benches in the theatre for the Equestrian order. This gave offence to the People, so that Roscius was commonly hissed when he appeared at any of the public assemblies. On some one of these occasions the Consul interposed; and, in a popular harangue, secured the attachment of the Knights to himself, and even reconciled the People to the distinction which had been made in favour of that body.

There happened under the same Consulate a business of greater difficulty, being a motion to restore the sons of the proscribed to the privilege of being chosen into the offices of State, of which they had been deprived by an ordinance of Sylla. Their fate was undoubtedly calamitous and severe. Many of them who had been too young to have incurred the guilt of their party, were now come of age, and found themselves stript of their birthright,

[1] It is probable that Cicero did not write in order to speak, but wrote after he had spoken, for the use of his friends. Epist. ad Atticum, lib. ii. c. 1.

right, and stigmatized with this mark of dishonour. It was proposed, in their behalf, to take away this cruel exclusion. But Cicero, apprehending that this proposal tended to arm and to strengthen persons, who, from long use, had contracted an habitual disaffection to the established government at Rome, powerfully opposed the motion, and succeeded in having it rejected [1].

Though the orations on the two subjects last mentioned have perished, great part of that which he spoke on the trial of C. Rabirius still remains. This man, of a great age, a respectable Senator, after an interval of six-and-thirty years, was brought to trial as an accomplice in the death of Apuleius Saturninus, the factious Tribune, who, as has been related, having seized the Capitol, was, by the Consuls Marius and Valerius Flaccus, acting under the authority of the Senate, and attended by all the most respectable citizens in arms, forced from his strong-hold, and put to death as a public enemy.

Titus Atius Labienus, one of the Tribunes, was the declared prosecutor of C. Rabirius; but historians agree, that this Tribune acted at the instigation, and under the direction, of C. Cæsar. The intention of the popular party was, by making an example of this respectable person in so strong a case, where the authority of the Senate, and the commands of the most popular Consul, where even the prescription of so old a date should have repelled every danger, effectually, for the future, to deter

[1] Plin. lib. vii, c. 30.

CHAP. XVII. deter every perfon from acting in fupport of the Senate, or from lending any force or oppofition to the defigns of factious Tribunes, however turbulent or dangerous.

The Senate, and all the friends of eftablifhed authority, were greatly alarmed, and united in defence of Rabirius. The popular party, as already defcribed, the ambitious, the profligate, the bankrupt, who were earneft to weaken the hands of government, and in hafte to bring on fcenes of confufion and trouble, took the oppofite fide.

The profecutor laid his charge for treafon of the moft heinous nature, which muft have led the convicted, though a freeman, to die on the crofs, the ordinary manner of executing the fentence of death on flaves. " The executioner ftalks in the " forum," faid Cicero, " and the crofs is erected " for a Roman citizen in the field of Mars." The accufation was firft brought before the Prætor, who poffeffed the ordinary jurifdiction in fuch cafes. And this magiftrate empannelled two judges, who were to determine in this mighty caufe. Thefe were Caius Julius and Lucius Cæfar. At this court the defendant was condemned; and with appearances of animofity on the part of Caius Cæfar, that greatly increafed the public alarm. This rifing citizen had always courted the populace, and was ftrongly fupported by them. That he fhould aim at honours and power, it was faid, is common; but that he wifhed to provide impunity for the difturbers of the commonwealth, was dreadful.

dreadful. The crime of Rabirius, even if he could be convicted of it, had been committed the year before Cæsar was born. In the perfon of the accufed every circumftance, even on the fuppofition of a true charge, pleaded for compaffion, and even for refpect: the fact, at the fame time, was denied, and a pofitive evidence was brought, that another had received a reward for killing Saturninus: but the policy of the faction required this victim; and the fentence muft have been executed, if the condemned had not fled, by appeal, to the judgment of the People, where indeed his caufe might be reckoned more defperate than it had been before a felect court. The parties attended this trial with great ardour. Hortenfius conducted the appeal and defence. Cicero pleaded in behalf of juftice and government; painted the age, the infirmities, the forlorn ftate of the defendant, who had furvived his relations and his friends. He pointed out the danger to government and to order from this precedent, in terms that muft have melted every heart, not callous from ambition, faction, or profligacy of manners: but in vain. Even in the affembly of the Centuries, the majority was haftening to affirm the fentence, when Q. Cæcilius Metellus Celer, then Prætor, and one of the Augurs, haftened to the Janiculum, and tore down the enfign which was planted there as a fign of peace. And a filly piece of fuperftition ftopt the proceedings of thofe whom neither juftice nor compaffion, nor regard to government, could reftrain.

strain. This form took its rise, as has been formerly mentioned[1], in the first ages of Rome, when the enemy inhabiting villages in the neighbourhood were suppofed at the gates, and the people convened in the field on one fide of the city might be affailed on the other. When the Centuries were formed, therefore, in the field of Mars, a guard was always pofted on the Janiculum, and an enfign difplayed. If any enemy appeared, the enfign was taken down, the affembly difmiffed, and the People took to their arms. This ceremony, like many other cuftoms both of fuperftition and law, remained after the occafion had ceafed; and it was held illegal or impious in the People to proceed in any affair without the enfign in view. By this means the trial of Rabirius was put off, and the profecutors, defpairing of being able to work up the People again into an equal degree of violence, dropt the profecution. The caufe ftill remained undecided, and the power of the Senate, to defend its own authority, continued in a ftate of fufpence.

The Tribune Labienus laid afide thoughts of renewing this invidious profecution, in order to purfue the object of fome other more popular acts; one in particular, to repeal the almoft only remaining ordinance of Sylla; that which conferred on the College of Priefts the power of filling up vacancies in their own order. The right of election was again taken from the college, and, according to

[1] See vol. i. c, 1.

to the law of Domitius, given to seventeen of the Tribes, who were to be drawn by lot. This change was intended to open the way of Caius Cæsar into that office; and he was accordingly promoted to it in the following year.

Others of the Tribunes likewise endeavoured to distinguish themselves by acts of turbulence and sedition. Metellus Nepos endeavoured to repeal that clause of the act against bribery and corruption, which declared the party convicted to be disqualified for any of the offices of State. This Tribune, though sufficiently disposed to disorderly courses, had many connections among the most respectable citizens, and was persuaded, in this instance, to drop his design.

But of all the cabals into which the popular faction was distributed, none was more desperate, nor supposed more dangerous, than that of Cataline, the late disappointed candidate for the Consulship. His rival Cicero had intimation, before the elections, of a design formed by this desperate party against his own person, and still continued to observe their motions. For this purpose he entered into a correspondence with a woman of the name of Fulvia, already mentioned, and who had given the first hints of a dangerous conspiracy; by means of this woman, he procured the confidence of Curius, who gave him minute information of all the proceedings of the party.

In public, Cataline again professed himself a candidate for the office of Consul, in competition with

CHAP.
XVII.

with Servius Sulpicius, P. Muræna, and J. Silanus. He boasted of support from Antonius; but Cicero, to divert his colleague from this dangerous connection, made him every concession. Having, in casting lots for the provinces of Gaul and Macedonia, drawn the latter, which was thought to be preferable, he yielded it up to Antonius; and by this, and every other means in his power, persuaded him to rest on the secure possession of dignities and honours, lawfully obtained, in preference to expectations formed on the projects of a few desperate men.

In secret, Cataline encouraged his adherents by pretending to have many resources, and to be supported by numbers who were ready to take arms at his command. In a formal meeting of his party in October, a few days before the Consular elections, he opened the whole of his design; and in the speech which he made on that occasion, is said to have used expressions to the following purport: "The distressed can rely for relief on those "only who have a common cause with themselves. Whoever is at ease in his own fortune, "will not regard the suffering of others. If you "would know how I stand affected to the parties "which now divide the republic, *rich creditors*, "and *needy debtors*, please to consider, what every "one knows, that I have no safety but in the destruction of the one, and in the relief of the "other: that my interest is the same with your own,

"and

" and that I have courage to attempt what may be
" neceſſary for our common relief and ſecurity."

From the ſtrain of this paſſage, the deſcription of a party to whom it was with propriety addreſſed, may be eaſily collected. Cicero, who had frequently taxed Cataline with dangerous deſigns, now determined to lay the whole of his intelligence before the public; and for this purpoſe deferred the Conſular elections, which were to have been held on the eighteenth of October, to a future day, and aſſembled the Senate. Cataline having, with the other members, attended, and hearing the charge, did not pretend to deny or to palliate his words. " There are," he ſaid, " in this " republic, two parties; one weak both in its " members and head; the other ſtrong in its " members, but wanting a head: while I have " the honour of being ſupported by this party, it " ſhall have a head." Upon theſe words, a general cry of indignation aroſe in the Senate; but no reſolution was taken. Many, who were there preſent as members, were pleaſed to ſee the Senate itſelf inſulted; and Cataline, as if in condition to brave all his enemies, was, in all his expreſſions, equally unguarded in the ſtreets and in the Senate. To Cato, who, in the public Forum, ſome days before this meeting, had threatened to have him impeached: " Do," he ſaid; " but if you " light a flame in my fortunes, I will extinguiſh " it under the ruins of the commonwealth [1]."

[1] Cicero Orat. pro Murænа.

CHAP. XVII.

A prosecution was actually raised against him in the name of Lucius Paulus, a young man of distinction, for carrying arms against the public peace. On this occasion, however, he thought proper to soften his tone, and offered to submit to voluntary confinement, until his innocence should be made to appear. "No one," he said, "who knows my rank, my pretensions, and the interest I have in the preservation of the commonwealth, will believe, that its destruction is to be apprehended from me, and that its safety is to come from a native of Arpinum [1]." He offered to commit himself to the custody of Cicero, of Metellus, or of any other magistrate, till this injurious aspersion were removed. To this offer the Consul replied, That he who did not think himself safe within the same ramparts with Cataline, would not receive him into his house [2].

By one effect of the unparalleled licence enjoyed by citizens of Rome, persons accused of the most heinous crimes were at large, during the dependence of their trial, and might either proceed in the execution of their designs, or withdraw from justice. Such was the effect of the laws of Valerius and Porcius, which secured against violence, or the power of the magistrate, the person of every citizen, however accused, until he were finally condemned by the People. In support of this privilege, which was salutary, when the abuse of power in the magistrate

---

[1] The town of which Cicero was native.
[2] Cicero in Catalinam, i. c. 8.

giftrate was more to be dreaded than the licence of crimes in the fubject, the Romans perfifted even after the depravity of manners was become too ftrong for the laws, and when exemption from every juft reftraint was fatally miftaken for liberty. The State had now been thrown, on many occafions, into the moft violent convulfions, becaufe there was not any regular method of refifting diforders, or of fuppreffing them on their firft appearance.

Cataline, foon after the elections, at which, by the preference given to his competitors Muræna and Silanus, he received a frefh difappointment in his hopes of the Confulfhip, fent Mallius, or Manlius, an experienced foldier, who had ferved with himfelf under Sylla, to prepare for an infurrection in the diftrict of Etruria. This officer, in the end of October, under pretence of giving refuge to debtors from the oppreffion of their creditors, had actually affembled a confiderable body of men [1]. Sufpicions at the fame time arofe againft Publius Sylla, who was making a large purchafe of gladiators at Capua, and infurrections were apprehended on the fide of Campania and Apulia. In this ftate of affairs, continual informations being brought of Cataline's defigns, the Senate gave in charge to the Confuls to watch over the fafety of the State; and thefe officers accordingly put chofen bodies of men under arms, and fecured all the pofts of confequence in the city. Metellus, the conqueror of Crete, who ftill remained without the

[1] Cicero in Catalinam, i. c. 3.

the walls in hopes of a triumph, was appointed to command on the fide of Apulia. The Prætor Metellus Celer was fent into the Cifalpine Gaul, in order to fecure the peace of that province [1]; and the Conful Antonius was deftined to fupprefs the infurrection of Mallius at Fæfulæ [2].

Cataline mean while remained in the city, and had frequent confultations for the arrangement and the execution of his plot. At a meeting of the party, held in the beginning of November, in the houfe of M. Porcius Lecca [3], a general maffacre of the principal Senators was projected. The confpirators feverally chofe their ftations, and undertook their feveral parts. Two in particular, who were familiar in Cicero's houfe, undertook in the morning, under pretence of a vifit, to furprife and affaffinate the Conful. But he being the fame night apprifed of his danger by Fulvia, gave the proper orders, and the intended affaffins, upon their appearance at his door, were refufed admittance. He immediately after affembled the Senate in the temple of Jupiter. Cataline prefented himfelf with his ufual prefumption; and Cicero, as appears from an oration which he then delivered, inftead of laying the matter in form before the Senate, accofted Cataline in a vehement invective, urging him to be gone from the city, where all his fteps were minutely obferved, where his meaning was underftood, and precautions taken againft all his

---

[1] Cicero in Cat. i. c. 11.   [2] Now Florence.
[3] Cicero pro Pub. Sylla, c. 16.

his designs. "I told you," said the Conful, "that
" your emiffary Mallius would be in arms by the
" firft of November; that you intended a maffacre
" of the Senators about the fame time. I now re-
" peat the memorable words you made ufe of
" when you were told, that many of the Senators
" had withdrawn from the city. You fhould be
" fatisfied, you faid, with the blood of thofe who
" remained. Were you not furrounded, hemmed
" in, and befet on every fide by the guards pofted
" to watch you? Did your intention to furprife
" Prænefté, on the night of the firft of November,
" efcape me? Did you not find precautions taken
" that implied a knowledge of your defign? There
" is nothing, in fhort, that you do, that you pre-
" pare, that you meditate, which is not heard,
" which is not feen, which is not felt by me in
" every circumftance. What of laft night? Were
" you not at the houfe of Porcius Lecca? Deny
" it! I have evidence. There are here prefent
" perfons who were of your company. But where
" are we? What manner of government or re-
" public is this? The enemies and deftroyers of
" the commonwealth make a part in its higheft
" councils! We know them, and yet they are fuf-
" fered to live! But, be gone. The time of en-
" during you is paft. The world is convinced of
" your guilt. Stay only till there is not a fingle
" perfon that can pretend to doubt of it; till your
" own partizans muft be filent, and till the cla-
" mour, which they would willingly raife againft

" every

"every neceffary act of government, be fuppref-
"fed."

This being the general tendency of the Conful's fpeech, fraught with fuch alarming matter, and urged with fo much confidence, the audience was feized with terror, and numbers, who happened to be on the fame bench with Cataline, withdrew from his fide. He himfelf arofe, and attempted to vindicate his character, but was filenced with a general cry of indignation; upon which he left the Senate; and, after concerting farther meafures with thofe of his party, not thinking that a longer ftay in the city could be of any ufe to his affairs, he withdrew in the night, leaving letters behind him to fome of the Senators, in which he complained, that, by a combination of his enemies, he was driven into exile; and that, rather than be the occafion of any difturbance in the commonwealth, he was willing to retire. While thefe letters were handed about in the city, he took his way, preceded by the ufhers and enfigns of a Roman Proconful, ftraight for the camp of Mallius, and entered into a ftate of open war. The features of this man's portrait are poffibly exaggerated by the vehement pencils and lively colourings of Cicero and of Salluft. He is reprefented as able to endure hardfhips of any kind, and as fearlefs in any danger; as, from his youth, fond of difcord, affaffinations, and bloodfhed; as ftained with the blood of his own brother, whom he murdered to have his eftate, and with the blood of his own child,
whom

whom he murdered, to remove the objection made to him by a woman who refused to marry him with the profpect of being a ftep-mother. He is reprefented as rapacious, prodigal, gloomy, impetuous, unquiet, diffembling, and perfidious; a defcription, of which the horrors are probably amplified: but for which it cannot be doubted there was much foundation, as he far exceeded in profligacy and defperation all thofe who, either in this or the former age, were, by their ambition or their vices, haftening the ruin of the commonwealth.

Cicero always profeffed to have particular information of the progrefs of Cataline. This, according to Salluft, he owed to Fulvia, by whofe means he obtained a correfpondence with Curius; but he himfelf, in none of his orations, gives any intimation of the manner in which he obtained his intelligence. It is probable that Curius defired to be concealed, that he might not be expofed to the rage of the confpirators as an informer and a traitor. On this account the Conful, although he was minutely apprifed of particulars, was obliged to adopt the plan he had hitherto followed, to urge the confpirators themfelves into open hoftilities, and into a full declaration of their purpofe. He had fuccceded with refpect to Cataline; but his accomplices were yet very numerous in the city, and were taking their meafures to co-operate with thofe who were in arms abroad.

In this ftate of affairs Fabius Sanga, a Roman citizen of diftinction, came to the Conful, and informed

CHAP. XVII.

formed him, that the ambaſſadors of the Allobroges, a people then inhabiting what is now called the territory of Geneva, and part of Savoy, whoſe patron he was, had made him privy to a very momentous affair; that, upon being diſappointed in a ſuit, on which they had been employed to the Senate, they had been carried by P. Umbrenus to Publius Cornelius Lentulus the Prætor, who condoled with them on the ſubject of the wrong they had received, aſſured them of redreſs if they would merit the favour of thoſe who were ſoon to have the aſcendant at Rome; and propoſed, that they ſhould immediately, upon their return to their own country, prevail on their nation to be prepared with an army, to co-operate with their friends in Italy. Cicero immediately laid hold of this intelligence, as affording means to bring the plot to light, in a proper manner, and with ſufficient evidence, to convict the conſpirators. He deſired Sanga to encourage this correſpondence; to adviſe the ambaſſadors to require proper credentials to be ſhown to their countrymen; to procure a liſt of the Roman citizens who, in caſe they ſhould riſe in rebellion againſt the Romans, were to become bound to protect them; and when they ſhould be thus provided, and about to depart, he inſtructed Sanga to bring him intimation of their motions, that they might be ſecured, with their writings, and other evidence of the facts to be aſcertained. Sanga, having inſtructed the ambaſſadors accordingly, gave notice of their

motions

motions to the Consul. In the evening before they were to depart, Cicero ordered the Prætors, L. Flaccus and C. Pontinus, to march by different ways, and in small parties, after it was dark, to place a sufficient armed force to intercept the ambassadors of the Allobroges. The parties were stationed on different sides of the river, at the bridge called Milvius, without knowing of each other, and without having any suspicion of the purpose for which they were posted, farther than arose from their having been told, that they were to seize any person who should attempt to pass in either direction. About three o'clock in the morning the ambassadors from the Roman side entered on the bridge with a numerous retinue; and being challenged, and commanded to stop by the party that was placed to intercept them, they endeavoured to force their way; and some blood was shed. But on the appearance of the Prætors, with their ensigns of office, the travellers ceased to resist. Their dispatches were secured. Volturcius, a Roman citizen, who was found in their company, was taken and searched. Letters were found upon him, in different hands, and under different seals, addressed to Cataline. These, together with the prisoners, were immediately carried back to the city.

The Consul being apprised of the success which attended this part of his design, sent, before any alarm could be taken by the party, messages to Gabinius, Statilius, Cethegus, and Lentulus, desiring to see them at his own house. The three former

mer came with the messenger; but Lentulus was newly gone to bed, and, by his delay, gave some cause to suspect that he was aware of his danger. He too, however, came before it was day; and the house of Cicero was presently crowded, not only with numbers of the Equestrian order that were in arms for the defence of his person, but likewise with many Senators whom he desired to be present. The ambassadors of the Allobroges, now prisoners, were likewise conducted thither, and the letters found in their possession, were produced unopened. Cicero declared his intention to assemble the Senate without delay, in order to lay the whole matter before them. Many of the company were of opinion, that the letters should be first opened, in order to see, whether they contained any matter of so much moment, as to require assembling the Senate, at a time when so great an alarm was likely to be taken. Cicero, however, having no doubt of the contents of the letters, and of the importance of the matter, over-ruled those scruples, and the Senate was accordingly called. Mean time the Allobroges dropt some expressions which implied, that some arms were concealed in the house of Cethegus. This occasioned a search being then made, and a considerable quantity of daggers and swords were accordingly found.

At the meeting of the Senate, Volturcius was first examined; he denied his knowledge of any treasonable designs, but appeared disconcerted; and, upon being reminded of the reward that had been

been offered for the discovery of any plot against the State, and of the danger to which he himself would be exposed in prevaricating, he confessed, that the letters seized in his custody were sent by the Prætor Lentulus and others: that he had besides a verbal message to Cataline, informing him, that the plan was now ready for execution; that the station of every person was assigned; that some were appointed to set fire to the city in different places, and some to massacre their enemies in the midst of the confusion that was likely to be occasioned by the fire; and desiring that Cataline, in order to support his friends, and to profit by the diversion they were to make in his favour within the walls, should issue a proclamation to arm the slaves, and that he himself should march directly to Rome.

The deputies of the Allobroges being next introduced, acknowledged, that they had been charged by Lentulus, Cethegus, Statilius, and Cassius, with assurances of support to the council of their nation, confirmed by oath, accompanied with directions to march, without delay, a body of horse into Italy, where they should be joined by a numerous infantry, and receive proper instructions in what manner they should farther proceed: that, to encourage them, Lentulus quoted a prophecy, found in the collection of the Sibyls, by which he himself was pointed out as the third of the Cornelii[1] destined to arrive at the sovereignty of Rome: that

---

[1] The former two were Cinna and Sylla.

CHAP. XVII.

that the conspirators had differed about the time of executing their design. Lentulus was of opinion it should be deferred to the holy-days in December; that Cethegus, notwithstanding, and the others, were impatient, and desired a nearer day.

The supposed conspirators were next called in their turns; and the letters, with the seals unbroken, were exhibited before them. Cethegus, being the first examined, persisted in denying his knowledge of any conspiracy; accounted for the arms which were found in his house, by saying, He was curious of workmanship of that nature, and always bought what he liked. He preserved his countenance undisturbed, till his own letter was produced, and then fell into great confusion, as the seal was immediately known to be his.

Lentulus next, with great confidence, denied the charge; affected not to know either Volturcius or the ambassadors; asked them upon what occasion they ever could pretend to have been admitted into his house? He, however, supposing that nothing in the contents of the letter that was now produced could convict him, acknowledged the seal. It was the head of his grandfather. But the letter being opened, was found to be unsigned, and in the following general terms: " The bearer will inform you who I am. Fear nothing. Remember where you stand; and neglect nothing. Call in every aid, even the meanest." While he persisted in his denial, some one asked him, If he had never quoted the Sybilline oracles

to

to these Gauls? Confounded with this question, he forgot his disguise, and confessed.

Gabinius too was at last brought to own his guilt; and in this manner the conspiracy was fully laid open. Lucius Cæsar, the Consul of the former year, in the presence of Lentulus, who was married to his sister, gave his opinion, that this unhappy man should be immediately put to death. " This," he said, " is no unprecedented mea" sure. My grandfather, Fulvius Flaccus, taken in " open rebellion as this man is, was slain by " order of the Consul Gabinius. His son was ta" ken into custody and put to death in prison." In the mean time Lentulus was ordered to divest himself of the office of Prætor, and, together with his accomplices, was committed to close imprisonment. This Cornelius Lentulus was distinguished by the addition of Sura to his name. He had been Consul about eight years before, and was afterwards, for his debaucheries, struck off the rolls of the Senate. He had now again condescended to accept of the office of Prætor, in order to recover, in the capacity of a magistrate, his seat in the Senate.

A proclamation was issued to apprehend M. Cæparius, who had been sent to procure an insurrection in Apulia, together with P. Furius, Magius Chilo, and P. Umbrenus, who had first introduced the Gaulish ambassadors to Gabinius. The Senate voted thanks to the Consul Cicero for his great vigilance, and for the consummate ability he had shewn in the discovery and suppression of this

treasonable

CHAP. treafonable defign; to the Prætors, for the faithful
XVII. execution of the Conful's orders; and to Antonius, his colleague, for having detached himfelf from men with whom he was known to have been formerly connected. A public thankfgiving to the gods was likewife decreed in honour of the Conful, and in confideration of this deliverance of the city from fire, of the People from maffacre, and of Italy from devaftation and war.

An affembly of the People being called, Cicero gave this account of the proceedings of the Senate, in a fpeech which is ftill extant [1], and early on the following day affembled that body again, to deliberate on the farther refolutions to be taken with refpect to the prifoners. An agent had been bufy in the night to raife fome difturbance in favour of Lentulus; but the defign of fetting fire to the city gave fo great an alarm, that not only fuch as were poffeffed of confiderable property, but every inhabitant, whatever might be his effects, trembled for his own perfon, and for the fafety of his houfe. The avenues to the Senate, the Capitol, the Forum, all the Temples in the neighbourhood, by break of day, were crowded with armed men. The Conful had fummoned the Equeftrian order in arms to fupport the government, and citizens of every rank came forth to have a part in what might be required for the fafety of their families.

When the Senate was affembled, the members differed in their judgment. Junius Silanus, one of the Confuls-elect, being called up firft in order, declared

[1] In Cat. 3.

clared himself for a sentence of death. Tiberius Nero differed from him, and proposed perpetual imprisonment. The majority, however, joined Silanus, until Caius Cæsar spoke. This able advocate declared against the opinion of Silanus, not as too severe, but as contrary to law; and insisted on the danger of a precedent which might set the life of every citizen at the mercy of a vote in the Senate. Death, he said, was the common destination of all men; what no one could avoid, and what the wise frequently coveted. It was not, therefore, to be used as a punishment; and he was disposed, in this case, not to mitigate, but to increase, the severity of the sentence. He proposed, therefore, that the estates of the prisoners should be confiscated; that their persons should be committed for life to the keeping of the most secure and best affected corporations in Italy; and that it should be declared treason for any one hereafter to move the Senate or the People for any mitigation of their punishment.

Cæsar might be considered as appearing on the side of the popular faction, and as laying the ground upon which the proceedings of the Senate, and the conduct of any particular member, might be afterwards arraigned before the People. The terrors of the Porcian and Sempronian laws, when likely to be urged by so powerful an advocate, alarmed the greater part of the Senate. Silanus himself retracted his opinion. In this fluctation the Consul submitting the question to the judgement

ment of the Senate, for his own part declared his willingness to execute any decree they should form. He treated Cæsar with great respect, and with some art laid hold of the severe terms in which this popular citizen had spoken of the conspiracy, as a pledge of his future conduct, in case the proceedings of government, with respect to the matter now before them, should hereafter be questioned or brought under review. "The Senate," he observed, "had
"no cause to dread the imputation of cruelty. It
"was mercy to prevent, in the most effectual man-
"ner, a crime to be perpetrated in so much blood.
"If this crime were not prevented, they were to
"see that city, the resort of nations, and the light
"and ornament of empire, perish at one blow.
"They were to see heaps of her citizens unbu-
"ried, and lying in their blood: they were to see
"the fury of Cethegus let loose in murder; to
"see Lentulus become a king, Cataline command-
"ing an army, and every where to hear the cries
"of mothers, to see the flight of children, and the
"rape of virgins.—If the father of a family,"
he continued, "should spare a slave who had shed
"the blood of his children, who had murdered
"his wife, and set fire to his dwelling, how should
"such a father be considered—as cruel, or as void
"of affection?

"He desired them not to regard what was given
"out, of their not being in condition to attempt
"any thing vigorous against these men. He him-
"self, as first magistrate, had not neglected the
"necessary

OF THE ROMAN REPUBLIC.

"necessary precautions; and the general ardour with which all ranks of men concurred in the defence of their families, their properties, and the seat of empire, rendered every resolution they could take secure of the utmost effect. The forum is full, all the temples in its neighbourhood are full, all the streets and avenues to this place of assembly are full of citizens of every denomination, armed for the defence of their country. But he requested that the Senate would issue their orders before the sun went down, and seemed to apprehend dangerous consequences, if these matters were left undetermined, and the city exposed to the accidents of the following night. For himself, he professed to have taken his resolution. Although he felt the occasion full of personal danger, he would execute the orders of the conscript fathers," he said; "but, if he fell in the attempt, implored their protection for his wife and his children¹."

All this appears to have passed in debate before Cato spoke. This virtuous citizen, then about thirty-three years of age, had, in the former part of his life, taken a very different course from the youths of his own time, and, both by his temper and education, was averse to the libertine principles which had crept into the politics and the manners of the age. He spoke chiefly in answer to Caius Cæsar, who, he observed, seemed to mistake

---

1 Cicero in Catalinam, orat. iv.

take the question. "We are not enquiring," he said, "what is the proper punishment of a crime "already committed, but how we may defend the "republic from an imminent danger with which "it is threatened. It is proposed to send the pri- "soners to safe keeping in the country. Why "into the country? Because perhaps the faction "of profligate citizens is more numerous in Rome, "and may rescue them. Is Rome the only place "to which profligate men may resort, or are pri- "soners of State most secure where the force of "government is least? This proposal is surely an "idle one, if the author of it professes to entertain "any fear of these men. But if, in this general "alarm of all the city, he and such persons be not "afraid, so much the more cause have we to be "on our guard. We are beset with enemies, "both within and without the walls. While Ca- "taline with fire and sword is hastening to your "gates, you hesitate, whether you will cut off or "spare his associates, who are taken with the torch "in their hands and the dagger at your breast! "You must strike those who are now in your "power, if you mean to intimidate those who are "coming to support their designs. The remiss- "ness or the vigour which you now show, will "be felt in the camp of Cataline, and will be at- "tended with suitable effects. I am therefore of "opinion, that we order these men, agreeably to "the practice which our ancestors have followed

"in

OF THE ROMAN REPUBLIC.

"in all cafes of treafon and of open war againſt the commonwealth, to immediate death."

Such is faid to have been the fpeech of Cato, by which the Senate was determined in the very momentous refolution which was taken on the prefent occafion; and however little we may be inclined to confider fuch compofitions in many parts of ancient hiſtory as records of fact, much credit is due to this reprefentation, as it is given by a perfon who himſelf became a partizan of Cæ-far, and as the words which he aſcribed to thefe fpeakers muſt have come in the perufal of his work under the infpection of many who were prefent to the delivery of them[1]. The execution of the prifoners was accordingly determined, and Cornelius Lentulus, in the beginning of the following night, was, by order of the Conful, committed to a vaulted dungeon under ground, and ſtrangled. His accomplices had the fame fate; and the minds of men, though fomewhat quieted of their fears, were nevertheleſs ſtunned with the fcene, and beheld with amazement a Patrician of the Cornelian family, of the firſt rank in the commonwealth, who himſelf had been Conful, fuffering, without any formal trial, by the hands of the common executioner of juſtice [2].

[1] The more credit is due to this account of Cæfar's and of Cato's fpeech, that the fpeech which is afcribed to Cicero by the fame hiftorian, is a faithful extract, or contains the purport of the oration which ſtill remains among his works.

[2] Saluſt. Bell. Catal. Cur ergo in fententiam Catonis? quia verbis luculentioribus et pluribus, rem eandem comprehenderat. Cicer. ad Atticum, lib. xii. epiſt. 21.

CHAP. XVII.

While these things were in agitation at Rome, Cataline was endeavouring to augment his force in the field. He found about two thousand men under Mallius. These he formed into two legions, and as his party increased he completed their numbers. He refused for some time to enrol the fugitive slaves, of whom many took refuge in his camp; thinking it would discredit and weaken his cause to rest any part of it on this support. But the freemen that joined him being ill armed, he was obliged to keep in the neighbourhood of the mountains, and frequently to change his ground, to avoid an engagement with the Consul; and he endeavoured to gain time, in hopes that, the intended blow being struck at Rome, a general defection of the opposite party would ensue. But when accounts came that his design had failed in the city, and that his principal associates were no more, those who were inclined to his cause were discouraged, and numbers who had already joined him began to fall off; he determined to remove to a distance from his enemies; and for this purpose directed his march to a pass in the Apennines, by which he might escape into Gaul. This design the Prætor Metellus had foreseen, made a forced march to prevent the effect of it, and Cataline at last, finding himself beset on every quarter, determined to hazard a battle. Of the armies that were in the field against him, he chose to face that of Antonius; either because it lay on his route to Rome, and, if defeated or removed, might open

open his way to the city, or becaufe he hoped to meet in the commander of it fome remains of inclination in his favour. In whatever degree thefe hopes were at firft reafonably conceived, they ceafed to have any foundation; as Antonius, being taken ill, had left the army under the command of Petreius. With this commander Cataline engaged in battle, and, after many efforts of valour and of conduct, fell, with the greater part of his followers, and thus delivered the State from a defperate enemy, whofe power was happily not equal to his defigns, and who has owed much of his celebrity to the orator and the hiftorian, who have made him the fubject of their eloquent compofitions. Salluft appears to have been fo intent on raifing and finifhing particular parts of his work, that he neglected the general order of his narrative. I have, therefore, in moft parts of the relation, preferred the authority of Cicero to his. This great man was undoubtedly beft informed, and he refted fo much of his reputation on this tranfaction, that he lofes no opportunity of returning to it, and in different parts of his writings, when collected, has furnifhed a pretty full narration of circumftances refpecting the origin and termination of this wild and profligate attempt to fubvert the government of the republic.

CHAP. XVIII.

Character of the Times.—Philosophy.—Opposite Tenets and Votaries.—Proceedings of the Senate.—Tribunate of Metellus, Nepos, and of Cato.—Proposal to recal Pompey at the head of his Army frustrated.—His arrival in Italy.—And Triumph.

IT may appear strange, that any age or nation should have furnished the example of a project conceived in so much guilt, or of characters so atrocious as those under which the accomplices of Cataline are described by the eloquent orator and historian [1], from whose writings the circumstances of the late conspiracy are collected. The scene, however, in this republic was such as to have no parallel, either in the past or in the subsequent history of mankind. There was less government, and more to be governed, than has been exhibited in any other instance. The inhabitants of Italy, as citizens of Rome, were become masters of the known world. They pretended to govern in a body, but it was impossible they ever could meet in a fair and adequate convention. They were represented, therefore, by partial meetings or occasional tumults in the capital; and to take the sense of the People on many a subject, was little better than to occasion a riot. Individuals were vested with powers almost discretionary in the provinces,

[1] Cicero in Sallust.

vinces, or continually aspired to such situations. At home they were impatient of government, and in haste to govern. Ruined in their fortunes by private prodigality, or by the public expence in soliciting honours; tempted to repair their ruins by oppression and extortion where they were intrusted with command; or by desperate attempts against the government of their country, if disappointed in their hopes of sharing its profits. Not only were many of the prevailing practices disorderly, but the law itself was erroneous [1]; adopted indeed at first by a virtuous people, because it secured the persons and the rights of individuals against the possibility of injustice, but now anxiously preserved by their posterity, because it gave a licence to their crimes.

The provinces were to be retained by the forces of Italy; the Italians themselves by the ascendant of the capital; and in this capital all was confusion and anarchy, except where the Senate, by its authority and the wisdom of its councils, prevailed. It was no doubt expedient for the People to restrain abuses of the aristocratical power; but when they assumed the government into their own hands, or when the sovereignty was exercised in the name of the collective body, abuses were multiplied,

---

[1] Lex Valeria & Porcia de tergo Civium lata. Liv. lib. ii. c. 8. lib. iii. c. 55. lib. x. c. 9. By these laws a Roman citizen could not be imprisoned any more than suffer punishment, before conviction; he might stop any proceeding against himself by an appeal to the People; and, being at large during his trial, might withdraw whenever he perceived the sentence likely to be given against him.

tiplied, and the confusion or anarchy which prevailed at Rome spread from one extremity of her dominion to the other. The provinces were oppressed, not upon a regular plan to aggrandize the State, but at the pleasure of individuals, to enrich a few of the most outrageous and profligate citizens. The People, under pretence of exerting their own powers, were perpetually violating the laws which had been made to restrain usurpations; and the public interests and the order of the State were in perpetual struggle with the pretensions of demagogues, or of single and profligate men. In such a situation there were many temptations to be wicked; and in such a situation likewise, minds that were turned to integrity and honour had a proportionate spring and scope to their exertions and pursuits. The range of the human character was great and extensive, and men were not likely to trifle within narrow bounds; they were destined to be good or to be wicked in the highest measure, and, by their struggles, to exhibit a scene interesting and instructive beyond any other in the history of mankind.

Among the causes that helped to carry the characters of men in this age to such distant extremes, may be reckoned the philosophy of the Greeks, which was lately come into fashion, and which was much affected by the higher ranks of men in the State [1]. Literature, by the difficulty and expence

[1] Vid. Cicero's Philosophical Works.

pence of multiplying copies of books [1], being confined to perfons having wealth and power, it was confidered as a diftinction of rank, and had its vogue not only as an ufeful, but as a fafhionable accomplifhment [1]. The leffons of the fchool were admitted as the elements of every liberal and active profeffion, and they were quoted at the bar, in the field, in the Senate, and every where in the conduct of real affairs. Philofophy was confidered as an ornament, as well as a real foundation of ftrength, ability and wifdom, in the practice of life. Men of the world, inftead of being afhamed of their fect, affected to employ its language on every important occafion, and to be governed by its rules fo much as to affume, in compliance with particular fyftems, diftinctions of manners, and even of drefs. They embraced their forms in philofophy, as the fectaries in modern times have embraced theirs in religion; and probably in the one cafe honoured their choice by the fincerity of their faith and the regularity of their practice, much in the fame degree as they have done in the other.

In thefe latter times of the Roman republic the fect of Epicurus appears to have prevailed; and what Fabricius, on hearing rehearfed the tenets of this philofophy, wifhed for the enemies of Rome, had now befallen her citizens [2]. Men were glutted

[1] The grandees had their flaves fometimes educated to ferve as fecretaries to themfelves, or as preceptors to their children.

[2] See Plutarch, in Pyrr. The philofopher Cyneas, in the hearing of Fabricius, entertained his prince with an argument, to prove that pleafure was the chief good. Fabricius wifhed that the enemies of Rome might long entertain fuch tenets.

glutted with national prosperity; they thought that they were born to enjoy what their fathers had won, and saw not the use of those austere and arduous virtues by which the State had increased to its present greatness. The votaries of this sect ascribed the formation of the world to chance, and denied the existence of Providence. They resolved the distinctions of right and wrong, of honour and dishonour, into mere appellations of pleasure and pain. Every man's pleasure was to himself the supreme rule of estimation and of action. All good was private. The public was a mere imposture, that might be successfully employed, perhaps to defraud the ignorant of their private enjoyments, while it furnished the conveniences of the wise[1]. By persons so instructed, the care of families and of states, with whatever else broke in upon the enjoyments of pleasure and ease, were classed among the follies of human life. And a sect under these imputations might be considered as patrons of licentiousness, both in morality and religion, and declared enemies to mankind. Yet the Epicureans, when urged in argument by their opponents, made some concessions in religion, and many more in morality. They admitted the existence of gods, but supposed those beings of too exalted a nature to have any concern in the affairs of men. They owned that, although good and pleasure were synonymous terms, yet, among the varieties of pleasure, those of virtue were the chief,

[1] Cicero in Pisonem.

OF THE ROMAN REPUBLIC.

chief. A conceſſion after which they ought to have ſaid that virtue or the chief pleaſure was alſo the chief good; yet they ſtill returned to the general appellation of pleaſure, at the hazard of miſleading the vulgar and even themſelves in their choice [1]; and while they contended that their difference with other ſects conſiſted in a mere diſpute about words, thoſe they were pleaſed to employ, ſerved to ſuppreſs the ſpecific ſentiments of conſcience and elevatoin of mind, and to change the reproaches of criminality, profligacy, or vileneſs, by which even bad men are reſtrained from iniquity, into mere imputations of miſtake, or variations of taſte.

Other ſects, particularly that of the Stoicks, maintained, almoſt in every particular, the reverſe of theſe tenets. They maintained the reality of Providence, and of a common intereſt of goodneſs and of juſtice, for which Providence was exerted, and in which all rational creatures were deeply concerned. They maintained, that although it be evident that happineſs or the chief good is pleaſant; yet it were abſurd converſely to ſay, that every pleaſure is happineſs or the chief good. In the

---

[1] Even the leader of this ſect himſelf, though more pure in the choice of his pleaſure than many of his followers, yet was far from being regulated in the choice he made by the more important occaſions of human life. To him the rearing of a family, without which the human race muſt ſpeedily periſh; the offices of State, without which ſociety cannot exiſt; were not only ſuperfluous, but expreſsly precluded from the choice of a wiſe man. His virtue was to be found in the peaceful retirement of a garden, in exemption from pain or trouble, in contemplation and ſerenity of mind, in the ſociety of a few ſelect friends, with ſobriety and moderation of diet, and other ſenſualities.

CHAP. XVIII. the application of these terms we must attend to the exemption from suffering, as well as the measure of enjoyment; and as our understanding cannot reach every possible effect upon which to estimate the least measure of pain, and the greatest of pleasure, Providence has not left us to the effect of such a discussion: we are taught to choose, on the first inspection of things, the part of the innocent, of the praise-worthy and just: Of this choice the pleasure is most delightful, and the sense of having failed in it, the most grievous pain; in so much, that although in the nature of things there are many grounds upon which we prefer or reject the objects that present themselves to us, yet the choice which we make, and our own actions, not the event of our efforts, decides our happiness or our misery; that right and wrong are the most important and the only grounds upon which we can at all times safely proceed in our choice, and that, in comparison to this difference, every thing else is of no account; that a just man will ever act as if there was nothing good but what is right, and nothing evil but what is wrong; that the Epicureans mistook human nature when they supposed all its principles resolvable into appetites for pleasure, or aversions to pain; that honour and dishonour, excellence and defect, were considerations which not only led to much nobler ends, but which were of much greater power in commanding the human will; the love of pleasure was groveling and vile, was the source of dissipation and

of

of sloth; the love of excellence and honour was aspiring and noble, and led to the greatest exertions and the highest attainments of our nature. They maintained that there is no private good separate from the public; that the same qualities of the understanding and the heart, wisdom, benevolence, and courage, which are good for the individual, are so likewise for the public; that these blessings every man may possess, independent of fortune or the will of other men; and that, whoever does possess them has nothing to hope, and nothing to fear, and can have but one sort of emotion, that of satisfaction and joy; that his affections, and the maxims of his station, as a creature of God, and as a member of society, lead him to act for the good of mankind; and that for himself he has nothing more to desire, than the happiness of acting this part. These, they said, were the tenets of reason leading to a perfection, which ought to be the aim of every person who means to preserve his integrity, or to consult his happiness, and towards which every one may advance, although no one has actually reached it.

In these disputes the celebrated fable of Prodicus seemed to be realized; and as virtue and pleasure there contended for the ear of youth, integrity and corruption now strove for acceptance with a pampered and restless people.

Among those on whom the public fortune seemed to depend, Cæsar is said to have embraced the doctrines of Epicurus; Cato those of Zeno. The first,

first, from indifference to moral distinctions, in compliance with fashion, or from the bias of an original temper. The other, from the force of conviction, as well as from the predilection of a warm and ingenuous mind. When such characters occur together, it is impossible not to see them in contrast. And Sallust in relating what passed in the Senate, on the subject of the Cataline conspiracy, seems to overlook every other character, to dwell upon these alone. Cæsar, at the time when this historian flourished, had many claims to his notice [1]; but Cato could owe it to nothing but the force of truth. He was distinguished from his infancy by an ardent and affectionate disposition. This part of his character is mentioned on occasion of his attachment to his brother Cæpio, and the vehement sorrow with which he was seized at his death. It is mentioned, on occasion of his visit to the Dictator Sylla, when he was with difficulty restrained, by the discretion of his tutor, from some act or expression of indignation against this real or apparent violator of public justice. He had from his infancy, according to Plutarch, a resolution, a steadiness, and a composure of mind, not to be moved by flattery, nor to be shaken by threats. Without fawning or insinuation, he was the favourite of his companions, and had, by his unaffected generosity and courage, the principal place in their confidence. Though in appearance stern and

---

[1] Sallust attached himself to Cæsar, and was employed by him in the civil wars.

and inflexible, he was warm in his affections, and zealous in the cause of innocence and justice. Such are the marks of an original temper, affixed by historians as the characters of his infancy and early youth. So fitted by nature, he imbibed with ease an opinion, that profligacy, cowardice, and malice, were the only evils to be feared; courage, integrity, and benevolence, the only good to be coveted; and that the proper care of a man on every occasion is, not what is to happen to him, but what he himself is to do. With this profession he became a striking contrast to many of his contemporaries; and to Cæsar in particular, not only a contrast, but a resolute opponent; and although in these times he could not furnish a sufficient counterpoise, yet he afforded always much weight to be thrown into the opposite scale. They were both of undaunted courage, and of great penetration; the one to distinguish what was best; the other to avail himself of the most effectual means for the attainment of any end on which he was bent. It were to mistake entirely the scene in which they were engaged, to judge of their abilities from the event of their different pursuits. Those of Cato were by their nature in direct opposition to the current of manners, and they were a series of struggles with almost insurmountable difficulties: those of Cæsar went with the stream, and except when he was jostled in the competition with others who ran the same course with himself, he had only to seize the advantages of which the

vices

vices and weaknesses of the times gave him an easy possession. Cato endeavoured to preserve the order of civil government, however desperate, because this was the part it became him to act, and in which he chose to live and to die. Cæsar hastened its ruin; because he was eager for power, and wished to dispose of all the wealth and honours of the State at his own discretion.

Cæsar, as versatile in his genius, as Cato was steady and inflexible, could personate any character, and support any cause; in debate he could derive his arguments from any topic; from topics of pity, of which he was insensible; from topics of justice and public good, for which he had no regard. His vigour in resisting personal insults or attacks appeared in his early youth, when he withstood the imperious commands of Sylla to part with his wife, the daughter of Cinna, and when he revenged the violence done by the pirates to himself; but while his temper might be supposed the most animated and warm, he was not involved in business by a predilection for any of the interests on which the People was divided. So long as the appetites of youth were sufficient to occupy him, he saw every object of State, or of faction, with indifference, and took no part in public affairs. But even in this period, by his application and genius, in both of which he was eminent, he made a distinguished progress in letters and eloquence. When he turned his mind to objects of ambition, the same personal vigour which appeared in his youth, became still more conspicuous; but,

but, unfortunately, this paffion, the moft energe- tic and powerful in the human mind, inftead of urging to genuine greatnefs, and elevation of nature, was in him a mere principle of competition among the leaders of faction at Rome. He had attained to feven-and-thirty years of age before he took any confiderable part as a member of the commonwealth. He then courted the populace in preference to the Senate or better fort of the People, and made his firft appearance in fupport of the profligate, againft the forms and authority of government. With perfons of defperate fortune and abandoned manners, he early bore the characters of liberality and friendfhip; was received among them as a generous fpirit, come to explode the morofe feverity of thofe who would reftrain the freedom of youth within the limits of fobriety and public order. Though himfelf a perfon of the greateft abilities, and the moft accomplifhed talents, having an opportunity to live on terms of equality with the greateft men that have yet appeared in the world, he chofe to ftart up as the chief among thofe who, being abandoned to every vice, faw the remains of virtue in their country with diftafte and averfion. In proportion as he emerged from the avocations of pleafure, or from the floth which accompanies the languor of diffipation, his defire to counteract the eftablifhed government of his country, and to make himfelf mafter of the commonwealth, became more and more evident. To this paffion he facrificed every fen- timent

CHAP.
XVIII.
timent of friendship or animosity, of honour, interest, resentment, or hatred. The philosophy which taught men to look for enjoyment indiscriminately wherever it pleased them most, found a ready acceptance in such a disposition. But while he possibly availed himself of the speculations of Epicurus to justify his choice of an object, he was not inferior to the followers of Zeno, in vigorous efforts and active exertions for the attainment of his ends. Being about seven years younger than Pompey, and three years older than Cato; the first he occasionally employed as a prop to his own ambition, or at least, in the early part of his career, did not seem to perceive him as a rival; the other, from a fixed animosity of opposite natures, and from having felt him as a continual opponent in all his designs, he sincerely hated.

Cato began his military service in the army which was employed against the gladiators, and concluded it as a legionary Tribune, under the Prætor Rubrius, in Macedonia; while Pompey remained in Syria. He was about three-and-thirty years of age when he made his speech in the Senate, relating to the accomplices of Cataline; and by the decisive and resolute spirit he had shown on this occasion, came to be considered as a principal support of the government and authority of the Senate [1]. To this body, as usual, every flagrant disorder repressed, brought an accession of power; and the discovery of a design, so odious as that of Cataline,

[1] Plutarch, in Catoh. edit. Londin. p. 236.

taline, covered under popular pretences, greatly served to difcredit the fuppofed popular caufe. One of the firft ufes the Senate propofed to make of their advantage, was to have Cato elected among the Tribunes of the fubfequent year. His fervices were likely to be wanted in oppofition to the fchemes of Metellus Nepos, who was then arrived from the army in Syria, with recommendations to public favour as a candidate for the office of Tribune; and if he fhould prevail in the election by the influence of Pompey, it was not doubted, he came charged with fome meafure to gratify the ambition or vanity of this infatiable fuitor for perfonal confideration and honour. It had not yet appeared what part he was to take in the difputes which were likely to arife on the legality or expedience of the late fummary executions; but it is not to be doubted, that he wifhed to hold the balance of parties, and that he would come prepared for the part that was moft likely to promote his own importance. Metellus was fent on before him to be fupported by his friends in the competition which was expected, and with his inftructions to take fuch meafures as were likely to favour his pretenfions.

The leading men of the Senate were now, for fome time, aware of the intrigues of Pompey, and bore, with impatience, the perfonal fuperiority which he affected even to the firft and moft refpected men of their order. They took occafion, in the prefent crifis, to mortify him, by admitting

CHAP XVIII. Lucullus and Metellus Creticus to the triumphs to which, by their respective victories in Pontus and in Crete, they were long entitled. Hitherto the claims of these officers had been over-ruled by the popular faction, either to annoy the Senatorian party, to which they were attached, or to flatter Pompey, who was supposed to be equally averse to the honours of both. They had waited in Italy about three years, and, in the manner of those who sue for a triumph, still retaining the fasces or ensigns of their late command [r], had refrained from entering the city.

Lucullus, having obtained the honour that was due to him, seemed to be satisfied with the acknowledgment of his right; and, as if merely to show with what sort of enemy he had fought, he entered the city with a few of the Armenian horsemen cased in armour, a few of the armed chariots winged with scythes, and about sixty of the officers and courtiers of Mithridates, who were his captives. He ordered the spoils he had gained, the arms and ensigns of war, the prows of the gallies he had taken, to be displayed in the great circus, and concluded the solemnity with giving a feast to the People. The Senate hoped for his support against the ambition of Pompey, and the factious designs of the popular leaders; but he was disgusted, and from thence forward scarcely ever took a part in the affairs of State.

The triumph of Metellus Creticus did not take place till after the accession of P. Junius Silanus and

[r] Cicero in Lucullo.

and Lucius Muræna, Confuls of the following year, after whofe election, Cicero, before he had vacated the office, or laid down the fafces, had occafion to defend his intended fucceffor Muræna, againft a charge of corruption brought upon the ftatute of Calpurnius, by Servius Sulpicius, one of his late competitors, fupported by Cato and others. The oration of Cicero on this occafion is ftill extant, and is a curious example of the topics which, under popular governments, are recurred to even in judicial pleadings. Great part of it confifts in a ridicule of law terms; becaufe Sulpicius, one of the profecutors, ufed to give counfel to his friends who confulted him in matters of law; and in a ridicule of the Stoic philofophy, becaufe Cato, another profecutor, was fuppofed to have embraced the doctrines of that fect. Cato made no other remark on this pleading, but that the republic was provided with a merry Conful. The argument however appeared fufficiently ftrong on the fide of Muræna, and he was acquitted.

At the clofe of this trial, Cicero, about to abdicate his power, and being to make the ufual affeveration, upon oath, That he had faithfully, and to the beft of his abilities, difcharged his truft; propofed to introduce this folemnity with a fpeech to the People, but was ordered by Metellus, already elected, and acting in the capacity of Tribune, to confine himfelf to the fimple terms of his oath. He accordingly refrained from fpeaking; but inftead of fwearing fimply, That he had been faithful to his trust, he took an oath, That he had preserved the republic[1]. It was on this occasion, probably, that Cato, now another of the Tribunes, addressing himself to the People, and alluding to the suppression of the late conspiracy, called Cicero the father of his Country[2]; and from this time entered upon an opposition to his colleague Metellus, which was not likely to drop while they continued in office.

U. C. 691.
D. Junius Silanus, L. Murena.

Soon after the accession of the new magistrates, a storm began to gather, which, though still aimed at the party of the Senate, burst at last in a personal attack upon the late Consul, who had been the prompter or instrument of the Senate in the late summary proceedings against the accomplices of Cataline. Metellus Nepos seems to have come from Asia, and to have entered on the office of Tribune, with a particular design to bring about the reception of Pompey with his army into Rome; and in this project he was joined by Caius Cæsar[3], now in the office of Prætor, who chose to support the Tribune in this measure, as an act of hostility to the Senate, if not as the means of obtaining a precedent of which he might in his turn avail himself.

In consequence of a plan concerted with Cæsar, the Tribune Metellus moved in the Senate, as had been usual in the times of its highest authority, for leave to propose a decree in the assembly of the People

---

[1] Plutarch. in Cicerone.
[2] Cicer. in Pisonem. c. 3.
[3] Sueton. in Jul. Cæs. c. 16.

People recalling Pompey from Afia at the head of his forces, in order to reftore the conftitution of the commonwealth, which, in the terms he afterwards employed to the People, had been violated by the arbitrary adminiftration of Cicero. This was the firft attempt of the party to inflame the minds of the People on the fubject of the late executions; and Pompey was, in this manner, offered to the popular party as their leader to avenge the fuppofed wrongs they had received. Cato, when the matter was propofed in the Senate, endeavoured to perfuade Metellus to withdraw his motion, reminding him of the dignity of his family, which had been always a principal ornament and fupport of the State. This treatment ferved only to raife the prefumption of Metellus, and brought on a violent altercation between the Tribunes. The Senate applauded Cato, but had not authority enough to prevent the motion which was propofed from being made to the People.

Metellus, apprehending an obftinate refiftance from his colleague, endeavoured to fill the place of affembly with his own partizans; and, on the evening before the meeting, in order to intimidate his opponents, paraded in the ftreets with a numerous attendance of men in arms. The friends and relations of the other Tribunes earneftly befeeched them not to expofe themfelves to the dangers with which they were threatened. But, on the following day, the other party being already affembled by Metellus, at the temple of Caftor, and the place having been in the night occupied by perfons under his direction, armed with clubs, fwords, and other offenfive weapons [f], Cato went forth attended only by Minucius Thermus, another of the Tribunes, and a few friends. They were joined by numbers in the ftreets, who could not accompany them to their place, being prevented by the multitude of armed men who already crowded the avenues and the fteps of the temple. But they themfelves, from refpect to their office, being fuffered to pafs, dragged along with them through the crowd, as an aid, in cafe any violence were offered, Munatius, a citizen much attached to Cato. When they came to the bench of Tribunes, they found that Metellus, with the Prætor Julius Cæfar, had taken their places there; and that, in order to concert their operations in the conduct of this affair, they were clofely feated together. Cato, to difappoint this intention, forced himfelf in betwixt them, and, when the ordinary officer began to read the intended decree, interpofed his negative, or forbade him to proceed. Metellus himfelf feized the writing, and began to read; but Cato fnatched it out of his hands. Metellus endeavoured to repeat the fubftance of it from his memory. Thermus clapt a hand to his mouth. A general filence remained in the affembly, till Metellus, having made a fignal concerted with his party to clear the comitium of their enemies, a great tumult and confufion arofe; and the Tribunes who oppofed

[f] Plutarch in Catone, edit. Londin. p. 141, &c.

opposed Metellus were in imminent danger. The Senators had met in mourning, to mark their sense of the evils which threatened the commonwealth; and now, under the apprehension of some signal calamity, gave a charge to the Consuls to watch over the safety of the State, and empowered them to take such measures as might be necessary to preserve or to restore the peace [1].

In consequence of this charge, the Consul Muræna appeared with a body of men in arms, had the good fortune to rescue Cato and Minucius Thermus; and probably by this seasonable interposition effaced any remains of misunderstanding which might have subsisted between Cato and himself, on account of the prosecution for bribery, which followed the late elections [2].

Metellus, after the tumult was composed, having again obtained silence, began to read the proposed decree; but the Senatorian party, headed by the Consuls, being then in the comitium, he found it impossible to proceed; and, together with the Prætor Caius Cæsar, retired from the assembly. From this time, these officers made no attempt to resume their motion, but complained that the government was usurped by a violent faction, under whom even the persons of the Tribunes were unsafe; and Metellus, as if forced to break through the rules which obliged the Tribunes to constant residence at Rome, abandoned the

[1] Plutarch. in Catone, edit. Londin. p. 241, &c.
[2] Plutarch, ibid.

the city, even left Italy, and fled to the camp of Pompey in Afia, from which he had but lately fet out on his journey to Rome [1]. He had already threatened his opponents in the city with the refentment and military power of his general, and now endeavoured to excite the army and their commander to follow the example which had been fet to them by Sylla and his legions, when oppreffed citizens, a defcription which he now affumed to himfelf, fled to them for protection and revenge.

It may well be fuppofed, that Cæfar, remembering his own efcape from the ruin of the Marian faction, and confidering Pompey as the head of an oppofite intereft, and a principal obftacle to his own ambition, muft look upon him with fome degree of perfonal diflike and animofity; but his conduct on this occafion fufficiently fhowed how little he was the dupe of any paffion or fentiment which had a tendency to check his purfuits. Meaning for the prefent only to weaken the Senate, and to partake in the favour which Pompey enjoyed with the People; he undertook the caufe even of a rival, and would have joined the populace, in delivering the commonwealth into his hands, rather than remain under a government which he confidered as the principal bar to his own elevation. But if he really meant to overthrow the Senate by force, he miftook his inftrument. Pompey, no doubt, afpired to be the firft among citizens, and wifhed for the oftentation of military power at Rome;

---

[1] Dio. Caff. lib. xxxvii. c. 43.

Rome; but even this he defired to receive as the fruit of confideration and perfonal refpect; and he ever hoped to make the People beftow it, and even force him to accept of it as their gift. For this purpofe he encouraged fo many agents and retainers to found his own praife; and for this purpofe he had recently fent Metellus Nepos from his camp in Afia to take upon him the functions of a popular Tribune at Rome; but having failed in the project of vanity, his mind mifgave him in the project of force. No one ever courted diftinction with a more inceffant emulation to his rivals; but he was entirely dependent on the public opinion for any fatisfaction he enjoyed in the poffeffion of power. Trufting perhaps to this part of his character, Cæfar, though no way remifs as a rival, was not yet alarmed at the elevation of Pompey, and thought that he was fafe in admitting him to govern with the fword at Rome. Pompey was, at this conjuncture, with his army moving towards Italy, and his approach was matter of great apprehenfion to the friends of the commonwealth, who feared that, in return to the affront of his not being invited, upon the motion of Metellus, to come with his army, he would employ it in perfon to enforce his commands. Upon his arrival at Brundifium, however, as formerly upon his return from Africa, he difpelled thofe fears by an immediate difmiffion of the troops, with inftructions, merely that they fhould attend at his triumph. He himfelf came forward to Rome with the fingle equipage of his Proconfular

fular rank. Multitudes of every condition went forth to receive him, and with shouts and acclamations recompensed the moderation with which he acquiesced in the condition of a citizen.

Cæsar, from whatever motive he acted in regard to Pompey, gave every other sign of disaffection to the Senate, and employed the name of this rising favourite of the People, to mortify such of the members in particular as were objects of personal animosity to himself. The repairs or rebuilding of the Capitol being finished about this time, the honour of dedicating the edifice, and of being named in the inscription it was to bear, was, by a resolution of the Senate, conferred on Catulus, under whose inspection the work had been executed. But Cæsar, affecting to obtain this honour for Pompey, alleged that Catulus had embezzled the money allotted for the service; that much yet remained to be done; and moved, that the inscription of Catulus should be erased; that the completion of the work being left to Pompey, should carry an inscription with his name [1]. Here he probably acted as much from antipathy to one, as from an intention to flatter the other. But the design being extremely odious to the whole body of the Nobles, who saw, with indignation, in that proposal, an attempt to affront a most respectable citizen, in order to flatter the vanity of one person, and to gratify the profligate resentments of another;

[1] Sueton. in Jul. Cæsare, c. 15.

another; under this aspect of the business, Cæsar was obliged to withdraw his motion [1].

It was probably during this year in which Cæsar was Prætor, and before the arrival of Pompey from Asia (although historians refer it to an earlier date), that Cæsar promoted, as has been already mentioned, prosecutions upon a charge of assassination against some of the persons concerned in the execution of Sylla's proscriptions. The Prætors had in charge by lot to superintend the application of particular laws. The law respecting assassination appears to have been the lot of Cæsar; and he was entitled, in virtue of his office, the jurisdiction of which was still very arbitrary, to extend, by his edict or plan of proceeding for the year, the description of the crime under his cognizance to any special case.

While he seemed to have formed so many designs against the peace of the commonwealth, and in the capacity of Prætor supported them with the authority of a magistrate, the Senatorian party made a powerful exertion of their influence to have him suspended, and actually obtained a decree for this purpose. He affected at first to slight their authority; but finding that a power was preparing to enforce it, perhaps at the hazard of his life, he laid aside for some time the robes and badges of magistracy, dismissed his Lictors, and abstained from the functions of Prætor, until, having rejected an offer of the People to restore him by force,

[1] Dio. Cass. lib. xlvii. c. 44.

force, he was, with proper marks of regard, for this instance of moderation and duty, reinstated by an act of the Senate itself.

The aristocratical party, meanwhile, to confirm and perpetuate the evidence on which they had proceeded against the accomplices of Cataline, continued their prosecutions on this subject, and obtained sentence of condemnation, in particular against a citizen of the name of Vergunteius, and against Autronius, who, about two years before, having been elected Consul, was set aside upon a charge of bribery; and who, from the disgust which he took to the Senate upon that occasion, had connected himself with the more desperate party. Publius Sylla, as has been mentioned, was also tried; but upon the pleading and testimony of Cicero, who possessed all the information obtained on this subject, was honourably acquitted.

Cæsar likewise was accused by Vectius as accessary to the conspiracy of Cataline; but it is not likely that he was concerned farther than by the general encouragement he gave to every party at variance with the Senate. Opposition to this body was reputed the cause of the People, and was pretended by every person who had any passions to gratify by crimes of State, or who wished to weaken the government, to which they themselves were accountable. Among the supporters of this interest, Crassus also was accused, but probably on no better grounds than Cæsar.

The

---

1 Sueton. in Jul. Cæsare, c. 16.

The whole of thefe proceedings, however, were fufpended by the approach of Pompey. This leader had now drawn the attention of all men upon himfelf, was quoted in every harangue as the great fupport of the empire, and courted by multitudes, who, without inquiry, or knowledge of his perfon affected to be claffed with his admirers and friends. While the contagion fpread, like a fafhion, among the People. He himfelf affected indifference to this mighty tide of renown; though not without much dignity and ftate, which he tempered with affability and grace; employing the greatnefs he poffeffed to give the more value to his condefcenfions. His manner, though acceptable to the People and the army he commanded, was difagreeable to the Senate. Having previoufly fent Pifo, one of his lieutenants, before him to ftand for the Confulate; he had the prefumption to defire that the Senate would defer the elections until he himfelf could be prefent to canvafs for his friend. The Senate, according to Dio, complied with his defire; but, according to Plutarch, rejected the propofal with difdain. This author imputes the refolution, which they took upon this occafion, to Cato, and fubjoins, that Pompey afterwards endeavoured to gain this opponent by a propofed marriage with one of his near relations; and that Cato declined the connection, faying, That he fhould not be caught in a female fnare. Pifo, however, was elected together with Valerius Meffala, and entered on his office before the folemnity of Pompey's triumph.

This

This followed foon after; and, though continued for two days, could not make place for all the magnificent fhews which had been provided to adorn it. The lift of conquefts exceeded that which had ever been produced at any other triumph. Including Afia, Pontus, Armenia, Cappadocia, Paphlagonia, Medea, Colchis, Iberia, Albania, Syria, Cilicia, Mefopotamia, Phænicia, Judæa, Arabia, Scythia, Crete[1], with the fea on all its coafts. Among the nations or potentates fubdued, were the Bafterni, Mithridates, and Tigranes. Among the captures, a thoufand fortreffes, nine hundred cities reduced, eight hundred galleys taken, above two millions of men in captivity. Towns repeopled, not lefs than three hundred and ninety-nine. To this pompous lift, it was fubjoined by his friends, that, this being his third triumph, he had now made a round of the known world, or had triumphed over all the three parts of the earth, Africa, Europe, and Afia.

After rewarding the foldiers, of whom none received lefs than fifteen hundred denarii[2], he carried to the treafury twenty thoufand talents[3]. Among his principal captives, were led, befides the chief pirates, Tigranes, fon to the king of Armenia, with his wife and his daughter,—Zozimé, the queen of Tigranes the father,—Ariftobulus, king of the Jews,—a fifter of Mithridates with five fons, and fome Scythian women;—the hoftages of the Iberii,

---

[1] Plin. Nat. Hift. lib. vii. c. 26.
[2] About 50 l.
[3] About 3,860,000 l.

rii, and the Commageni, together with trophies for every battle he had fought, making in all a more splendid exhibition than any that was to be found on the records of the State.

The triumphal proceffions of Pompey merit more attention than thofe of any other perfon, becaufe they exhibit his character as well as military fuccefs. Others took the benefit of an eftablifhed practice to publifh and to ratify the honours they had acquired; but Pompey, it is likely, would have invented the triumph, even if it had not been formerly thought of; and it is not to be doubted, that he over-ran fome provinces in which the enemy were fubdued, or in which they were fo weak, as not to be able to make any refiftance, merely to place them in the lift of his conquefts; and that he made fome part of his progrefs in Afia merely to accumulate trophies and ornaments for this pompous fcene.

The triumph, in its ordinary form, confifted only of fuch exhibitions as had a reference to the fervice in which it was obtained; the captives and fpoils of the enemy, with effigies or reprefentations of the firft, where the originals, by any accident, could not be difplayed. But in the folemnities inftituted for the honour of Pompey, were admitted whatever could diftinguifh or fignalize the occafion. Among thefe, according to the record tranfcribed by Pliny[1], there were many coftly ornaments of gold and of precious ftones, not taken from the enemy,

[1] Nat. Hift. lib. xxxvii. c. 2.

enemy, but fabricated on purpose to be shown. Plates, used for some species of game or play, made of one entire crystal; a model of the moon in gold, weighing thirty pondo; tables, utensils, statues, crowns adorned with precious stones, the representation also of an entire mountain in gold, with its herds of deer, and other animals, haunted with lions: and what serves as an evidence that these exhibitions were not limited to the spoils actually taken in war, there is mentioned an effigy of Pompey himself incrusted with pearls. The whole conducted with more arrangement and order, than were necessary, perhaps, in the disposition made for any of the battles which the triumph was intended to celebrate.

Among the images, representations, and memorials which were carried before the victor on this occasion, there was held up to view a state of the public finance, from which it appeared, that before Pompey's time the revenue amounted to no more than fifty millions [1]; and that the addition which he alone brought to it amounted to eighty-five millions [2].

Soon after this pomp was over, an assembly of the People was called in the Circus Flaminius, to receive an address from the victorious commander; but, from an extreme caution not to offend any party, the speech which he made, upon this occasion, was acceptable to none. " It gave no hopes," says Cicero,

(1) 416,666 l.
(2) 708,333 l. Plutarch. in Pompeio, edit. Lond. p. 470.

Cicero [1], "to the poor; no flattery to the rich; no satisfaction to the good; no encouragement to the profligate." Pompey was suffered to possess the highest place in the consideration of the public, merely because he assumed it; and he preserved his dignity, by never committing his reputation without being prepared, or without having concerted a variety of arts by which it might be supported [2].

---

[1] Cicer. ad Atticum, lib. i. ep. 14.

[2] Sallust in Catalin. c. 54. in contrasting the characters of Cæsar and Cato, does not propose to decide on the comparative merit of their objects: for this he assumes to have been consideration or glory, and the same in both; but in reality he seems to have mistaken the object of either. That of Cæsar was not consideration: for although he courted the public opinion, when subservient to his power; yet he slighted it also, when it stood in his way to dominion. In the object of Cato, consideration had no share. His life was distinguished by the general tenor of reason, integrity, humanity and justice, in the public cause, whatever the world might think of his conduct. And his resolution often led him into measures, unsuccessful from the want of co-operation in a corrupt or misguided age. The great distinction of Pompey, if we insert his character into this comparison, was the prevailing attention to consideration or glory, in preference to either virtue or power.

CHAP. XIX.

Transactions at Rome, and in the Provinces.—Julius Cæsar appointed in the Quality of Proprætor to his first Province of Lusitania.—Trial of Clodius.—Proposed Adoption into a Plebeian Family, to qualify him for the Office of Tribune.—Cæsar, a Candidate for the Consulship.—The Triumvirate of Cæsar, Pompey, and Crassus.—Consulship of Cæsar.—Motion of Vatinius, to confer on Cæsar, for five Years, the Command in Gaul.—Marriage of Pompey to Julia.—Of Cæsar to Calpurnia.—Plot of Vettius.—Consulate of Lucius Calpurnius and A. Gabinius.—Attack made upon Cicero.—His Exile.

POMPEY, at his departure from Syria, left that province with two legions under the command of M. Æmilius Scaurus, one of his lieutenants. This officer occupied the country from the Euphrates to the frontier of Egypt, and continued the war which his predecessor had begun with the Arabs.

Caius Antonius, the late colleague of Cicero in the Consulate, soon after the defeat of Cataline, proceeded to the province of Macedonia, of which, by the arrangements of the year, he had been appointed the governor. He entered his province with the ensigns of victory, which had been obtained by the defeat of Cataline; but these he soon forfeited by his misconduct in a war against the

OF THE ROMAN REPUBLIC.

CHAP. XIX.

the Thracians, and by the disgrace which he otherwise incurred in the mal-administration of his province. Complaints were exhibited against him for extortion. On this occasion, it had been reported by himself, or by some of his family, that, having agreed to divide the profits of his government with Cicero, part only of his exactions was made on his own account. This allegation, Cicero, in a letter to Atticus, mentions with scorn; and, being asked to undertake the defence of Antonius, questions whether he can decently do so under this imputation [1]. But as he soon afterwards undertook the cause, and employed his interest to have the Proconsul continued in his province, it is probable that this imputation either gained no credit, or was entirely removed [2].

The Allobroges, though deprived of the support they were made to expect from the party of Cataline, nevertheless took arms, and invaded the Roman province of Gaul. After a variety of events, they were repulsed by Pontinius, who then commanded the legions in that quarter, and forced to retire into their own country [3].

About the same time, Caius Julius Cæsar, upon the expiration of his term in the office of Prætor, obtained his first military command, being appointed by lot to the government of Lusitania, where, under different pretences, he found an opportunity

[1] Vid. Cicero ad Atticum, lib. i. ep. 12.
[2] Ad Familiar. lib. v. ep. 5.
[3] Dio. lib. xxxvii.

portunity to quarrel with the natives, to shew his own capacity for war, and to lay some ground for his claim to a triumph [1]. In pushing his way to the preferments which he now held in the State, he had ruined his fortune by largesses, public shews, and entertainments to the People, by his lavish bounty in private to needy and profligate citizens, and in supporting every desperate cause against the Senate and the government; and is reported to have said of himself, when he set out for his province, that he needed one hundred and fifty millions Roman money, or one million two hundred thousand pounds sterling, to be worth nothing [2]. When about to depart from the city, he was pressed by his creditors, and had recourse to Crassus, who became his surety for great sums [3].

A person who, in any other state than that of Rome, could suppose such a fortune reparable, must have thought of means alarming to the State itself; but Cæsar had now quitted the paths of pleasure for those of ambition; and, in an empire which extended over so many opulent provinces, needed only to have power, in order to become rich. Although the province which now fell to his lot was not the most wealthy, or was only a step to somewhat farther, more considerable, and more likely to supply him with the means of pursuing his objects, he was nevertheless reported,

even

[1] Dio. c. 52, &c.
[2] Appian. de Bell. Civ. lib. ii. p. 715.
[3] Ibid. About 160,000 l. Plutarch. in Cæsare.

even there, to have supplied his own wants, and to have enriched his army [1].

In passing the Alps, on his way into Spain, at a village on the way, one of his company having observed, that "*Here too there might be parties and contests for power.*" "*Ay,*" said Cæsar, with a characteristical confession, "*and I would rather be the first man in this place, than the second, at Rome* [2]." Upon his arrival in Lusitania, he made the necessary augmentation of the army, and soon over-ran all the districts that were disposed to resist his authority. With the same ability with which he conducted his military operations, he supported the dignity of a Roman governor, no less in the civil than in the department of war. Historians, upon an idea which occurred to them, that the disorder in his own affairs might have rendered him partial to insolvent debtors, and being at pains to acquit him of any such charge, observe that he gave proofs of the contrary, among which they specify a rule which he followed, in ordering two thirds of the debtor's effects to be sequestered for the use of his creditors [3].

While these things passed in the provinces, the People being indulged in their favourite gratifications, suffered an increase of the political distempers with which the public had been for some time infected. The expence and dissipation attending the public shews, in particular, were augmented to a great degree. Lucius Domitius Ahenobarbus,

[1] Plutarch. in Cæsare, edit. Lond. p. 111.   [2] Ibid.   [3] Ibid. p. 112.

nobarbus, exhibited the baiting of an hundred bears by African huntſmen [1] ; and whereas ſuch entertainments had formerly ended at one meeting, they were now continued through many acts [2], and were intermitted only while the ſpectators retired to their meals.

The office of Cenſor, as appears from the tranſactions which are mentioned relating to the farms of the revenue and the rolls of the Senate, was in actual exertion at this time, although the names of the perſons by whom it was exerciſed are not recorded. Theſe officers are ſaid to have let the revenues of Aſia at a rate, of which the farmers afterwards complained, alleging, that their own avidity in graſping at the profits to be made in this new province had miſled them [3]. The Cenſors likewiſe put upon the rolls of the Senate all who had ever held any office of magiſtracy, and by this addition increaſed the number of members beyond the former and ordinary rate [4].

About the ſame time happened the memorable trial of Publius Clodius, for the ſcandal he had given by profaning the ſacred rites in Cæſar's houſe. This debauchee was ſuppoſed, for ſome time, to have ſought for an opportunity of a criminal correſpondence with Pompeia, Cæſar's wife; but to have been prevented, if not by her own diſcretion, at leaſt by the attention and vigilance of
her

---

[1] Plin. Nat. Hiſt. lib. viii. c. 36.
[2] Dio. Caſſ. lib. xxxvii. c. 47.
[3] Cicer. ad Atticum, lib. i. ep. 17.
[4] Dio. lib. xxxvii. c. 46.

her family¹. In these circumstances, during the preceding year, it fell to the lot of Pompeia, as being wife to one of the Prætors in office, to celebrate, at her house, the festival of a certain female deity² worshipped by the Romans; and at whose rites women alone were admitted. Every male domestic, even the husband, was obliged to absent himself from home while the rites were administered. Clodius took this opportunity to carry on his intrigue; put himself in a female dress, and, being young and of an effeminate aspect, expected to pass for a woman³. Pompeia was supposed to be apprised of the design, and to have stationed a female slave to receive and conduct her paramour through the apartments. But being met by another slave who was not in the secret, his voice betrayed him. A cry of amazement and horror was immediately communicated through all the apartments, and the occasion of it discovered to the matrons, who were met to celebrate the rites. Clodius escaped, but not without being known. The college of Pontiffs made a report, that the sacred rites had been profaned. The Senate resolved, that inquiry should be made into the grounds of the scandal; and that the People should be moved to authorise the Prætor in office to select, without drawing lots, proper judges for the trial of the accused.

Clodius,

---
1 Plutarch. in Cæsare, edit. Lond. p. 109.
2 Called the Bona & Dea.
3 Cicero ad Atticum, lib. i. ep. 12, 13.

CHAP. XIX.

Clodius, by the suspicion of an incestuous commerce with his own sister, the wife of Lucullus; by his perfidy in seducing the troops of that general to mutiny, and by his profligacy on every occasion, had incurred a general detestation; and many of the Senators, as the likeliest way of removing him from the commonwealth, combined in urging the present prosecution against him.

He himself, foreseeing the storm, had taken refuge in the popular party, and endeavoured to silence the voice of infamy, by professing extraordinary zeal for the People, and vehement opposition to the Senate. These parties accordingly became interested in the issue of his cause. The popular leaders endeavoured to preserve him as an useful instrument, and the Senate to remove him, as a vile and dangerous tool, from the hands of their enemies. Even Cæsar, though personally insulted, and so far moved by the scandal which had been given in his own house as to part with his wife, still affected to consider as groundless the charge which was laid against Clodius; and being asked, why he had parted with a woman who, upon this supposition, must appear to be innocent, said, that his wife must not only be innocent, but above imputation. Pompey, to avoid giving offence, declined to favour either party; but being called upon in the assembly of the People to declare his opinion, whether this trial should proceed according to the decree of the Senate; made a long speech, full of respect to the Nobles, and of

submission

submission to the Senate, whose authority, in all questions of this sort, he said, should ever with him have the greatest weight. He afterwards, in the Senate itself, being called upon by Messala the Consul, delivered himself to the same purpose; and when he had done, whispered Cicero, who sat by him, that he thought he had now sufficiently explained himself; intimating probably, that he meant to comprehend, in this declaration, also his judgment with respect to all the acts of the Senate which had passed relating to the accomplices of Cataline [1].

The Consul Piso was instructed to carry to the People, for their assent, an act for the better conduct of the trial of Clodius, dispensing with the usual mode of draughting the judges by lot, and authorising the Prætor to select them, that he might name the more respectable persons. On the day on which this motion was to be made, a numerous party of young Nobility appeared for the defendant. His hirelings and retainers crowded the Comitium. Even Piso, who moved the question, dissuaded the People from passing the law, and allowed the friends of Clodius to put a ridiculous trick on the assembly, by distributing to the People, as they came forward to vote, two ballots, which, instead of being, as usual, one negative and the other affirmative, were both negative. This trick being observed, Cato, with the authority of Tribune, suspended the ballot, and strongly remonstrated against the proceeding of the Consul [2].

In

[1] Cicero ad Atticum, lib. i. epist. 13. 14. 16.
[2] Ibid.

In this he was supported by Hortensius and Favonius. The assembly broke up, and the affair again returned to the Senate. The members were importuned by Clodius, who cast himself at their feet as they entered; they, nevertheless, confirmed their former resolution by a majority of four hundred to fifteen [1].

Hortensius, however, having proposed that, instead of the motion which the Consuls had been instructed to make for the selection of the judges, the Tribune Fusius should move the People to grant commission for the trial, leaving the judges, as usual, to be drawn by lot; an edict was accordingly framed and passed to this effect. Hortensius, who conducted the trial, was confident that no jury could acquit the accused. And the court, in all their proceedings, seemed at first inclined to severity. They even applied for a guard to protect their persons against the partizans of the criminal; but the majority, nevertheless, it was alleged, suffered themselves to be corrupted, or took money in the course of the trial. Of fifty-six judges that were inclosed, twenty-five gave their voice to condemn, and thirty-one to acquit. Catulus, on this occasion, asked the majority to what purpose they had desired a guard? "Was it," he said, with a sarcasm, which modern juries could ill endure, "to secure the money you expected to "receive for your votes [2]?"

Soon after this judgment the Senate resolved that inquiry should be made concerning those judges

---

[1] Cicer. ad Att. lib. i. epist. 13, 14, 16.
[2] Dio. Cass. lib xxxvii. c. 46. Cicero ad Att. lib. i. ep. 16.

judges who had been corrupted in the trial. And by this refolution gave a general offence to the Equeftrian order, who confidered it as an imputation on their whole body [1].

Pompey, in the courfe of this tranfaction, had been obliged to declare himfelf for the Senate; but his object was to be on good terms with all parties, and to manage his intereft, by having fome of his creatures always chofen into the higheft offices of State. He offered, as candidate for the Confulate of the following year, Afranius, one of his dependants, who is reprefented by Cicero as a perfon of mean character, and who, having no perfonal dignity, nor any credit with the People, was to be fupported in his canvafs by money alone. Pompey himfelf, and the Conful Pifo, openly employed bribery in obtaining votes in his favour [2].

A variety of refolutions were obtained in the Senate to reftrain thefe practices. Two of them were propofed by Cato and Domitius. The firft was levelled againft the Conful Pifo himfelf, and gave permiffion, on the fufpicion of illicit practices refpecting elections, to vifit the houfe even of a magiftrate. By the other it was declared, that all thofe who were found diftributing money to the People fhould be confidered as enemies to their country [3].

The Senate, at the fame time, encouraged Lurco, one of the Tribunes, to propofe a new claufe to corroborate the laws againft bribery. By this claufe

[1] Dio. Caff. lib. xxxvi. c. 46. Cicero ad Att. lib. i. ep. 17.
[2] Cicero ad Att. lib i. ep. 16.
[3] Ibid.

clause promises of money made to the People, if not performed, did not infer guilt; but, if performed, subjected the guilty person from thenceforward to pay to each of the Tribes an annual tax of three thousand Roman money, or about twenty-four pounds sterling; and there being thirty-five Tribes, this tax amounted in all to about eight hundred and forty pounds of our money. That the Tribune might not be interrupted in carrying this law, the Senate farther resolved, that the formalities or restrictions of the Lex Ælia and Fufia[1] should not be opposed to him[2]. It appears, however, that the liberality or other influence of Pompey prevailed against these precautions, as Afranius was elected, together with Q. Cæcilius Metellus Celer.

Soon after the election of these officers the farmers of the revenue of Asia, supported by the whole Equestrian order, complained, as has been mentioned, of the terms of their contract, in which they alleged that they had greatly exceeded what the funds of that province could afford, and made application to the Senate for relief. Their plea was contested for some months with great animosity on both sides[3].

Upon the accession of the new Consuls, several other matters, tending to innovation and public disturbance, were introduced. Metellus Nepos, late Tribune, being now in the office of Prætor, procured

---

[1] These were formalities and restrictions provided to check the precipitate passing of laws.
[2] Cicer. ad Atticum, lib. i. ep. 16.
[3] Cicero ad Att. lib. i. ep. 17, 18.

procured a law to abolish the customs payable at any of the ports of Italy. The Romans, as has been observed, upon the accession of wealth derived from Macedonia, had exempted themselves from all the antient assessments, and they now completed the exemption of all the Italians from every tax besides that of quit-rents for public lands, and the twentieth penny on the value of slaves when sold or emancipated. They were become the sovereigns of a great empire, and as such, thought themselves entitled to receive, not obliged to pay, contributions [1].

The Tribune Herennius, at the same time, made a motion for an act to enable Publius Clodius to be adopted into a Plebeian family, which, though an act of a more private nature than any of the former, tended still more to embroil the parties of the Senate and the People. This factious and profligate person had entertained great resentments against many of the Senators on account of the prosecution he had lately incurred, and against Cicero in particular, who, having been called as an evidence on his trial, gave a very unfavourable account of his character. The summary proceedings against the accomplices of Cataline, in which Cicero presided as Consul, exposed him to the resentment of the popular faction; and Clodius now proposed to qualify himself to be elected Tribune of the People, in order to wreck his vengeance on that magistrate in particular, as well

[1] Cicero ad Att. lib ii. ep. 16. Dio. Caſſ. lib. xxvii. c. 51.

well as on the other abettors of the Senatorian party. The motion, however, for the prefent was rejected, though not finally dropt, either by Clodius himfelf, or by the popular faction, whofe caufe he profeffed to efpoufe [1].

Two other motions were made in which Pompey was deeply interefted: one, to ratify and confirm all his acts in the province of Afia: another, to procure fettlements for the veterans who had ferved under his command. The firft, as it implied a reflection on Lucullus, many of whofe judgments Pompey had reverfed, roufed this ftatefman from the care of his houfehold and his table, to that of the republic [2]. He oppofed this motion with vigour, and infifted that the acts of Pompey fhould be feparately examined, and not confirmed in a fingle vote. In this he was fupported by Catulus, by Cato, by the Conful Metellus, and by the Senate in general. Afranius, though vefted with the Confulate, and acting almoft as the agent of Pompey, had neither dignity nor force to fupport fuch a meafure; and Pompey, finding it rejected by the Senate, declined carrying it to the People [3].

The other propofal, relating to the allotment of fettlements for the foldiers of Pompey, was, by L. Flavius, one of the Tribunes, moved in the affembly of the People, under the title of an Agrarian Law. In this act, to guard againft the imputation of partiality

---

[1] Dio. Caff. lib. xxxvii. c. 51.
[2] Plutarch. in Lucullo, edit. Lond. p. 297.
[3] Dio. lib. xxxvii. c. 49.

partiality to any particular class, certain means of relief were projected for the indigent citizens in general[1]; and, to enable the commonwealth to extend its bounty, it was proposed first of all to revoke the conveyance of certain lands, which, having belonged to the public in the Consulate of P. Mucius and L. Calpurnius, were sold by the Senate; and that the price should be restored to the purchasers. It was proposed, likewise, to seize certain lands which had been confiscated by Sylla, but not appropriated to any particular use; and to allot, during five years, the fruits of the recent conquests in Asia to purchase settlements, which should be distributed in terms of this act[2].

The Consul Metellus Celer, supported by the Senate, strenuously opposed the passing of this law. But the Tribune persisted with great obstinacy, and, to remove the obstruction he met with, committed the Consul to prison. The whole Senate would have attended him thither, and numbers accordingly crowded to the place, when the Tribune, vested with the sacred defences of his person, to bar their way, planted his stool or chair of office in the door of the prison; and, having seated himself upon it, "This way," he said, "you cannot pass; if you mean to enter, you must pierce through the walls[3]." He declared his resolution to remain all night where he sat. The parties were collecting their strength, and matters were

[1] Dio. lib. l. [2] Cicer. ad Att. lib. i. ep 19.
[3] Dio. lib. xxxvii. p. 50.

likely to end in greater extremities than suited the indirect and cautious conduct of Pompey. This politician, although he engaged all his friends to support the motion of Flavius, affected to have no part in the measure, and now probably in secret instructed the Tribune to remove from the doors of the prison. This at least might be suspected from the sudden resolution of the Tribune, to give way, saying that he did so at the request of the prisoner, who begged for his liberty [1].

It is supposed that Pompey, on this occasion, severely felt the checks which his ambition received from the Senate; that he regretted, for a moment, the dismission of his army, and wished himself in condition to enforce what his craft or his artifice had not been able to obtain. The error he had committed in resigning the sword, if he conceived it as such, might have still been corrected by recovering the possession of some considerable province, which would have given him the command of an army and of proper resources to support his power. He, nevertheless, appears to have preferred the scene of intrigue in the city and the capital of the empire; a choice in which he was probably confirmed by Cæsar, who professed great attachment to him, and who was about this time returned from the government which he held as Proprætor in Lusitania.

This officer, according to Dio, had found some pretence for a war with the nations on the frontier

---

Dio. lib. xxxvii. p. 56.

tier of the Roman province; had obliged them to take refuge in some of the islands on the coast, and afterwards subdued them in that retreat. His object was to return to resign his command with the reputation of victory, to obtain a triumph, and to offer himself as a candidate for the Consulship of the following year. For this purpose he quitted his province without waiting for a successor, and, upon his arrival at Rome, halted, as usual, with the ensigns of his military rank at the gates of the city, applied for a triumph; and at the same time made interest for votes at the approaching election [1]. The Senate, and the friends of the republic in general, were already become extremely jealous of his designs, and of his credit with the People. From a libertine he was become an ardent politician, seemed to have no passion but emulation or animosity to the more respectable orders of the State; without committing himself, he had abetted every factious leader against them, and seemed to be indifferent to consideration or honours, except so far as they led to power. Cicero and Cato were at this time the principal, or most conspicuous, members of the Senate. The first was possessed of consular rank, great ingenuity, wit, and accomplished talents: the other, possessed of great abilities and an inflexible resolution, embraced the cause of the republic with the same ardour that others displayed in conducting their interests or pursuing their pleasures. He had penetration enough to perceive

---

[1] Dio. Cass. lib. xxxvii. c. 50, &c.

in Cæsar, long before the Senate in general was alarmed, a difpofition to vilify the ariftocracy, and, in conjunction with needy and profligate citizens, to make a prey of the republic. Under this apprehenfion, he oppofed him with a degree of keennefs which Cæsar endeavoured to reprefent as a mere perfonal hatred or animofity to himfelf.

The Senators, in general, now aware of their danger from Cæsar, were difpofed to refift his applications, whether made for honours or for public truft. They, on the prefent occafion, difputed his pretenfions to a triumph; and, while he remained without the city in expectation of this honour, refufed, according to the forms of the commonwealth, to admit him on the lift of candidates for the office of Conful. But the day of election being fixed, Cæsar, without hefitation, preferred the confulate to the triumph, laid down the enfigns of his late military character, affumed the gown, and entered the city as a candidate for the Confulfhip [1].

'The People were at this time divided into a variety of factions. Pompey and Craffus diftrufted each other, and both were jealous of Cæsar. Their divifions ftrengthened the party of the Senate, and furnifhed that body with the means of thwarting feparately many of their ambitious defigns. This Cæsar had long perceived, and had paid his court both to Pompey and to Craffus, in order to hinder their joining the Senate againft him. The expedience.

[1] Sueton. in Cæfare, c. 18. Dio. lib. xxxvii. c. 54.

dience of this precaution now appeared more clearly than ever, and he is supposed to have separately represented to these rivals the advantage which their enemies derived from their misunderstanding, and the ease with which, if united, they might concert among themselves all the affairs of the republic, gratify every friend, and disappoint every enemy. Upon this representation, Pompey and Crassus were reconciled, and agreed to act in concert with Cæsar, and in particular to support him in his pretensions at the approaching elections [1].

This private combination, which remained some time a secret, was afterwards, by a kind of mockery, called the Triumvirate, alluding to the designation by which certain collegiate offices were known, derived from the numbers which were joined in the commission [2]. In the mean time, these leaders of supposed opposite factions, in abating their violence against one another, took a favourable aspect of moderation and candour. They paid their court separately to persons whom they wished to gain, and flattered them with hopes of being able to heal the divisions of their country. This sort of court they paid in particular to Cicero; and by their flatteries, and real or pretended admiration of his talents, seem to have got entire possession of his mind. Pompey affected to place the merits of Cicero greatly above his own.

" I,

[1] Dio. Cass. lib. xxxvii. c. 54, 55. Plutarch. in Pompeio, Cæsare, & Crasso.

[2] As the Decemvirs, Septemvirs, &c.

"I, indeed," he said, "have served my country, but this man has preserved it [1]." At this time it appeared that Cicero, though a fine genius, was but a weak man. The Senators, with whom he had hitherto acted, were alarmed: Atticus, it seems, had taxed him with leaving his party, to commit himself into the hands of their enemies. In his answer to this imputation, he seems to have flattered himself that he had made an acquisition of Pompey, not surrendered himself into his power; at least, that he had reclaimed or diverted him from the dangerous projects in which he had been lately engaged, and that he thought himself likely to succeed in the same manner with Cæsar: so much, that he triumphed in the superiority of his own conduct to that of Cato, who, by his austerity and vehemence, he said, had alienated the minds of men otherwise well disposed to the republic [2], "While I," he said, "by a little discretion, disarm, or even reclaim its enemies [3]."

Few persons, where his vanity did not blind him, were possessed of more penetration than Cicero; but it will afterwards appear how egregiously he was mistaken on this occasion; he chose not to see what checked his vain glory, or prevented his enjoying the court which was paid to him

---

[1] Cicero ad Atticum, lib. ii. epist. 1.

[2] Alluding to the opposition which Cato gave to the farmers of the revenue, in their petition for an abatement of their rent. But Cato followed his judgment in this matter; and there is no reason to prefer the judgment of Cicero to his.

[3] Cicero ad Atticum, lib. ii. epist. 1.

him by such eminent men as Pompey and Cæsar. His own importance, for the most part, intercepted every other object from his view, and made him the dupe of every person who professed to admire him, and incapable of any serious regard for any one who did not pay him, on every occasion, the expected tribute of praise; a description under which Cato, though his most sincere well-wisher and friend, appears at this time to have fallen.

Cæsar, to the other arts which he employed to secure his election, added the use of money, which he obtained by joining his interest, in opposition to Bibulus, with that of Lucceius, another of the candidates possessed of great wealth. He himself having squandered his fortune, as has been observed, was still greatly in debt, and Lucceius willingly furnished the money that was given to the People in the name of both. This illegal proceeding, together with the menacing concerts of which he began to be suspected with Pompey and Crassus, greatly alarmed the friends of the republic. They determined to support Bibulus against Lucceius; and, in order to give Cæsar a colleague who might occasionally oppose his dangerous intentions, they even went so far as to contribute sums of money, and to bid for votes as high as their opponents. In this crisis, it is said, that even Cato owned it was meritorious to bribe [s].

[s] Sueton. in Caio Cæsare, c. xix. Appian. de Bell. Civil. lib. ii.

CHAP.
XIX.

During the dependence of this conteſt, the Senate, by the death of Lutatius Catulus, was deprived of an able member, and the People of a fellow-citizen of great integrity, moderation, fortitude, and ability; a model of what the Romans in this age ſhould have been, in order to have preſerved the State. He partook with Cato in the averſion which Cæſar bore to the moſt reſpectable members and beſt ſupports of the Senate, and would probably have taken part with him likewiſe in the continual efforts he made to maintain its authority. The ariſtocratical party, notwithſtanding this loſs, prevailed in carrying the election of Bibulus againſt Lucceius; and though they could not exclude Cæſar from the office of Conſul, they hoped, by means of his colleague, to oppoſe and to fruſtrate his deſigns [*].

Cæſar, well aware of their purpoſe, opened his adminiſtration with a ſpeech in praiſe of unanimity, and recommending good agreement between thoſe who were joined in any public truſt. While he meant to vilify the Senate, and to foſter every diſorderly party againſt them, he guarded his own behaviour, at leaſt in the firſt period of his Conſulſhip, with every appearance of moderation and candour, paid his court not only to leaders of faction, but to perſons of every condition; and while he took care to eſpouſe the popular ſide in every queſtion, was active likewiſe in deviſing regulations for the better government of the Empire: ſo that

[*] Plutarch. Appian. Dio. Sueton. &c.

that the Senate, however inclined to counteract his designs, as calculated to raise himself on the ruins of the commonwealth, could scarcely, with a good grace, oppose him in any particular measure. He set out with a project for the relief of such indigent citizens as had numerous families, including the veterans and disbanded soldiers of Pompey; these he proposed to settle on some of the public lands in Italy. He gave out that he expected the concurrence of Cicero in this measure, sent him a message by Balbus [1], with assurances *that he meant to consult with Pompey and himself in all matters of importance*, and *that he had hopes of bringing Crassus also into the same mind*: words, from which it is manifest that the coalition of these persons was not yet publicly known. "What "a fine prospect I have before me," says Cicero to Atticus; "a perfect union with Pompey, even "with Cæsar if I please; peace with my enemies, "and tranquility in my old age." But his heart soon after misgave him; the honours of his former life recurred to his mind. With his eminent talents, he was destined to transmit a more honest fame to posterity, and to become the lamented victim of his country's betrayers, not the detestate associate of their crimes [2].

This Consulate is distinguished by the passing of many laws, particularly this, which was devised for the settlement of citizens on certain parts of the public

---

[1] Dio Cass. lib. viii. initio. Plutarch. in Cæsare. In Pompeio, Lucullo, Catone, &c. &c. Sueton. in Cæsare. Appian. de Bell. Civil. lib. ij.
[2] Cicero ad Atticum, lib. ii. ep. 3.

blic domain; and therefore known by the title of an Agrarian Law. On this act Cæsar was to rest his popularity, and his triumph over the Senate. He gave out that he was to make a provision for twenty thousand citizens, without any burden to the revenue. But he well knew that his antagonists would perceive the tendency of the measure, or not suffer it to pass without opposition; and he affected great moderation in the general purpose, and in framing every part of his plan; affecting solicitude to obtain the consent of the Senate; but, in reality, to make their opposition appear the more unreasonable and the more odious to the People. He declared, that he did not mean to strip the revenue of any branch that was known to carry profit to the public; nor to make any partial distribution in favour of his friends; that he only meant to plant with inhabitants certain unprofitable wastes, and to provide for a number of citizens, who, being indigent and uneasy in their circumstances, filled the city itself with frequent disorders and tumults; and that he would not proceed a step without consulting the Senate, and every person of credit and authority in the State.

In a way to save these appearances, and with these professions, Cæsar formed the first draught of an act which he brought to the Senate for their approbation, and in hopes to obtain their support in proposing it to the People. It was difficult to find topics on which to oppose a measure so plausible, and conducted with so much appearance of moderation

moderation and candour. But the tendency of the act itself was evidently not to promote the peace of the commonwealth, but to constitute a merit in the person who procured it, and to confer high measures of power on those who were to be intrusted with its execution.

CHAP. XIX.

In great and populous cities, indigent citizens are ever likely to be numerous, and would be more so, if the idle and profligate were taught to hope for bounties and gratuitous provisions, to quiet their clamours and to suppress their disorders. If men were to have estates in the country because they are factious and turbulent in the city, it is evident that public lands, and all the resources of the most prosperous state, would not be sufficient to supply their wants. Commissioners appointed for the distribution of such public favours would be raised above the ordinary magistrates, and above the laws of their country. They might reward their own creatures, and keep the citizens in general in a state of dependence on their will. The authors of such proposals, while they were urging the State and the people to ruin, would be considered as their only patrons and friends. " It is not this law I dread," said Cato; " it is the reward expected for obtaining it."

Odious as the task of opposition on such difficult ground might appear to the People, this Senator did not decline it. Being asked his opinion in his turn, he answered, That he saw no occasion for

for the change that was now proposed in the state of the public domains; and entered on an argument with which he meant so to exhaust the whole time of the sitting, as to prevent the Senate from coming to a question. He was entitled, by his privilege as a member in that assembly, to speak without interruption, and might, if he chose to continue speaking, persist until all the members had left the house. Cæsar suspecting his design, and finding it impossible otherwise to silence him, ordered him into custody. The whole Senate instantly rose in a tumult. "Whither go you be"fore the meeting is adjourned?" said Cæsar to Petreius, who was moving from his side. "I go," said the other, "into confinement with Cato. "With him a prison is preferable to a place in ", the Senate with you." The greater part of the members were actually moving away with Cato, and Cæsar felt himself at once stript of the disguise of moderation he had assumed, and dreaded the spirit which he saw rising in so numerous a body of men, who, on former occasions, had maintained their authority with a vigour too fatal to those who opposed it. He had relied on their want of decision, and on their ignorance of their own strength. But his rashness broke the charm. He wished that the prisoner would procure some friend among the Tribunes to interpose; but Cato, seeing him embarrassed, and the Senate engaged in the cause, went off in the custody of the Lictor without any signs of reluctance. Cæsar immediately

immediately recollecting himself, and never hurried too far by any passion, dispatched a Tribune of his own party with secret directions to rescue the prisoner ; and this being done, the Senators again returned to their places. "I meant," said Cæsar, "to have submitted this law to your judg-
"ment and correction ; but if you throw it aside,
"the People shall take it up [1]."

Cæsar, upon this occasion, increased his own popularity, and diminished that of his enemies in the Senate, who were supposed in this, as in some other instances, to withstand with keenness every measure that was devised for the comfort of the People. The imputations cast out against him by Cato and others, were supposed to proceed from malice or cynical prejudices. He found himself strong enough to extend his bounty to the People, so as to comprehend the lands of Campania, which were hitherto considered as unalienable, and the richest demesne of the public, together with a valuable district near the confluence of the Vulturnus and the Sabbatus, formerly consecrated to pious uses. In these valuable tracts of land there was sufficient subject for an ample provision for the soldiers of Pompey, and for the retainers of those who, together with Crassus and Cæsar himself, were proposed to be commissioners for carrying this law into execution.

At the first assembly of the People, Cæsar proposed his scheme to impropriate the lands of Campania,

---

[1] Dio. lib. xxxviii. c. 1, 2, 3. Plutarch. Sueton. Appian, &c.

pania, with the above additions; and first of all called on his colleague Bibulus to declare his mind on the subject. Bibulus spoke his diffent; and in vehement terms declared, that no such alienation of the public demesne should be made in his Consulate. Cæsar next called upon Pompey, though in a private station; and the audience, ignorant of the concert into which these leaders had entered, were impatient to hear this oracle on the subject of a measure which was likely to elevate a supposed rival so high in the favour of the People. To the surprise of all who were present, Pompey applauded the general design, and, in a speech of considerable length, discussed all the clauses of the act, and with great approbation of each. When he had done speaking, Cæsar, alluding to what had dropt from his colleague, and affecting to fear the interposition of force; " Will you support us," he said to Pompey, " in case we are attacked?"— " If any one," said the other, " shall lift up a " sword against you, I shall lift up both sword " and shield [1]." Crassus being called upon, also spoke to the same effect. The concurrence of all these leaders portended the unanimous consent of all parties; and a day being fixed for finally deciding the question, the assembly adjourned.

To oppose a measure so popular, and from which such numbers had great expectations, no means remained so likely to succeed as superstition. To this

---

[1] Cicero ad Att. lib. ii. Plutarch. in Pompeio. Dio. Cass. lib. xxxviii. c. 5.

this aid Bibulus accordingly had recourse, and, by virtue of the authority with which he was vested, proclaimed a general fast, and a suspension for the present year of all the affairs of State. The design of this suspension, and the extravagant length of time to which it was extended, probably enabled his colleague to treat it with contempt, and to proceed in the design of putting his question, as if no such proclamation had been issued. The assembly was accordingly summoned in the temple of Concord. Cæsar, early in the morning, secured all the avenues and the steps of the portico, where he had Vatinius, one of the Tribunes of the People, who was entirely devoted to his interest, and even in his pay [1], stationed with a party, and prepared to take the odium of all violent measures on himself. Bibulus, however, attended by numbers of the Senate, and three of the Tribunes, who were engaged, by their negative, to put a stop to every proceeding, came into the place of assembly, with all the forms of office, and protested against the legality of any meeting to be held in a time of general fast; but the opposite party being in possession of the temple, forced him from the steps, broke the ensigns of the Lictors, wounded the Tribunes who interposed in his defence, and effectually removed all farther obstruction to their own designs. The question then being put, the law passed with-

out

[1] Cicero in Vatinium. Cæsar was reported to have said at Acquileia, some time after this date, when Vatinius was disappointed of the Edileship, that he had no business with honours, being intent on money only; and that he was paid for all his services in the Tribunate.

out opposition, including a clause to oblige every Senator, under pain of exile or death, to swear to the observance of it.

This oath was probably a snare laid by Cæsar for the most resolute of his opponents, like that which had been formerly laid by Marius, on a like occasion, for Metellus Numidicus, and by means of which that virtuous citizen was actually for some time removed from the commonwealth [1].

Metellus Celer, the late Consul, together with Cato and Favonius, unaware of the snare which was laid for them, at first declared their resolution not to swear to the observance of any such ruinous law; but, on farther deliberation, they became sensible that in this they were serving the cause of their enemies. "You may have no need "of Rome," said Cicero, now awake from his dream, to Cato, " and may go into exile with " pleasure; but Rome has need of you. Give " not such a victory to her enemies and your own." Upon view of the matter, it was determined to comply [2].

Bibulus, on the day following that of his violent expulsion from the assembly of the People, convened the Senate, represented the outrage he had received, and submitted the state of the republic to their consideration. But even this assembly, though consisting of above six hundred of the most powerful citizens of Rome, not destitute even

[1] See vol. ii. c. 13.
[2] Plutarch, in Catone. Appian. de Bell. Civil. lib. ii.

even of perſonal courage, were declined in their ſpirit, and became averſe to exertions of vigour. Being occupied with their villas, their equipages, and the other appurtenances of wealth and of high rank. "They appear," ſaid Cicero upon this occaſion, "to think, that even if the republic ſhould "periſh, they will be able to preſerve their fiſh-"ponds."

The Conſul Bibulus, even Cato, though far removed from any ambiguity of conduct, ſaw no poſſibility of withſtanding the torrent. The firſt retired to his own houſe, and from thenceforward during the remainder of his term in office, did not perſonally appear in his public character, and even Cato abſented himſelf from the Senate [1].

While Cæſar engroſſed the full exerciſe of the conſular power, Bibulus was content with iſſuing his edicts or manifeſtos in writing, containing proteſts, by which he endeavoured to ſtop all proceedings in public affairs on account of the religious faſt, or continuation of holidays, which, according to the forms of the commonwealth, he had inſtituted to reſtrain his colleague. In theſe writings, he publiſhed violent invectives againſt Cæſar, in which, among other articles, he charged him with having had a part in the conſpiracy of Cataline [2]. The Tribune Vatinius, in return, iſſued a warrant to commit the Conſul Bibulus to priſon; and, in order to ſeize his perſon, attempted to break into his

---

[1] Cicero pro Sexto. Plutarch. in Catone.
[2] Sueton. in C. Cæſare.

CHAP. XIX.

his house; but in this he was foiled, and the parties continued, during the remainder of this Consulate, in the same situation with respect to each other.

In dating the year, instead of the Consulate of Cæsar and Bibulus, it was called by some wag the Consulate of Julius and Cæsar [1]. This able adventurer, though suspected of the deepest designs, went still deeper in laying his measures for the execution of them than his keenest opponents supposed. He found means to tie up every hand that was likely to be lifted up against himself; as those of Pompey and Crassus, by their secret agreement, of which the articles were gradually disclosed in the effect. He confirmed to Pompey all the acts of his administration in Asia, and, by putting him on the commission for dividing the lands of Campania, and for settling a colony at Capua, gave him an opportunity, which the other earnestly desired, of providing for many necessitous citizens of his party. He flattered Crassus sufficiently, by placing him on the same commission, and by admitting him to a supposed equal participation of that political consequence which the Triumvirs proposed to secure by their union. He gained the Equestrian order, by granting a suit which they had long in dependence, for a diminution of the rents payable by the revenue farmers in Asia [2]. These he reduced a third; and by this act, acquired with that

[1] Sueton. in C. Cæsare, c. 20. Dio. Cass. lib. xxxvii. c. 6. 8.
[2] Cicero ad Att. lib. ii. ep. 1. Appian. de Bell. Civil. lib. ii. p. 435.

OF THE ROMAN REPUBLIC.

that order of men the character of great liberality and candour. He himself was the only person who, in appearance, was not to profit by these arrangements. He was occupied, as his retainers gave out, in serving the republic, and in promoting his friends; was the general patron of the diftreffed and the indigent, and had nothing to propose for himself.

With his confent, and under his authority, Fufius, one of the Prætors, and Vatinius, one of the Tribunes, obtained two laws, both of them equitable and falutary: the first, relating to the use of the ballot in the Comitia, or affembly of the People: the other, relating to the challenge of parties in the nomination of judges or juries. The introduction of the ballot in political queftions had greatly weakened the influence of the ariftocracy over the determinations of the People; and refolutions were frequently carried in this manner, which no party, nor any particular order of men, were willing to acknowledge as their meafure. The Nobles imputed abfurd determinations to the majority which was formed by the People, and thefe in their turn retorted the imputation. To leave no doubt in fuch matters for the future, Fufius propofed, that the feparate orders of Patrician, Equeftrian, and Plebeian, fhould ballot apart [1]. This regulation had fome tendency to reftore the influence of the fuperior claffes.

Vatinius

[1] Dio. Lb. xxxviii. c. 2.

CHAP. XIX.

Vatinius proposed that in criminal actions, when the judges were drawn by lot, the defendant and prosecutors might, in their turns, challenge, or strike off from the list, persons to whom they took a particular exception [1].

Cæsar himself was busy in devising new regulations to reform the mode of elections, and to improve the forms of business in some of the public departments. By one of his acts the priests were to be elected agreeably to the former laws of Atius and Domitius, with this difference, that candidates might be admitted even in absence. By another of his acts, regular journals were to be kept in the Senate and in the assemblies of the People, and all their proceedings recorded for the inspection of the public. By a third, persons convicted of treason were subjected to new penalties, and governors of provinces to additional restraints in the exercise of their power. Such officers were not allowed to receive any honorary gift from their provinces, until their services being considered at Rome, were found to have entitled them to a triumph [2]. They were restrained from encroaching on the right of any State or principality beyond the limits of their province. They were obliged to leave copies of their books and of their acts at two of the principal towns in their government [3], and, immediately upon their arrival at Rome, to give in a copy of the same accounts to the treasury.

---

[1] Dio. lib. xxxviii. c. 8. Appian.
[2] Cicero ad Att. lib. v. ep. 16. & lib. vi. ep. 7.
[3] Cicero ad Famil. lib. ii. ep. 17. & lib. v. ep. 20.

fury. They were doomed to make reſtitution of all ſubjects received in extortion, not only by themſelves, but by any of their attendants [1].

With theſe acts Cæſar adorned his Conſulate, and in ſome meaſure diſcountenanced the party which was diſpoſed to traduce him. He is, nevertheleſs, accuſed of having ſtolen from the treaſury, to which he had acceſs in the capacity of Conſul, bars of gold weighing three thouſand pondo, and of having concealed the theft, by ſubſtituting braſs gilt, and of the ſame form, in its ſtead [2].

Whatever foundation there may have been for this report, it ſoon appeared that Cæſar had objects of a more ſerious nature, could copy, on occaſion, the example of Pompey, and, in his manner, cauſe what was perſonal to himſelf to be propoſed by others, whom he might be free to ſupport or diſavow according to the reception which his propoſal ſhould meet from the public. It cannot be doubted that he now conceived the deſign of having a military force, if neceſſary to ſupport his pretenſions in the city. Hitherto kingly power being odious at Rome, whoever had aſpired to it had always periſhed in the attempt, and the mere imputation, however ſupported, was fatal. The moſt profligate party among the populace were unable

or

---

[1] Cicero. in Vatinium pro Sext.

[2] Sueton. in Jul. c. 54. Cæſar is ſaid to have ſold the gold bullion he brought from Spain at 3000 H. S. or about 25 l. of our money the pondo. This will make his ſuppoſed theft about 75,000 l.

or unwilling to support their demagogues to this extent; and the People in general became jealous of their most respectable citizens, when it appeared that merit itself approached to monarchical elevation. Marius, by the continued possession of the highest offices, and by the supreme command of armies, had acquired a species of sovereignty which he knew not how to resign. Cinna came into partnership with Marius, and wished to govern after his decease. Sylla, to avenge his own wrongs and those of his friends, to cut off a profligate faction, and restore the republic, took possession of the government. He led his army against usurpers, and had the power to become himself the most successful usurper, as he was put in possession of a sovereignty which he no doubt might have retained. So far in him, therefore, every ambitious adventurer found a model, and was instructed in the means which could insure to a single person the sovereignty of Rome. Cataline, with his accomplices Lentulus and Cethegus, by means of a profligate party among the populace or citizens of desperate fortune, had vainly attempted to overturn the State, or usurp its government [1]. Cæsar was become head of the same party; but an army like that of Sylla, a convenient station, and the resources of a great province, were necessary to support the contest, and to carry it against his rivals,

---

[1] Speaking of the imaginary danger to a State of being overturned by the rabble; we might as much fear, said a witty writer of the present age, that a city would be drowned by the overflowing of its own kennels.

rivals, as well as againſt the republic itſelf, to any favourable iſſue.

The republic had taken many precautions to prevent the introduction of military power at Rome. Although the functions of State and of war were intruſted to the ſame perſons, yet the civil and military characters, except in the caſe of a Dictator, were never united at once in the ſame perſon. The officer of State reſigned his civil power before he became a ſoldier, and the ſoldier was obliged to lay aſide his military enſigns and character before he could enter the city; and if he ſued for a triumph in his military form, muſt remain without the walls till that ſuit was diſ‑cuſſed. The command of armies and of pro‑vinces in the perſon of any officer was limited to a ſingle year at a time, at the end of which, if the commiſſion were not expreſsly prolonged, it was underſtood to expire, and to devolve on a ſuccſſ‑for named by the Senate.

That no leader of party might have an army at hand to overawe the republic, no military ſta‑tion was ſuppoſed to exiſt within the limits of Italy. The purpoſe, however, of this precaution was in ſome meaſure fruſtrated by the ſituation of a province in which an army was kept with‑in the Alps. Italy was underſtood to extend on‑ly from the ſea of Tarentum to the Arnus and the Rubicon: beyond theſe boundaries, on the northweſt, all thoſe extenſive and rich tracts on both ſides of the Apennines, and within the Alps,

CHAP. XIX.

which now make the dutchies of Ferrara, Bologna, Modeno, Milan, the States of Piedmont and Venice, with the dutchy of Carniola, and the whole of Lombardy, and part of Tuscany, were considered, not as Italy, but as a province termed the Cisalpine Gaul, and, like the other Roman provinces, was to be held by a military officer, supported by an army.

This then was the most commodious station at which a political adventurer might unite the greatest advantages; that of having an army at his command; and that of being so near the city of Rome, as not only to influence the public councils, but to be able also, by surprise, to occupy the seats of government whenever his designs were ripe for such an attempt.

Sylla had an army devoted to his pleasure; but, having the seas of Asia and Ionia to pass in his way to Italy, could not, without giving an alarm from a great distance, and without putting his enemies on their guard, approach to the capital. He therefore, when he had this object in view, made no secret of his purpose.

Cæsar, from his native disposition, could not restrain his ambition short of the sovereignty, and without any signal incitement or singular circumstances, like those of Sylla, was prepared to obtain it. He arranged his measures like the plan of a campaign, which he had ability to digest, and the patience to execute with the greatest deliberation. He

proposed

proposed to make himself master of an army at the gates of Rome, and to have the resources of a province contiguous to the capital. He proposed to secure the possession of these advantages by an unprecedented prolongation of the usual appointments for five years; so that after an appointment in these terms, the People themselves could not, without a breach of faith, recal their grant upon any sudden alarm of the improper use he might propose to make of their favours.

The Cisalpine Gaul, or that part of Italy which extended from the Rubicon to the Alps, was thus peculiarly suited to the purpose of Cæsar. But the distribution of the provinces was still within the prerogative of the Senate; and the provincial governments were filled by their nomination, in pursuance of an express regulation ascribed to Caius Gracchus, and known, from his name, by the title of the Sempronian Law[1]. Cæsar had ever been at variance with the greater part of the Senate. In the office of Prætor he had been suspended by their authority. In his present office of Consul he had set them at open defiance. He had no prospect of being able to obtain from them the choice he had made of a province; and the proposal to put him in possession of the Cisalpine Gaul for a term of years, joined to the preceding parts of his conduct, would have given a general alarm, and opened at once the whole extent of his design.

It

[1] Lex Sempronia, Vid. vol. ii. c. 10.

CHAP. XIX.

It was neceſſary, therefore, in order to obtain this object, to ſet aſide the authority of the Senate, and to procure his nomination by ſome degree of ſurpriſe. The Tribune Vatinius accordingly, upon a rumour that the Helvetii, or the nations inhabiting the tracts or valleys from Mount Jura to the Alps, were likely to cauſe ſome commotion on the frontier of Gaul, moved the People to ſet aſide the law of Sempronius, and, by virtue of their own tranſcendent authority, to name Cæſar as Proconſul of the Ciſalpine Gaul and Illyricum for five years, with an army of three legions. The ſenatorian party, as might have been expected, were greatly alarmed at this propoſal. They vainly, however, hoped to evade it by ſubſtituting another appointment for Cæſar in place of this province. It was propoſed to make him ſuperintendant of the public foreſts throughout the empire; a charge which, though not, in our acceptation of the word, a province, was however, like every other public department in that empire, known by this name. This ſubſtitute for the government of the Ciſalpine Gaul was thought to be the better choſen, that it neither implied nor required the command of an army, and was to withhold the engine of military power from a perſon ſo likely to abuſe it. This weak attempt, however, againſt ſo able an adverſary, only tended to expoſe the meaning of thoſe by whom it was made, and by ſhewing to the Senate their own weakneſs, hurried them into conceſſions which perhaps might have been other-

wiſe

OF THE ROMAN REPUBLIC.

wife avoided. In order that Cæsar might not owe every thing to the People and nothing to them, they extended his command at once to both sides of the Alps. On the one side of these mountains he had a station from which to overawe the city: on the other, he had a great extent of territory, and a theatre of war on which he might form an army and inure them to service. The Senate, seeing he had already, by a vote of the People, obtained the first with an army of three legions for five years; and imagining that it was no longer of any use to oppose him; or hoping to occupy his attention, or to wear out the five years of his command in wars that might arise beyond the Alps, they joined to his province on the Po that of the Transalpine Gaul also, with an additional legion. In this manner, whether from these or any similar motives, it is affirmed by some of the historians [1], that the Senate even outran the People in concessions to Cæsar; and to this occasion is referred the memorable saying of Cato: " Now you have taken to yourselves a king, and " have placed him with his guards in your Ci-" tadel [2]."

Cæsar, at the same time, on the motion of the Tribune Vatinius, was empowered to settle a Roman colony on the Lake Larius at Novum Comum, with full authority to confer the privilege of

[1] Sueton. in Jul. Cæsare, c. 22.
[2] Plutarch. in Catone. Dio. Cass. lib. xxxviii. Appian. de Bell. Civil. lib. ii.

of Roman citizens on those he should settle in this place. Having obtained the great object of his Consulate, in his appointment for a term of years to the command of an army within the Alps, he no longer kept any measures with the Senate, nor allowed them any merit in the advantages he had gained. He was aware of their malice, he said, and had prevailed in every suit, not by their concession, but in direct opposition to their will. Though capable of great command of temper, and of the deepest dissimulation, when in pursuit of his object, he appears, on this and other occasions to have had a vanity which he idly indulged, in braving the world when his end was obtained [1]. As he insulted the Senate when no longer depending on their consent for any of his objects; so he no longer disguised his connection with Pompey and Crassus, or the means by which, in his late measures, the concurrence of these rivals had been obtained.

As such combinations and cabals generally have an invidious aspect to those who are excluded from them, the Triumvirate, for so it began to be called in detestation and irony [2], notwithstanding the popularity or influence enjoyed by those who had formed it, became an object of aversion and general abuse [3]. They were received at all public places

---

[1] Sueton. in Cæsare, lib. ii. c. 22.

[2] The titles of Duumvirs, Triumvirs, and so on, were the designations of legal commissions at Rome acting under public authority; such title was given to the private coalition of these adventurers in mere irony.

[3] Cicer. ad Att. lib. ii. ep. 16.

ces with groans and expreſſions of hatred. An actor, performing on the public theatre, applied to Pompey the Great, a ſentence of reproach, which occurred in the part he was acting. The application was received with peals of applauſe, and called for again and again [1].

The edicts that were publiſhed by Bibulus in oppoſition to Cæſar were extolled, and received with avidity. The places of the ſtreets at which they were poſted up were ſo crowded with multitudes aſſembled to read them, that the ways were obſtructed. Cæſar and Pompey endeavoured to leſſen the effect of theſe edicts in ſpeeches to the People, but were ill heard. Pompey loſt his temper and his ſpirit, and ſunk in his conſideration as much as Cæſar advanced in power. It became manifeſt, even to the People, that Cæſar was the only gainer by this coalition, that he had procured it for his own conveniency [2]; but Pompey himſelf probably felt that he was too far advanced to recede.

The Senate, and all the moſt reſpectable citizens of Rome, though unanimous in their deteſtation of the deſign that was formed by Cæſar, Pompey, and Craſſus, to diſpoſe of the republic at their pleaſure, yet either were, or believed themſelves, unable

[1] " To our misfortune thou art great." He was called upon to repeat theſe words again and again innumerable times. " The time will come " when thou ſhalt rue this State;" likewiſe repeated with peals of applauſe, &c. Cicero ad Att. lib. ii. epiſt. 19. Val. Max. lib. vi. c. 2.

[2] One of the ſentences, ſo much applauded in its application to him at the theatre, was, " Eandem virtutem tempus veniet cum graviter gemes."

CHAP.
XIX.

unable to cope with the power of so many factions united. Cæsar, in order to hold by force what he gained by artifice, and by some degree of surprise, filled the streets with his retainers in arms, and showed, that, in case of any attempt to recal what had been so weakly given up to him, he was in condition to resist, and to lay the city in blood. If he were driven from Rome, he had provided within the Alps an army of two or three complete legions, with which he could maintain his province, or even recover his possession of the city. Every one censured, complained and lamented; but there was little concert, and less vigour, even among the members of the Senate.

Cato, with his declared disapprobation of the late measures, was reduced to the single expedient of assisting Bibulus in drawing up the edicts or manifestos against the proceedings of Cæsar, which, as has been mentioned, were at this time received with so much avidity by the People.

Cicero now declined taking part in any affair of State; but being known for an advocate of the greatest ability, was courted in this capacity by many citizens, who had affairs in dependence before the courts of justice; but apprehending an attack which was likely to be made upon himself, on account of the transactions of his Consulate, he avoided, as much as possible, giving offence to any of the parties which divided the commonwealth. The storm was to be directed against him by Publius Clodius, under whose animosity to the government

ment of the Nobles, and to Cicero in particular, it was perceived for some time to be gathering[1].

This bustling profligate having, in the former year, in order that he might be qualified for Tribune of the People, got himself adopted into a Plebeian family, could not obtain the necessary ratification of the deed of adoption in the assembly of the Curiæ, until his cause was espoused by Cæsar, who seems to have taken his part, in resentment of some insinuations thrown out against himself by Cicero in pleading for M. Antonius, his late colleague in the Consulate. Antonius being, as has been mentioned, on account of his administration in Macedonia, accused of extortion, was defended by Cicero, who took that occasion to lament the state of the republic, brought under subjection as it was by a cabal which ruled by violence, and in contempt of the laws. Cæsar was greatly provoked at these expressions: " This per- " son," he said, " takes the same liberty to vilify " the reputation of others, that he takes to extol " his own;" and considering this speech as a warning of the part which Cicero was likely to take in his absence, he determined not to leave him at the head of the Senatorian party to operate against him. His destruction might be effected merely by expediting the formality of Clodius's adoption into a Plebeian family, to qualify him for Tribune of the People[2]; and Cæsar, on the very day in which

[1] Cicero ad Att. lib. ii. epist. 19, 20, 21, 22, 23.
[2] Dio. Cass. lib. xxxviii. c. 10. &c. Plutarch. In Cicerone. Cicero pro domo sua, de Provinciis Consularibus, &c.

which he received this provocation from Cicero, permitted the act of adoption to pass, in the assembly of the Curiæ.

Pompey likewise concurred in executing this deed of adoption for Clodius, and assisted in the quality of Augur to carry it through the religious forms. Clodius, in the mean time, gave out, that he had no design on the Tribunate, but was soliciting an embassy to Tigranes king of Armenia. Cicero was so much blinded by this pretence, that he was merry in his letter to Atticus on the absurdity of Clodius, in having himself degraded into a Plebeian, merely to qualify him to appear at the court of Tigranes. He was merry likewise with his not being put on the commission of twenty for the execution of Cæsar's Agrarian Law. "Strange!" he said, " that he who was once the only male creature in Cæsar's house, cannot now find one place among twenty in the list of his friends [1]."

The more effectually to impose upon Cicero and his friends, Cæsar affected to believe, that the intention of Clodius was against himself, and taken up with the animosity of a person who had already attempted to dishonour his house [2]; and he pretended to dispute the validity of his adoption, and of consequence, his qualification to be elected a Tribune. Pompey joined also in the same vile artifice. "Nay," says Cicero, upon hearing of
" their

---

[1] Cicero ad Att. lib. ii. epist. 7.
[2] In the intrigue with Cæsar's wife.

their pretended oppofition to Clodius, "this is "vexation merely. Send but the proper officers to "me, and I will make oath, that Pompey told me "himfelf he had affifted as Augur in paffing that "decree!."

With thefe tranfactions the year of Cæfar's Confulate drew to a clofe. He ratified his treaty with Pompey, by giving him his daughter Julia in marriage. During the former part of the year, this lady had been promifed to Servilius Cæpio, and had been of great ufe to her father, by fecuring the fervices of Cæpio againft Bibulus. But now it was found more expedient to attach Pompey; and Servilius, on his difappointment, was pacified by the promife of Pompey's daughter. Cæfar himfelf married the daughter of Calpurnius Pifo, who, together with Gabinius, the creature of Pompey, was deftined to fucceed in the Confulate, and who was, by this alliance, fecured in the intereft of Cæfar. "Provinces, armies, and kingdoms," faid Cato on this occafion, "are made the dowries "of women [1], and the empire itfelf an appendage "of female proftitution."

In this fituation of affairs, and among parties who dealt in impofitions and artifices, as well as in open and daring meafures, fome particulars are recorded, which, to gain our belief, require fome acquaintance with the intrigues of popular faction. Vettius, a citizen of fome note, who had been employed

[1] Cic. ad Att. epift. 10. Vul. 12.
[2] Plutarch. in Catone.

ployed by Cicero in the time of his Conſulſhip to gain intelligence of the Cataline conſpiracy, now himſelf appeared as the author of a plot, of which the origin and the iſſue were matter of various conjecture. Knowing that Curio, a young man of high rank, and a declared enemy of Cæſar, was on bad terms likewiſe with Pompey, Vettius told him in confidence, that he himſelf had determined to aſſaſſinate Pompey, and propoſed to Curio to join with him in that deſign. The young man communicated the matter to his father, and the father to Pompey, who laid it before the Senate. Vettius being examined in the Senate, at firſt denied any intercourſe with Curio, but afterwards confeſſed, that he had been drawn into a conſpiracy in which this young man was concerned with Lucullus, Brutus, Bibulus, and ſome others, who had formed a deſign on Pompey's life.

It was ſuſpected, that Cæſar had employed Vettius to pretend this deſign againſt Pompey, and by opening himſelf to theſe perſons to engage ſome of them in a concert with himſelf; and that it was intended, as ſoon as he had laid ſome foundation for an imputation of guilt againſt any of them, that he ſhould, attended by a party of ſlaves, armed with daggers, put himſelf in the way of being taken; that he ſhould at firſt deny the plot, but afterwards ſuffer himſelf to be forced, by degrees, to confeſs, and to declare his accomplices; but that this plan was diſconcerted by the early intimation which Curio gave to his father, before all the circumſtances

cumstances projected to give it an air of probability were in readiness.

It was scarcely credible, however, that Cæsar should have committed his reputation to the hazard of detection in so infamous a project. He laid hold of it indeed with some avidity, and endeavoured to turn it against his opponents. After Vettius had been examined before the Senate, and was committed to prison for farther examination, Cæsar presented him to the People, and brought him into the rostra, to declare what he knew of this pretended most bloody design. The prisoner repeated his confession, but varied in the account of his accomplices, particularly in leaving Brutus out of the list; a circumstance likewise, in the scandal of the times, imputed to the partiality of Cæsar, and considered as proof of his clandestine relation to this young man. Vettius was remanded to prison, and a process commenced against him on the statute of intended assassination. A trial must have probably disclosed the whole scene, and for this reason was said to have been prevented, by the sudden death of Vettius, who was supposed to have been strangled, by order of Cæsar, in prison[1].

By the influence of Pompey and Cæsar, Gabinius and Piso were elected Consuls; and, by their connivance, Clodius became Tribune of the People. The ascendant they had gained, however, was extremely disagreeable to many of the other officers of State, and even to some of the Tribunes. L. Domitius

*U. C. 695.
L. Calpurnius Piso Cesonianus, A. Gabinius Nepos.*

[1] Cicero ad Att. lib. ii. epist. 24. Sueton. in Cæsare, c. 20.

CHAP. Domitius Ahenobarbus, and C. Memmius Gemellus, joined in a profecution againſt Cæſar, late Conſul, for proceedings in office contrary to law and religion. Cæſar, for ſome time, affected to join iſſue with them on the queſtions propoſed, and to ſubmit his cauſe to judgment; but at laſt, apprehending delay and trouble, without any advantage from ſuch an inquiry, he pleaded his privilege as a perſon deſtined for public ſervice; and accordingly, without ſtaying to anſwer the charge which was laid againſt him, withdrew from the city, continued to make his levies, and to aſſemble an army in the ſuburbs of Rome. In this poſture of affairs, one of the Quæſtors, who had ſerved under Cæſar in his Conſulſhip, was convicted of ſome miſdemeanor [1]; and the oppoſite party, as if they had of a ſudden broke the chains in which they were held, commenced ſuits againſt all the tools that had been employed by him in his late violent meaſures. Gabinius had been charged with bribery by Caius Cato, then a young man. But the Prætor, whoſe lot it was to exerciſe the juriſdiction in ſuch caſes, being under the influence of Pompey, evaded the queſtion. Caius Cato complained to the People, and, in ſtating the caſe, having ſaid that Pompey uſurped a Dictatorial power, ſo far incenſed part of his audience, that he narrowly eſcaped with his life [2].

Vatinius, the late mercenary Tribune, was accuſed before the Prætor Memmius, who willingly

---

[1] Sueton. in Nerone, c. ii. et in Cæſare, c. 23.
[2] Cicero ad Quint. Frat. lib. i. epiſt. 2.

ly received the accufation; but all proceedings in the matter were fuddenly ftopped by the interpofition of Clodius in his new fituation; and the attention of the People and of the Senate foon afterwards came to be more intenfely occupied with the defigns of this factious Tribune himfelf, than with any other bufinefs whatever.

The ruin of Cicero appears to have been the principal object which Clodius propofed to himfelf in foliciting the office which he now held; and this, though affecting to be of the popular party, he purfued chiefly from motives of perfonal animofity and refentment. Cicero had given evidence againft him on his late trial, and afterwards in the Senate made him the object of his wit and invective [1]. He is generally reprefented as effeminate and profligate, void of difcretion or prudence. On the prefent occafion, however, he feems to have managed with confiderable fteadinefs and addrefs. He acted evidently in concert with Cæfar, Pompey, and Craffus; but probably had not from them any particular direction in what manner he was to proceed.

Ever fince the fummary proceedings which were employed againft the accomplices of Cataline, the danger of this precedent was a favourite topic with the popular faction. Clodius profeffed that the whole object of his Tribunate was to provide a guard againft fuch dangers for the future. He began with paying his court to the different parties

[1] Cicer. ad Att. lib. 1.

ties and different orders of men in the republic, by proposing such acts as were favourable to each; and he stated his motion for better securing the People against arbitrary executions, without any application to Cicero, as but one of many regulations intended by him for the benefit of the public, and which he joined with some acts of gratification to private persons. He gained the present Consuls by procuring them lucrative appointments, at the expiration of their year in office; to Piso, Macedonia including Achaia; to Gabinius, Syria with a considerable addition beyond the usual bounds of that province [1]. He gained the indigent part of the People by an act to remit all the debts which were due for corn at the public granaries; and by ordering, for the future, gratuitous distributions to be made from thence [2]. He, at the same time, procured another act extremely agreeable to many of the citizens, for restoring and increasing the number of incorporated societies, which had been abolished about nine years before, on account of the troubles to which they gave rise.

The operation of corporate bodies, in a city so much addicted to faction and tumult, had been the cause of frequent disorders. As persons, affecting to govern the State, endeavoured to gain the People by indulging their humour in idleness and dissipation, with games, theatrical entertainments, combats of gladiators, and the baiting of wild beasts;

so

---

[1] Plutarch. in Cicerone.
[2] Pædianus in Pisoniaua. Dio. lib. xxxviii. Cicer. pro Domo sua.

fo the head of every corporate body, though upon a smaller scale, had his feasts, his entertainments, and shews, forming to himself a party of retainers, on occasion, to be employed as his faction might require. The renewal, therefore, of such establishments, a measure which carried to every ambitious tradesman in his stall the feeling and consequence of a Crassus, a Pompey, or a Cæsar, affecting to govern the world in their respective ways, was greedily adopted by the lower People. And Clodius took occasion, in the first ardour of such corporate meetings, to foment and to direct their zeal to his own purpose [1]. He even gained a considerable party in the Senate, by affecting to circumscribe the discretionary power of the Censors in purging their rolls. Many of the members had reason to dread the Censorial animadversions, and were pleased with an act which this Tribune obtained to provide, that, for the future, no one could be struck off the list of the Senate without a formal trial, and the concurrence of both the Censors [2].

Joined to so many arts practised to reconcile different parties to the measures he affected to take for the security of the People, Clodius promulgated his law of provision against arbitrary executions, and gave it a retrospect, which was undoubtedly meant to comprehend the summary proceedings which had been held against Cethegus and Lentulus,

[1] Dio lib. xxxviii. c. 13. Cicero in Pisonem, c. 4. et Ascanius, ibid.
[2] Ibid. See a summary of these acts. Cicero pro Sextio, from c. 15. to c. 28.

CHAP. Lentulus, in the Consulate of Cicero. While the
XIX. subject was under consideration, he thought of two
circumstances which might operate against his design, and which he was therefore determined to prevent. One was, the practice of recurring to the celestial auspices, by which the proceedings of the People were sometimes suspended; and the other was, the opposition which he might expect from Marcus Cato, who was likely to consider the cause of the Senate and the republic as involved in that of the magistrate, who had preserved the State by executing their decrees. To secure himself against the first, he procured an edict to prohibit all persons from observing the heavens while the People were deliberating on any affair of State; and to obviate the second, he thought of a pretence for a temporary removal of Cato from Rome.

In the preceding Consulate, Cato, though armed as he was solely with the reputation of integrity, unable to prevent the progress of a ruinous faction affecting popular measures, yet, by his unremitted opposition, he had forced them, on occasion, to show what Pompey in particular was extremely desirous to conceal, that they prevailed by corruption and force, not by what they pretended, the free choice of their fellow-citizens. Clodius, foreseeing if Cato remained at Rome, a like opposition; and possibly a disappointment in his design against Cicero, devised a commission to employ him in foreign service. Ptolomy, king of Cyprus, had put a personal affront on Clodius, by refusing to pay

his

his ranfom when taken by pirates on the coaſt of Afia near to that iſland. But now, in the wretched condition of nations, depending on the will of a ſingle profligate citizen, he took an opportunity to be revenged on this prince, by procuring an act to forfeit his kingdom and his treaſure; and by making Cato the inſtrument of his revenge, he propoſed to free himſelf at the ſame time from the interruption which this citizen was likely to give to his projects in the city [1].

At an interview with Cato, Clodius had the impudence to pretend great admiration of his virtue; told him, that the commiſſion to reduce Cyprus into the form of a province was ſolicited by many; but that he knew of none who, by his faithfulneſs and integrity, was ſo well qualified for the truſt as Cato, and that he meant to propoſe him to the People. "That," ſaid Cato, "I know is a "mere artifice; not an honour, but an indignity "intended to me."—"Nay," ſaid Clodius, "if "you do not go willingly, you ſhall go by force;" and on that very day moved and obtained his nomination from the People. Leſt the affair of Cyprus ſhould not detain him a ſufficient time, he was farther charged in his commiſſion to repair to Byzantium, to reſtore ſome exiles, and to quiet ſome troubles which had ariſen in that place.

Cæſar and Pompey likewiſe concurred in procuring this commiſſion to Cato, in order to remove a powerful ſupport from the Prætors Memmius and

[1] Cicero pro Sextio.

CHAP. XIX.

and Domitius, whofe propofal to repeal all the acts of Cæfar was yet in fufpenfe.

The ftorm was now ready to burſt upon the magiftrate who had prefided in the fuppreffion of Cataline's faction, and no man had any doubt of its direction. Cato, before he left Rome, feeing Cæfar in poffeffion of the gates with an army, and ready, in the event of any tumult, under pretence of repreffing diforders, to enter the city by force, and to feize on the government; or apprehending, that the caufe in queftion, however juft, was altogether defperate, earneftly exhorted Cicero, rather to yield and to withdraw from the city, than to bring matters to extremities in the prefent ftate of the republic [1].

Cicero, however, was for fome time undecided. Having fecured the fupport of L. Ninius Quadratus, one of the Tribunes, he propofed to obftruct the proceedings of his enemy, by oppofing the negative of a colleague, to all his motions. Afterwards, upon affurances from Clodius, that the purpofe of the act was altogether general, and had no fpecial relation to himfelf; he was prevailed on not to divide the college of Tribunes, nor to engage his friends in the invidious tafk of giving the negative to a law, which was intended merely to guard the People for the future againft arbitrary proceedings [2].

But Clodius, having thus made way for the declaratory act, which he had drawn up in general terms,

[1] Plutarch. in Catone.
[2] Dio. lib. xxxviii. c. 14.

terms, no longer made any secret of his design against the magistrate, who had dared to order the execution of Lentulus and Cethegus, and boasted of the concurrence of Cæsar and Pompey. In this neither of these professed friends of Cicero denied the imputation [1]; but excused themselves in private by pleading, that while their own acts of the preceding year were still questioned by the Prætor, it was necessary for them to keep terms with so violent a tribune as Clodius [2]; and Pompey, together with this apology for his present conduct, gave Cicero the strongest assurances of future protection. " This Tribune," he said, " shall kill me before he injure you." It is not credible that Pompey then meant to betray a person for whom he professed so much friendship; it was sufficiently base that, in the sequel, he did not perform his promise. On the contrary, when his aid came to be most wanted by his injured friend, he retired to the country, under pretence of business; and being at his villa near Alba, where Lentulus, Lucullus, and many of the most respectable Senators repaired to him with the warmest intreaties in behalf of a person to whose eloquence and panegyric he owed so many of his honours, he coldly referred them to the ordinary officers of State for protection, saying, That as a private citizen he could not contend with a furious Tribune at the head of an armed People [3].

In

---

[1] Cicero post Reditum in Senatum.
[2] Ibid. pro Sextio, c. 17. et 18.
[3] Cicero in Pisonem.

CHAP. XIX.

In the mean time, the Conful Gabinius, though under the abfolute direction of Pompey, promoted the attack againft Cicero, and checked every attempt that was made in his favour. When the Equeftrian order, together with numbers of the moft refpectable citizens from every quarter of Italy, crowded in mourning to Rome, and prefented a memorial to the Senate in his behalf; and when the members of the Senate itfelf propofed to take mourning, and to intercede with the People, Gabinius fuddenly left the chair, broke up the meeting, went directly from thence to the affembly of the People, where he threw out injurious infinuations againft the Senate, and mentioned the meetings which had been held by the Equeftrian order, as bordering on fedition and riot; faid, that the Knights ought to be cautious how they revived the memory of that part which they themfelves had acted in the violent meafures which were now coming under review, and which were fo likely to meet with a juft retribution from the People of Rome.

In this extremity Cicero attempted to fee Pompey in perfon at his country houfe; but while the fuppliant was entering at one door, this treacherous friend withdrew at another [1]. No longer doubting that he was betrayed by a perfon on whom he had fo fully relied, he began to be agitated by a variety of counfels and projects. He was invited by Cæfar to place himfelf in the ftation

[1] Plutarch. in Cicerone.

CHAP. XIX.

tion of lieutenant in his province of Gaul; and, in that public character abroad, to take refuge from the ſtorm that was gathering againſt him in Italy. But this, from a perſon who had ſo much contributed to raiſe the ſtorm, was ſuppoſed to proceed from a deſign to inſult or betray him; or at beſt to reduce him to a ſtate of dependence on himſelf. Being attended by a numerous body of citizens, chiefly of the Equeſtrian order, who had taken arms in his cauſe, he ſometimes had thoughts of defending himſelf by force; at other times, he ſunk in deſpair, and, as appears from his letters, propoſed to die by his own hands; an intention from which he was diverted only by the entreaties and anxious care of his friends.

Such was the ſtate of affairs, when Clodius aſſembled the People to paſs the act he had framed againſt arbitrary executions. He had ſummoned them to meet in the ſuburbs, that Cæſar, who, on account of his military command was then excluded from the city, might be preſent. This artful politician being called upon among the firſt to deliver his opinion, with an appearance of moderation, and unwillingneſs to bear hard on any perſon to whom the law might apply, referred the People to his former declarations; ſaid, that every one knew his mind on the ſubject of arbitrary executions; that he certainly approved the act which was now propoſed, as far as it provided againſt ſuch offences for the future; but could not concur

in

CHAP. XIX. in giving it a retrospect to any transaction already passed.

While Cæsar thus, in delivering his own opinion, affected to go no farther than consistency and a regard to his former conduct seemed to require, he permitted or directed his party to go every length with Clodius, and meant either to ruin Cicero, or force him to accept of protection on the terms that should be prescribed to him.

When the general law had passed, there was yet no mention of Cicero; and his enemies might have still found it a difficult matter to carry the application to him; but he himself, in the anguish of his mind, anticipated the consequence, went forth in mourning to the streets, and implored mercy of every citizen with an aspect of despondency, which probably did not encourage any party to espouse his cause. He was frequently met in this condition, and insulted by Clodius, who walked in the streets, attended by an armed rabble; and determined at last to abandon the city. Being escorted by a company of his friends, he passed through the gates in the middle of the night on the first of April, took the road of Lucania, and intended to have made his retreat into Sicily, where he flattered himself the memory of his administration in the quality of Quæstor, and the subsequent effects of his patronage at Rome, were likely to procure him a favourable reception [t]. But Clodius, immediately upon his departure, having carried a
special

[t] Vid. Actionem in Verrem.

special attainder, by which, in the language of such acts, he was interdicted the use of fire and water; and by which every person within five hundred miles of Italy was forbid, under severe penalties, to harbour him; Virgilius, the Prætor of Sicily, though his friend, declined to receive him. He turned from thence to Brundisium, passed into Macedonia, and would have fixed his residence at Athens; but apprehending that this place was within the distance prescribed to him by the act of banishment, he went to Thessalonica in his way to Cyzicum. Here he had letters, that gave him intimation of some change in his favour, entertained some prospect of being speedily recalled, and accordingly determined to wait the issue of these hopes.

We have better means of knowing the frailties of Cicero, than perhaps is safe for the reputation of any one labouring under the ordinary defects of human nature. He was open and undisguised to his friends, and has left an extensive correspondence behind him. Expressions of vanity in some passages of his life, and of pusillanimity in others, escape him with uncommon facility. Being at least of a querulous and impatient temper, he gave it full scope in his exile, perhaps not more from weakness, than from a design to excite his friends in redoubling their efforts to have him restored. He knew the value of fortitude as a topic of praise, and might have aspired to it; but would it not, he may have questioned, in the present instance,

encourage

encourage his party to sleep over his wrongs? In any other view, his complaints resemble more the wailings of an infant, or the strains of a tragedy composed to draw tears, than the language of a man supporting the cause of integrity in the midst of unmerited trouble. " I wish I may see the "day," he writes to Atticus, " in which I shall "be disposed to thank you for having prevailed " upon me not to lay violent hands on myself; " for it is certainly now matter of bitter regret to " me that I yielded to you in that matter [1]."

In answer to the same friend, who had chid him for want of fortitude, " What species of evil," he says, " do I not endure? Did ever any person " fall from so high a state? in so good a cause? " with such abilities and knowledge? with so much " public esteem? with the support of such a re- " spectable order of citizens? Can I remember " what I was, and not feel what I am? Stript of " so many honours, cut off in the career of so " much glory, deprived of such a fortune, tore " from the arms of such children, debarred the " view of such a brother, dearer to me than I was " to myself, yet now debarred from my presence, " that I may spare him what he must suffer from " such a sight, and myself what I must feel in be- " ing the cause of so much misery to him. I " could say more of a load of evils which is too " heavy for me to bear; but I am stopped by my " tears [2]."

From

[1] Cicero ad Att. lib. iii. epist. 3.
[2] Ibid. lib. iii. epist. 10.

OF THE ROMAN REPUBLIC.

CHAP. XIX.

From the whole of this correspondence of Cicero in his exile, we may collect to what degree the unjust reproaches which he had suffered, the desertion of those on whom he relied for support, the dangers to which he left his family exposed, affected his mind. The consciousness of his integrity, even his vanity forsook him; and his fine genius, no longer displayed in the Forum or in the Senate, or busied in the literary studies which afterwards amused him [1] in a more calamitous time of the republic, now, by exaggerating the distress of his fortunes, preyed upon himself. It appeared from this, and many other scenes of his life, that although he loved virtuous actions, yet his virtue was accompanied with so unsatiable a thirst of the praise to which it entitled him, that his mind was unable to sustain itself without this foreign assistance; and when the praise to which he aspired for his Consulate was changed into obloquy and scorn, he seems to have lost the sense of good or of evil in his own conduct or character; and at Thessalonica, where he fixed the scene of his exile, sunk or rose, even in his own esteem, as he seemed to be valued or neglected at Rome [2].

[1] See the Book of Tusculan Questions.
[2] Vid. Cicero ad Att. lib. iii.

END OF VOLUME SECOND.

www.ingramcontent.com/pod-product-compliance
Lightning Source LLC
Chambersburg PA
CBHW032003300426
44117CB00008B/879